FILMMAKERS SERIES
edited by
ANTHONY SLIDE

1. *James Whale,* by James Curtis. 1982
2. *Cinema Stylists,* by John Belton. 1983
3. *Harry Langdon,* by William Schelly. 1982
4. *William A. Wellman,* by Frank Thompson. 1983
5. *Stanley Donen,* by Joseph Casper. 1983
6. *Brian De Palma,* by Michael Bliss. 1983
7. *J. Stuart Blackton,* by Marian Blackton Trimble. 1985
8. *Martin Scorsese and Michael Cimino,* by Michael Bliss. 1985
9. *Franklin J. Schaffner,* by Erwin Kim. 1985
10. *D. W. Griffith and the Biograph Company,* by Cooper C. Graham et al. 1985
11. *Some Day We'll Laugh: An Autobiography,* by Esther Ralston. 1985
12. *The Memoirs of Alice Guy Blanché,* 2nd ed., trans. by Roberta and Simone Blanché. 1996
13. *Leni Riefenstahl and Olympia,* by Cooper C. Graham. 1986
14. *Robert Florey,* by Brian Taves. 1987
15. *Henry King's America,* by Walter Coppedge. 1986
16. *Aldous Huxley and Film,* by Virginia M. Clark. 1987
17. *Five American Cinematographers,* by Scott Eyman. 1987
18. *Cinematographers on the Art and Craft of Cinematography,* by Anna Kate Sterling. 1987
19. *Stars of the Silents,* by Edward Wagenknecht. 1987
20. *Twentieth Century-Fox,* by Aubrey Solomon. 1988
21. *Highlights and Shadows: The Memoirs of a Hollywood Cameraman,* by Charles G. Clarke. 1989
22. *I Went That-a-Way: The Memoirs of a Western Film Director,* by Harry L. Fraser; edited by Wheeler Winston Dixon and Audrey Brown Fraser. 1990
23. *Order in the Universe: The Films of John Carpenter,* by Robert C. Cumbow. 1990
24. *The Films of Freddie Francis,* by Wheeler Winston Dixon. 1991
25. *Hollywood Be Thy Name,* by William Bakewell. 1991
26. *The Charm of Evil: The Life and Films of Terence Fisher,* by Wheeler Winston Dixon. 1991
27. *Lionheart in Hollywood: The Autobiography of Henry Wilcoxon,* with Katherine Orrison. 1991
28. *William Desmond Taylor: A Dossier,* by Bruce Long. 1991
29. *The Films of Leni Riefenstahl,* 2nd ed., by David B. Hinton. 1991

30. *Hollywood Holyland: The Filming and Scoring of "The Greatest Story Ever Told,"* by Ken Darby. 1992
31. *The Films of Reginald LeBorg: Interviews, Essays, and Filmography,* by Wheeler Winston Dixon. 1992
32. *Memoirs of a Professional Cad,* by George Sanders, with Tony Thomas. 1992
33. *The Holocaust in French Film,* by André Pierre Colombat. 1993
34. *Robert Goldstein and "The Spirit of '76,"* edited and compiled by Anthony Slide. 1993
35. *Those Were the Days, My Friend: My Life In Hollywood with David O. Selznick and Others,* by Paul Macnamara. 1993
36. *The Creative Producer,* by David Lewis; edited by James Curtis. 1993
37. *Reinventing Reality: The Art and Life of Rouben Mamoulian,* by Mark Spergel. 1993
38. *Malcolm St. Clair: His Films, 1915–1948,* by Ruth Anne Dwyer. 1997
39. *Beyond Hollywood's Grasp: American Filmmakers Abroad, 1914–1945,* by Harry Waldman. 1994
40. *A Steady Digression to a Fixed Point,* by Rose Hobart. 1994
41. *Radical Juxtaposition: The Films of Yvonne Rainer,* by Shelley Green. 1994
42. *Company of Heroes: My Life as an Actor in the John Ford Stock Company,* by Harry Carey, Jr. 1994
43. *Strangers in Hollywood: A History of Scandinavian Actors in American Films from 1910 to World War II,* by Hans J. Wollstein. 1994
44. *Charlie Chaplin: Intimate Close-Ups,* by Georgia Hale, edited with an introduction and notes by Heather Kiernan. 1995
45. *The Word Made Flesh: Catholicism and Conflict in the Films of Martin Scorsese,* by Michael Bliss. 1995
46. *W. S. Van Dyke's Journal: White Shadows in the South Seas (1927–1928) and Other Van Dyke on Van Dyke,* edited and annotated by Rudy Behlmer. 1996
47. *Music from the House of Hammer: Music in the Hammer Horror Films, 1950–1980,* by Randall D. Larson. 1996
48. *Directing: Learn from the Masters,* by Tay Garnett. 1996
49. *Featured Player: An Oral Autobiography of Mae Clarke,* edited with an introduction by James Curtis. 1996
50. *A Great Lady: A Life of the Screenwriter Sonya Levien,* by Larry Ceplair. 1996
51. *A History of Horrors: The Rise and Fall of the House of Hammer,* by Denis Meikle. 1996
52. *The Films of Michael Powell and the Archers,* by Scott Salwolke. 1997

Wife of the Life of the Party

Lita Grey Chaplin
and Jeffrey Vance

The Scarecrow Press, Inc.
Lanham, Md., & London
1998

SCARECROW PRESS, INC.

Published in the United States of America
by Scarecrow Press, Inc.
4720 Boston Way
Lanham, Maryland 20706

4 Pleydell Gardens, Folkestone
Kent CT20 2DN, England

British Library Cataloguing in Publication Information Available

Library of Congress Cataloging-in-Publication Data

Chaplin, Lita Grey, 1908–1995
    Wife of the life of the party / Lita Grey Chaplin and Jeffrey Vance.
        p.   cm. — (Filmmakers series ; 61)
    ISBN 0-8108-3432-4 (cloth : alk. paper)
    1. Chaplin, Lita Grey, 1908–1995. 2. Chaplin, Charlie,
1889–1977. 3. Entertainers' spouses—Biography. 4. Comedians
—United States—Biography. 5. Motion picture actors and actresses
—United States—Biography. I. Vance, Jeffrey, 1970– . II. Title.
III. Series. IV. Series: Filmmakers series ; no. 61.
PN2287.C513A3   1998
791.43′028′092—dc21
[B]   97-42024
                                                    CIP

ISBN 0-8108-3432-4 (cloth : alk. paper)

Contents

Foreword

My mother was never happy with her first "autobiography," *My Life with Chaplin: An Intimate Memoir*, coauthored with Morton Cooper in 1966. The book was more Cooper than Mother—and more *An Intimate Memoir* than *My Life with Chaplin*. My mother's publisher had convinced her that exaggerating the more sensational and intimate details of her relationship with my father, Charlie Chaplin, would sell books. Of course, they were right, and, quite frankly, at the time Mother needed the money.

This was not the first time that my mother was convinced to let someone else sensationalize her story. In 1927, my great-uncle Edwin McMurray and his team of divorce lawyers drafted a complaint against my father that was a blockbuster in its day. An unprecedented forty-two pages in length, it accused my father of "solicit[ing], urg[ing] and demand[ing] that plaintiff [my mother] submit to, perform and commit such acts and things for the gratification of defendant's said abnormal, unnatural, perverted and degenerate sexual desires, as to be too revolting, indecent and immoral to set forth in detail in this complaint." Wow! That is certainly not the way my mother told the story. When asked about her celebrated "intimate" life with my father about a year before she died, she answered, "I can say this about my sex life with old Charlie: not good . . . but often!"

The lawyers' tactics worked, and Mother won from my father the largest divorce settlement in California history until that time—$825,000—a lot of money in 1927. The complaint was so shocking that copies of it were sold on the street to thousands who wanted to know the "truth" about the most famous man in the world. My parents' divorce was quite a story, and the first in a long line of scandalous Hollywood divorces that would follow.

ix

An example of my parents' strained dealings with one another was the fight they had over my name. My father wanted to hand down a family name and name me after my uncle, Sydney Chaplin. Mother wanted to name me Thomas Edward. They fought and fought, and eventually, as was often the case, my father won—and I was named Sydney Chaplin. My father did allow my mother to sneak in her father's middle name "Earl" as my middle name, but this did not appease her. For a long time, well after the divorce, she refused to call me "Sydney," declaring, "I don't care if that's your legal name or not!" So, for many years, I was called "Tommy" in her house. She finally gave up, however, in the last twenty years of her life. She realized that although my father had won the "name" battle, she had won the "money" battle. "Sydney" wasn't so bad after all!

Somehow, through it all, Lita Grey Chaplin remained an attentive mother. I remember after I left Lawrenceville (a posh college prep school near Princeton, New Jersey), I went to the less posh North Hollywood High for a time. This was the first public school that I had ever attended. One of my pals one day suggested that we "ditch school." Because I had always gone to boarding school, it never occurred to me that you could just cut class. One day I went to Mother, dressed as if I was going to school, and asked if I could have a dollar for lunch money. "What is it, a double feature?" she asked. Mother had caught me in the act, and needless to say I went to school that day.

As long as I can remember, my mother wanted to tell *her own story, in her own words.* Two years before she died, she set out to do just that. With the help of her friend and coauthor Jeff Vance, Mother began to write her story as she remembered it, without exaggeration, and perhaps surprisingly to some, painting a more balanced portrait of my father than either the Cooper book or the McMurray complaint would allow. Although Mother didn't spare my father his faults, she was fair. At the age of eighty-seven, with nothing to lose and only the truth to gain, my mother rewrote the story of her life with Charlie Chaplin.

The project totally consumed my mother until she finished this manuscript, nearly two months before she died. Mother was obsessed with setting the record straight—and set it straight she did. This book is a marvelous story, beginning with an innocent young girl's first encounter with the famous "Little Tramp," and ending with the scandal of her bitter divorce from him. It contains details that have never before appeared in print, and even fans of my father who are convinced that they know everything about Lita Grey and Charlie Chaplin will find something of interest in these pages.

The book ends with my mother, twenty years old and no longer Mrs. Charles Chaplin, embarking on a career of her own in show business. Mother wanted to be a movie star but settled instead for a fairly successful career as a vaudeville and nightclub singer.

Although I never saw my mother's stage act, I did hear her sing. I was always around the house, listening to her rehearse at home. She handled her special material, such as "I'm the Wife of the Life of the Party" (a knowing reference to my father that audiences loved) quite well. Even in the living room, Mother had a marvelous stage presence.

For my father, the divorce from my mother was a bitter period in his life that he decided was better left as a forgotten bad memory. In fact, he didn't discuss that part of his life at all. He barely mentions it in his own autobiography—dismissing it in a few terse lines. He never even talked to me about the marriage. Never. It is quite amazing if one thinks about it. After all, she was my mother, and I did work closely with my father. One would think he would say something like "We didn't get along," or "She was too young," or "It wasn't meant to be." Nothing. Not a single word. I never asked because it was clear that this was not a subject for discussion. He never even asked how she was doing. It really is difficult to imagine that if a man had a child by somebody that he would never ask vaguely about how the mother is doing or what is happening with her. It was just that painful for him.

It's clear from this book that Mother didn't share my father's hang-ups about the marriage. Following the bitter divorce, Mother picked herself up, dusted herself off, and moved on to start again—with a resilience not unlike my father's own famous character. She began her career in show business, lost a son to drink, and almost lost her own life to the same. In these pages, Lita Grey Chaplin finally comes full circle, back to the events that made her famous—and my mother finally gets her chance to tell *her own story, in her own words.*

Sydney Chaplin
Palm Springs, California
1997

Acknowledgments

My principal thanks are to Sydney Chaplin and Margaret Beebe for their kindness and patience and for rendering vital support and assistance.

A special thanks goes to Jon S. Bouker for his counsel and whose contribution to this book has been legion.

My thanks to Kevin Brownlow, David Robinson, and David Shepard for reading the manuscript and improving it with their suggestions.

My thanks also to Bonnie McCourt for her suggestions and assistance proofreading this text.

I am indebted to Steve Randisi for making available material he has collected over the years on Lita Grey Chaplin.

My gratitude to the Totheroh family, especially David Totheroh, for sharing with me their unpublished interview with Rollie Totheroh.

I am also grateful to the following individuals who spoke with me about Lita Grey Chaplin and/or Charles Chaplin from their various points of view, providing indispensable corroboration: Sydney Chaplin, Anthony Coogan, Alistair Cooke, Douglas Fairbanks Jr., Pat Longo, Virginia Cherrill Martini, Pamela Paumier, David Raksin, Dean Riesner, David Robinson, and Betty Chaplin Tetrick.

I would like to express my appreciation to Stephan Chaplin, Linda Frank, Sebastian Twardosz, and Sandra Vance for their support.

I wish to acknowledge the assistance I have received from officials and staff of the Margaret Herrick Library of the Academy of Motion Picture Arts and Sciences and the Los Angeles Superior Court Archives.

Finally, this project could not have been possible without the assistance of Roy Export Company Establishment, especially Pamela Paumier and her successor Kate Guyonvarch, who kindly provided photographs and papers from the Chaplin Archives (© Roy Export Company Establishment, Paris).

Introduction

> My life is an open book . . . in fact, it is two open books, and
> the second one is the corrected one.
>
> —*Lita Grey Chaplin*

Lita Grey Chaplin, the embattled second wife of Charles Chaplin,
began this, her second memoir, late in her long life of eighty-
seven years. Indeed, most of the writing for this book was completed in 1995, the year of her death. By the time Lita began the
actual process of putting pen to paper to record the remembrances
chronicled in this volume, she had come to terms with her bitter
divorce from Charlie Chaplin and her feelings of anger toward
him. Her acrimony had slowly eroded over the years through the
realization that the public's continued interest in her came through
her connection to Chaplin. This book, therefore, begun and completed at the end of Lita Grey Chaplin's life, is the result of nearly
seventy years of close and thoughtful reflection. It is the product
of a woman who had come to terms with her past and wanted
to leave an accurate accounting of her life's experiences for the
future.

Lita felt very strongly that before she died she should correct
the inaccuracies contained in her first "autobiography," *My Life
with Chaplin: An Intimate Memoir*, coauthored with Morton
Cooper. Cooper had rewritten and embellished Lita's rambling
manuscript at the instruction of the publisher, in an effort to make
the text coherent and to emphasize the more scandalous aspects
of her relationship with Chaplin. The publisher correctly gambled
that a lascivious, "tell-all" book would attract readers, but Lita

was never satisfied with the final product. This book does not demur from the intimate details of Lita's relationship with Charles Chaplin, but it presents them accurately and without exaggeration, as Lita would have done in 1966, had she not acceded to the publisher's marketing techniques and her own need for a large monetary return on the project.

In this memoir, Lita Grey Chaplin seizes her final opportunity to correct the many inaccuracies and embellishments of the 1966 text—a vital task given the continued fascination with Lita and her importance to the historical record of Charles Chaplin's life and work.

Charles Chaplin's relationship with Lita Grey was perhaps the most destructive relationship Chaplin had with a woman, ending in a bitter divorce that scandalized Hollywood of the 1920s. At the time of the divorce, public opinion regarding Lita was equally divided. Some people viewed Lita as a gold digger, out to bring down the most famous man in the world for her own financial gain; others were disgusted that a man of Chaplin's age would have an intimate relationship with such a young girl. When books and articles relating the sordid tale of Charlie Chaplin and Lita Grey began in earnest, starting in the early 1950s, Lita was not treated well by the authors, who were mostly prejudiced in Chaplin's favor, unaware of the basic facts of their relationship, which have been unavailable until now. It was also during the 1950s that Vladimir Nabokov published his novel *Lolita*, which many believe to be inspired by the story of Charlie Chaplin and Lita Grey.

Although it is clear that Lita's place in the Charlie Chaplin hagiography would have remained secure merely because of the difficult marriage and the fact that she is the mother of his two eldest sons, Charles Chaplin Jr. and Sydney Chaplin, it is incumbent upon film historians and aficionados alike to recognize a more textured contribution. Lita not only was an intimate witness to the events surrounding arguably Chaplin's greatest period—the 1920s—but she herself dramatically altered the course of three of Chaplin's most important works: *The Kid*, *The Gold Rush*, and *The Circus*.

Chaplin created Lita Grey by bestowing upon young Lillita MacMurray this appellation that he thought was better suited for cinema marquees. Many have speculated about what originally attracted Chaplin to the tall, big-boned little girl whom he cast as the flirting angel in *The Kid*. Lita's large, expressive eyes contributed to Chaplin's initial attraction. But Lita herself in one of her final interviews described a more complex, psychologically based attraction. She said, "He [Chaplin] was so creative that he even liked to create people. He liked to see the girl come alive. He was fascinated by the awakening of a girl . . . and he had a fetish for virgins."[1]

Many clues support this assessment. For example, with the signing of her first contract in 1920 for *The Kid*, Chaplin had twelve-year-old Lillita sit for a photograph in the pose of Joshua Reynolds's famous portrait of an angelic little girl, *The Age of Innocence*. Chaplin created the role of the flirting angel in *The Kid* for Lita and constructed the elaborate angel dream sequence in the film to accommodate this character—a performance both portentous of the difficult days to come and illustrative of Chaplin's fascination with awakening sexuality. The intertitles throughout the flirting angel sequence are steeped in irony and metaphor: "The trouble begins." "Vamp him." "Innocence." "Getting flighty." Roland Totheroh, Chaplin's longtime cameraman, corroborates this assessment, remembering Lita as a decidedly immature girl for whom Chaplin developed an immediate attraction. According to Totheroh:

> There was a big close-up [in *The Kid*] where she [Lita] ties this villain up, supposed to be—Chuck [Riesner]—up there in heaven. Boy, he'd [Chaplin] run that back and forth and look at it; Jesus, his mouth would drool, and I said, "Oh, Jeez," I said to Jack [Wilson, second cameraman on *The Kid*], "What the hell? That god-damn kid, a little bony-legged thing and that—what does he see in that?"[2]

Nearly concomitant with the start of their sexual relationship, Chaplin cast Lita in the role of the dancehall girl in *The Gold Rush*. Despite Lita's being the film's leading lady for over six months, Chaplin filmed only one important scene with her, three weeks after engaging her as the dance hall girl. The continuity reports from 24 March 1924 reveal Chaplin's preoccupation with his sexual attraction to Lita and the depth to which it was influencing his work. The scene evokes Chaplin's own fantasies of Lita as his "forbidden fruit":

---

1. This and all following quotes from Lita Grey Chaplin are from tapes recorded by Jeffrey Vance in 1995.
2. Roland H. Totheroh in a 1964 interview with his family.

Scene 14: Close-up. Dissolve. C. asleep in kitchen on couch. Lita
standing over him with cake—wakens him—he sits up—
she sits down beside him—smiles—takes berry—gives
it to him—he turns forward—eats it—smiles—she takes
another berry—starts to give it to him. She says: Close
your eyes and open your mouth. He does so and she
throws whole cake in his face and laughs. C. takes cake
off—face all smeared with cream—Fade out and fade
into close-up in cabin with C. asleep in cot—blanket over
body but not on head—snow on neck and face—snow
drops down from roof five times—he wakes up then sits
up—and looks around room—brushes snow off—gets
up—comes forward left of camera. O.K.

The dance hall girl does not appear until nearly halfway through
The Gold Rush. This odd structure reveals Chaplin's difficulty in
constructing scenes that he felt the immature Lita was capable of
playing. Indeed, most extant photographs of Lita from the production show her sitting idle, and the production records indicate that
Chaplin shot few scenes with her. All but one of these scenes were
taken on location at Truckee, California. The exception was the
"forbidden fruit" dream sequence, described earlier, which was
filmed at the Chaplin Studio.

During the production of *The Gold Rush,* Lita became pregnant
and Chaplin ceased production on the film for over three months.
With the growing child distorting her thin frame, and the constant
reminder that Lita was no longer forbidden, sexy, and virginal,
Chaplin began to lose interest. To quell looming legal threats and
scandal, Chaplin married the sixteen-year-old Lita Grey on 25 November 1924, although the relationship had lost all passion for
him. Lita was now his wife, totally compliant and not suited to the
intellectual pursuits of Chaplin and his circle of friends. When
Chaplin resumed production of *The Gold Rush,* he had a new leading lady, Georgia Hale, who had replaced his new wife in the film.
Chaplin discarded the only significant scene he had shot with Lita,
choosing not to reshoot the forbidden fruit sequence with Hale.

Lita's initial influence over Chaplin's next film, *The Circus,* was
her successful urging of Chaplin to cast Merna Kennedy—Lita's
closest girlfriend—in the leading female role of the young equestrienne. Lita described the events leading up to Merna Kennedy's
engagement in the role:

Merna Kennedy and I had been friends ever since dancing school together when we were small children. When Mr. Chaplin made it known that he was planning a film on the circus, it occurred to me that my friend Merna would be ideal for the leading lady and I asked him if he would consider testing her. He did not like me, or for that matter his crew even, to make suggestions about these matters, but he finally, after my pestering him, agreed to make a test of her. . . . Mr. Chaplin was very pleased with the test and paid me a compliment for suggesting that he consider her.[3]

At the heart of the plot of *The Circus*, the equestrienne becomes the cause of the Tramp's losing his ability to be funny. In real life, Chaplin believed his wife was inducing a similar effect. In her sensational divorce complaint, filed on 10 January 1927 during the creation of *The Circus*, Lita alleged that her husband once declared, "Go away some place for a while; I can't work or create when you are here. You are ruining my career." The divorce threatened the completion of the film, halting production for over eight months, as Lita's attorneys sought to attach all of Chaplin's property, including the uncompleted film and his studio.

Desperate to save his studio and his film, Chaplin had nine reels of cut positive and thirteen reels of uncut scenes of *The Circus* packed and removed to safety in New York. Learning from his earlier divorce from Mildred Harris during the filming of *The Kid*, when her lawyers had similarly attempted to seize his film, Chaplin had the foresight to protect *The Circus* before Lita's lawyers could get hold of it.

In the third week of January 1927, shortly after Lita's divorce complaint was filed in Los Angeles, Chaplin suffered a nervous breakdown at the New York apartment of his attorney, Nathan Burkan. The allegations between the two parties would make headlines over the next several months. Finally, on 22 August 1927, after eight months in which Chaplin did not work on *The Circus*, Lita was awarded an interlocutory decree of divorce, a settlement of $825,000 ($625,000 for herself and $100,000 for each son in the form of a trust), and custody of their two children. This volume contains the entire unedited divorce complaint, Chaplin's answer, Chaplin's cross-complaint, and Lita's an-

3. Lita Grey Chaplin in letter to Jeffrey Vance, 29 November 1993.

swer—a tragicomic black-and-white account of the bitter, interne-cine struggle between Charles Chaplin and his second wife.

The divorce from Lita during the production of *The Circus*—a production beset with problems—soured Chaplin's recollections of this difficult period of his life and the film itself. Despite its superb quality, Chaplin only mentions the film in passing in his principal volume of autobiography, *My Autobiography*. For de-cades Chaplin refused to reissue *The Circus*, associating the film with Lita. It was only in 1970, forty-two years after its initial re-lease, that Chaplin revived the film. When Chaplin saw how en-thusiastically modern audiences responded to the picture, his ill feeling toward the film disappeared.

Some of Chaplin's bitterness toward Lita began to fade as he became an octogenarian, but he was still loathe to discuss her. On the rare occasion when Lita came up in conversation, Chaplin reiterated, "I loved all the women in my life, except her."[4] At the same time, Lita took satisfaction in recounting to others her last meeting with Chaplin in the early 1940s, after his marriage to Oona O'Neill, when a tempered Chaplin comforted an ailing Lita in saying, "There are only two women I've really loved in my life, you and the girl I'm married to now."

The continued fascination with Lita may in part be owing to Chaplin's own public silence regarding the relationship, a posture that caused Lita to experience feelings of lifelong rejection, which she yearned to overcome through the accurate retelling of her life's story. "Charlie's autobiography was a purposeful elimina-tion of me from his life story," Lita said late in life, "because for him to include me would have made him look bad. He would have been unable to portray himself as a victim." Indeed, Chaplin makes scant reference to Lita in his two autobiographical volumes, *My Autobiography* and *My Life in Pictures*. In *My Autobiography*, he writes:

> During the filming of *The Gold Rush* I married for the second time. Because we have two grown sons of whom I am very fond, I will not go into any details. For two years we were married and tried to make a go of it, but it was hopeless and ended in a great deal of bitterness.[5]

---

4. Pamela Paumier to Jeffrey Vance, March 1994.
5. Charles Chaplin, *My Autobiography* (London: Bodley Head, 1964), p. 328.

Similarly, in *My Life in Pictures*, Chaplin avoids revealing any details of the marriage:

> My second marriage was even more disastrous than the first. The one good thing that came from it was the birth of two sons—Charles, Jr. and Sydney. Lita Grey had played a small part in *The Kid* before I engaged her for *The Gold Rush*. We were married in 1924 and only remained together two years. The divorce was surrounded by an atmosphere of bitterness and squalor. This period in my life was a time of great professional prosperity but also of private grief. In addition to the unpleasantness of my relations with Lita Grey, I had the deep sorrow of my mother's death.[6]

Despite Charles Chaplin's own bitter assessments of his marriage to Lita, her story is a vital component of the rich legacy of the Chaplin legend. This volume aims to shed light not only on Lita Grey Chaplin but also on Chaplin himself. Lita often remarked that she saw Chaplin as two people, Charles Chaplin the man and Charles Chaplin the artist. She explained, "Charles Chaplin the man was very serious. The artist, when he was in costume, was a humorous man. I love Chaplin the artist. I believe him to be a multifaceted genius. But I also knew the man—in every conceivable mood—and Charlie's real love was his work. Anything that threatened that would bring out the worst in the man." Although young Lita Grey had fallen in love with Chaplin the artist, it was the man she had married. This dichotomy would prove the couple's undoing.

In the final analysis, Lita herself may have provided the best explanation of why this volume is relevant and hopefully revelatory: "I had a unique perspective. I was a typical teenage girl thrown into the world of the Hollywood elite during the remarkable early days of the movies. I never lost my perspective as an outsider peering into a different world. This point of view, I believe, makes my memories all the more interesting."

Jeffrey Vance
Los Angeles, California
1997

---

6. Charles Chaplin, *My Life in Pictures* (London: Bodley Head, 1974), p. 228.

Note on the Text

I feel compelled to expound briefly on my contribution to this volume, as my name appears in tandem with Lita's on the jacket.

The main text was almost entirely written by Lita's own hand, and I believe the historical record is enhanced by that, while at times the fluidity of the writing may suffer for it. My own influence on the creation of the main text was at once editor and compiler, cajoler and alchemist. I can claim complete credit only for the introduction, notes, and other explanatory materials.

As with everything else in this book, Lita had the final say.

Jeffrey Vance

"I'm the Wife of the Life of the Party"

Words and Music by Pearl and Arthur Lippman
Property and Copyright of Lita Grey Chaplin

Verse:
My story has the charm of brutal brevity
I'm married to a man who lives for levity
I could have had a king, or aviator—
but no, I took a prestidigitator . . . magician!
And therein lies the point of my recessional
The poor slob isn't even a professional.
I could have had a famous decorator
I could have had a lightning calculator
But no—I picked a prestidigitator
And it serves me ga—well it really serves me
right!

Chorus:
I'm the wife of the life of the party
I'm the one guest he never would miss
While he's winning renown, as a clown about
town,
I'm sitting, and knitting and laughing—like this!
He makes sounds like the beasts of the forest
He gets laughs when he should get the *bird*!
At parties he's frisky and feted and fed, but
when I
get him home and I crawl in his bed . . . he's
left all
of his "life" at the party instead.
I'm the wife of the life of the party.

Meter change: No wonder I resemble a tragedian
I'm wedded to a drawing room comedian.
He's got a dozen suits, but I look frowzy!
Well—I'll have to take the good with the lousy.
A family, to him, is quite subordinate
He never even asks me to coordinate.
But when he's at a party he is merry!
He's quite the brightest parlor luminary!
You know, sometimes I think the guy's a fairy!
Well it serves me ga—it really serves me right.

Chorus: I'm the wife of the life of the party
I'm the drag on the wag they enjoy.
And while he's dripping wine, down some
    dowager's spine,
I sweetly remark, "Oh he's just a big *boy*!"
He'll be forty-three in December, and if he's a
    boy I'm a *duck*!
It was ten years ago, I came under his spell—
    and he pulled out a rabbit from—well I daren't
    tell.
But when I see a rabbit now . . . *I run like Hell*!
I'm the wife of the life of the party,
And that party is wrecking my life.

The Early Years and *The Kid*

My story begins in Hollywood. My family and I were there from the start. In the early 1900s, long before motor cars would be commonly seen on the streets of the cities, and when movie theaters were called nickelodeons, my grandfather, William E. Curry,[1] and his partner, a German man by the name of Schmitt, had been doing a brisk business in a downtown Los Angeles establishment called the Barrel House. It catered to the better element of the Los Angeles business section. It was a bar-luncheonette; the bar consisted of a row of sawed-in-half barrels strung together with brass fittings, the lower brass rail serving as a foot rest. The bar itself was a sheet of treated highly polished mahogany. A back bar held huge slabs of roast beef and ham, a large bowl of ready-mixed salad, breads, and drinks.

The customers preferred to sit at the bar rather than at the tables, which were freshly set with starched tablecloths and place settings, for here they could pick their choice of meats and have a quick lunch and still have leisure time before getting back to the office. Besides, the food at this "fast-food" bar was free with every stein of beer. A real bargain!

Of late, Wil Curry had not been feeling well. His partner, Schmitty, was a sober man who had taken care of the paperwork and such administrative details as would be needed to run an establishment of this type. Wil Curry was the public relations man, the friendly face who greeted the patrons and drank with them.

---

1. William Edward Curry (1858–1929) was the maternal grandfather of Lita Grey Chaplin. A pioneer of Hollywood real estate, Curry was born a British subject and educated at King's College, London. He became a U. S. citizen in 1885, the year he married Louisa Seymourfina Carrillo.

Wil had been diagnosed as having diabetes. It was now thought that he would have to retire. He sold out his half-interest in the Barrel House for $75,000, a substantial sum in those days. He took the money and purchased, on the advice of his son Frank Clober Curry, a real estate broker, a seven-and-a-half-acre plot of land in a remote area of Los Angeles. Many years later this land would be known as Whitley Heights, a fashionable residential area of Hollywood. At this time, it was populated only with cactus, rolling tumbleweed, sagebrush, and coyotes. Frank had promised his father that he would never regret the purchase; the land would soon be ready for parceling off and, should he wish to sell it, he would be making a substantial profit.

The Currys built a two-story stucco house on the land, bought a Great Dane to guard the premises, and planted palm tree shoots all over the hill. I remember my grandmother laughing in later years recalling such times as when an uninvited visitor lost his straw hat fleeing from the Great Dane down the hill, or when she used grandfather's hunting rifle to kill what she thought to be a skunk. It turned out to be grandfather's black-and-white striped socks lying in the sun, drying over a windowsill.

Wil and Louisa Curry hosted many interesting social gatherings in this house. Louisa, born Louisa Seymourfina Carrillo,[2] had several well-known relations—members of the Alvarado, Pico, and Gage families. Whenever any of these family members came to visit, Wil would get out his best whiskey and be the gracious host, just as he was at the Barrel House. Wil would imbibe a bit himself, in spite of the diabetes.

On one such occasion, a cousin of Louisa's brought along a tall, blond Scotsman named Robert Earl MacMurray[3] to be her dinner

---

2. Louisa Seymourfina Carrillo Curry (1868–1950) was the maternal grandmother of Lita Grey Chaplin. She was the great-granddaughter of Antonio María Lugo, illustrious California land baron. In 1929, nearly two years after the Chaplin–Lita Grey divorce, she helped reestablish relations between Charles Chaplin and his sons Charles Jr. and Sydney.

3. Robert Earl MacMurray (b. 1887) was the father of Lita Grey Chaplin. He was working as an accountant when his daughter was born. Lita seldom saw her father after her parents divorced in 1911. She later recalled seeing him on only two other occasions: in the early 1920s after the release of *The Kid* (1921) and again in the late 1940s. At the time of Lita's divorce from Charles Chaplin, MacMurray had remarried and was working as a printer in Wichita, Kansas.

partner. Wil and Louisa's daughter, Lillian,[4] and this handsome stranger were immediately attracted to each other and in no time were seeing each other on a regular basis. Finally, Robert asked Wil for permission to court his daughter. The two then, after receiving permission from Wil, began spending every evening in the Curry's parlor under the watchful eyes of their chaperones Wil and Louisa. They courted for one year—the unwritten requirement in those years—and were married in a simple ceremony. As a wedding present, Wil generously gave them the limited use of the house for a honeymoon.

The "limited use of the house" turned into many months. It was a big mistake, causing numerous family quarrels, a trial separation, a separation, and ultimately the divorce of a couple who had been very much in love.

I was born 15 April 1908 and named Lillita Louise MacMurray.[5] My parents' two-year marriage was already unsteady when I was born. Unfortunately, my birth did not bring them closer together. My father would leave my mother when I was eighteen months old. I saw my father on only two occasions, many years later. Grandfather Curry was to assume the role of surrogate father. Grandmother Curry, who had had a nervous breakdown before my birth, began to get well again with the cares and concerns of her first grandchild.

At last it was peaceful in the Curry household.

The Currys sold the Whitley Heights house in 1914, and we moved to the Navarro, an apartment building Grandfather had ordered built in the interim. The building was named after one of Grandmother's relatives, José Anton Navarro, who allegedly carried the flag the day Los Angeles was named the "City of Angels" in 1781. The building was located at 925 Alvarado Street—near

---

4. Lillian Grey (Lillie Curry) (1888–1985), the mother of Lita Grey Chaplin, would legally change her name to Lillian Grey after her daughter's public divorce from Chaplin, which became final in 1928. She was born and raised in California; at fourteen she was sent to France to spend a year in a convent in Fontainebleau. Later, she was in the first graduating class at Hollywood High School. She appears briefly as a maid, along with her daughter, in *The Idle Class* (1921) and marched the trail at Truckee as one of the prospectors in *The Gold Rush* (1925). Her marriages to Robert MacMurray and Robert Spicer were dissolved. She was widowed from her second husband, Hal Parker.

5. Her birth certificate, riddled with errors, records her name as Lillian Louisa McMurray. Lillita means "little Lillie" in Spanish.

9th and Alvarado Streets—in the Westlake district of Los Angeles, near Westlake Park.[6] It was during this time that Grandmother began taking me to the Westlake Theater, the popular local movie theater. On a Saturday we would see Pearl White in her popular serial, *The Perils of Pauline*,[7] Ruth Roland,[8] or perhaps Charlie Chaplin in one of his early two-reel comedies. After the movie we would go across the street to the park and feed the ducks. I loved those Saturdays.

It would not be long before Hollywood, considered at the time an outlying community, would become synonymous with Los Angeles. Back then no one ever imagined it as the future mecca for tourists enamored with film stars.

On my eighth birthday,[9] a warm day in the spring of 1916, my mother decided to take me to lunch in Hollywood and, perhaps, to see some movie stars. After a long ride on the trolley and a long walk to Hollywood Boulevard, my mother said she was tired and would be glad to sit down. We soon found a small tea shop where we could have lunch. We went in and sat down near a window where we could look out and see the people passing by on the boulevard. The proprietor of the shop came over to our table, greeted us, then handed my mother a menu. Mama told the proprietor this was my special birthday lunch.

"Before you order," he said, "Would you like me to take your little girl over to meet Charlie Chaplin?"

"Oh, that would be wonderful," said my mother. "That's why we came to Hollywood."

---

6. Westlake Park (present-day MacArthur Park) was a fashionable place for a leisurely stroll when Lita was a child.

7. *The Perils of Pauline* (1914), the Pathé serial of twenty episodes, starred Pearl White (1889–1938) and made her the quintessential serial queen of silent films.

8. Ruth Roland (1892–1937) was second only to Pearl White in popularity as a serial queen of the silent cinema. *The Red Circle* (1915) and *The Neglected Wife* (1917) were Roland serials Lita saw as a child. Lita and Roland were to become friends after her marriage to Chaplin ended in 1926.

9. In several interviews, as well as in *My Life with Chaplin*, Lita claimed to have first met Charles Chaplin on 15 April 1914. She only discovered late in life that this was most unlikely, as Chaplin had made only nine one-reel films and was not commonly known by name at that time. It would appear more likely that she met Chaplin on 15 April 1916, when Chaplin was working at the Lone Star Studio on the corner of Lillian Way and Eleanor Avenue, making nearby Hollywood Boulevard a likely location for Chaplin to be having lunch while in costume and make-up.

The proprietor took my hand and guided me through the tables over to where Charlie sat having lunch with a friend.

The proprietor introduced me. "This little girl wanted to meet you, Mr. Chaplin."

Charlie drew some matches from his vest pocket. "Well, look what we have here," he said. "A pretty little girl who would probably like to see a magic trick." He winked at his friend.

"Pay attention now," warned Charlie's friend. "He's good at this. Bet you won't be able to figure it out."

I stood transfixed. Was this the same man I saw often with Grandma at the movie theater? He looked the same: the baggy trousers, the derby hat, the tattered vest and coat. But it could not be—this was a real person; the one on the screen was not.

A bamboo cane hung on the clotheshorse next to the table, and this man had on his hat. I had been told that gentlemen always took off their hats when addressing people, or at least they tipped them. I was certain that a man should never wear his hat while eating. Who was this man with the fuzzy hair sticking out from under his hat?

I was not watching the magic trick but the strange man trying to entertain me. I had the sudden urge to run, and run I did. Breaking away from the proprietor's grasp, I ran back—threading my way through the tables to my mother.

My mother was astonished. "What's the matter, dear?" she said. "Didn't you like meeting Charlie Chaplin?"

The proprietor had followed me over. "You can never tell what kids will do or say," he explained to my mother, brushing the incident off with good humor. "Now what would you like for lunch?"

While we were waiting for lunch to be served, my mother questioned me. "Did you mind your manners with Mr. Chaplin? Why were you so frightened?"

"It was just spooky," I said.

"You're sure you weren't rude?" asked my mother.

"No, Mama, I wasn't rude. It was just spooky, that's all." And with that remark the waiter arrived with lunch.

That night at home we were told that some movie people were coming to dance in the Navarro's ballroom. Grandfather had one of only a few ballrooms in town, and for some reason it drew many of the film crowd.

Mama said I could stay up a little past my bedtime to watch the people arrive. I opened the door a slit, just enough to be able to see down the hall. I watched entranced by these people who, to me, inhabited a different world from the one I was living in with Mama.

"All right now," said my mother. "You've seen enough. It's almost nine o'clock. Close the door and get to bed."

In bed I stared at the ceiling. I was really puzzled at how I could see the real Charlie Chaplin at a tea shop and yet see an unreal Charlie Chaplin on a movie screen. I could not get the answer. I closed my eyes and finally fell asleep.

Around this time my mother had married again, which was cause for celebration. Mama's new husband was named Hal Parker. He was an assistant director to Cecil B. DeMille[10] at the Famous Players–Lasky Studio. Grandfather was not pleased with the union. To Grandfather, my mother's new husband appeared to be unambitious and without much energy. Moreover, like many business people, Grandfather was suspicious of show people. He used to say they were very unreliable.

Hal was a warm and humorous man who accepted Grandfather's thinking with grace, but he believed that living near Grandfather with his constant criticism would not make for comfort. Grandfather evidently felt the same way and offered us lodgings at the Aragon apartment house, another of my grandfather's investments. He had bought the apartment house with the remaining funds from the sale of his half-interest in the Barrel House. We moved into the Aragon. I was happy now, with a loving father and someone who was good to Mama.

Hal Parker was a wonderful father to me. He would never let Mama tell anyone I was not his real daughter. Even before Hal and Mama married, during their long courtship, Hal began to regularly take Mama and me to various film screenings, as well as to the Lasky Studio to watch the actual shootings. It was on one such

---

10. Cecil Blount DeMille (1881–1959) was the motion picture director and producer who cofounded Paramount Pictures. He directed *The Squaw Man* (1913), the first American feature film made in Hollywood; *Carmen* (1915); *Joan the Woman* (1916); and a succession of other important and influential silent films before turning to such spectacles as *The Ten Commandments* (1923, rem   ?   he is perhaps best known.

visit that I had the opportunity to watch Geraldine Farrar,[11] the great opera singer, slap Wallace Reid[12] in the face with a fish! Hal had tried to explain to me the process by which the film in a motion picture camera is transformed to the screen in a movie theater, but I did not quite understand. However, over a period of time my stepfather had increased my confidence in myself; I was no longer the easily frightened child of a short time before.

But it did not seem to be destined for me to have a tranquil existence for long. Hal Parker was not a well man. Lately there had been times when he called in sick—he was unable to go to work. Some time after his marriage to my mother he had gone to a doctor for a complete physical examination. The doctor advised that he go into the hospital where proper tests could be made.

At the hospital he was told that he should stay about three days to give the doctor time to analyze the results of the tests in case further investigation would be necessary. The doctor had determined that the cause of Hal's distress was in the lung area, and on the third day the results from the second tests confirmed what the doctor had suspected: Hal Parker had tuberculosis. It was the tuberculosis that had been sapping his strength.

Mama and I were standing next to Hal's bed in the hospital, and Mama was impressed with Hal's cheerfulness. The doctor was also in the room, as he had some information for Hal. "These tests tell us that your problems seem to be in the lung area," said the doctor. "No more smokes for you, son, and that's a must!"

"Well, if I must, I must," said Hal cheerfully.

The doctor left and a nurse entered the room. She gave Hal a sleeping pill. She had not heard the doctor's admonition. She put Hal's pack of cigarettes in the drawer next to his bed. Visiting hours were over, so Mama and I had a late dinner in the hospital's commissary and then we went home.

We were home and in bed several hours when the telephone

---

11. Geraldine Farrar (1882–1967), the prima donna of the New York Metropolitan Opera, was signed by Famous Players–Lasky in 1915 and acted in the Cecil B. DeMille films *Carmen* (1915) and *Joan the Woman* (1916).

12. Wallace Reid (1891–1923) was a popular actor of silent films, specializing in portraying young, upstanding American men. He made five films with Geraldine Farrar. The one that Lita saw being filmed was probably *Carmen* (1915), which Chaplin parody in his Essanay release *Charlie Chaplin's Burlesque on*

rang. It was nearly one o'clock in the morning. Mama answered the telephone. It was the doctor telephoning from the hospital. He gave no information but asked her to come to the hospital right away.

My mother got her clothes on immediately and told me to dress. She said something was wrong at the hospital. Mama went next door to our neighbors and asked if I could please stay over for the night. With Mama knowing I would be all right with our neighbors, she quickly rushed to the hospital. The first thing the doctor said, when he met her in the hospital lobby, was that she could not go up on the third floor, as the fire department was there cleaning up the mess. When Mama heard the word "fire," she fainted. The doctor caught her just in time before she collapsed to the floor. When Mama revived, the doctor explained to her the tragic news.

According to the doctor, he had been summoned from home, as there had been a terrible accident after he had left for the night. When he arrived, the firefighters were on the hospital premises, and the third floor, where Hal's room was located, was closed off. It seems that Hal wanted a last cigarette before he would have to give up the habit. Finding the half-smoked pack of cigarettes in the drawer beside his bed, he took one and lit up. The sleeping medication began to take effect, and he dozed off, dropping the lit cigarette on the bed. The mattress smoldered for some time, then the bedclothes caught fire. Smoke and fumes filled the room and were seeping out from under Hal's door. A night nurse eventually noticed the smoke and rang the alarm. Along with an intern, the nurse attempted to get Hal out of his room, risking their own lives to do so. But Hal had been inhaling smoke and fumes for far too long. The night nurse and intern attempted to revive him, but it was too late. Hal had died from smoke inhalation. It was little consolation to my mother to be informed by the doctor that Hal would not have lived long anyway, as he believed that Hal had an advanced case of tuberculosis.

Mama and I moved back to the Navarro, and Mama got a job as a bookkeeper in a small market in our neighborhood. Being at the Navarro, Grandmother could be with me when I came home from school. I was enrolled at a Catholic school called the Blessed Sacrament and later transferred to Grant School, a grammar school, where I graduated from the eighth grade.

The loss of Hal Parker had dealt Mama and me a severe blow. Mama had lost a good husband, and I had lost not only a father but a good friend. Grandfather felt terrible when he remembered accusing Hal of being a loafer. He attempted to console us, but it provided little comfort. These were melancholy days—the Great War, now called the First World War, was raging, and a great emptiness entered our lives as a result of Hal's death. It was not long, however, before our spirits were somewhat lifted by Grandfather's announcement that he was moving us to Hollywood.

"Don't get excited," Grandfather said. "It isn't going to be immediate. I have several matters of importance I must attend to before we can make the move. I have to sell off the apartment buildings, and I'm hoping the owner of a building I have my sights on will be able to accommodate me when I'm ready to come to Hollywood. It's located at the corner of De Longpre and Gower Streets."

It was the late autumn of 1918, and the celebrations as a result of the armistice caused the streets to be overrun with streamers and confetti. The celebrators danced in mad confusion, kicking up the dirt from the streets with their gyrations. My mother went to Hollywood and joined the crowd on Vine Street. In a few days she was down in bed with a bad case of influenza.

For a while, I was in great fear that I was going to lose Mama. She was very ill and living only on fruit juices. My mother was one of many who had contracted the Spanish flu, which had reached epidemic proportions. She was one of the lucky ones— after a long convalescence she recovered. Mama, however, was in the minority. More people died from the Spanish flu epidemic than were killed in the war.

Finally, Grandfather announced that the deals for the apartment houses were in escrow and we could begin preparations for the move. Mama and I had not previously had the opportunity to look over the area where we were going to live. It would all be new for us, as it was in the heart of Hollywood, with several film studios nearby. To the north, a few blocks away, was a small studio where comics chased one another about dilapidated sets, threw pies at one another, and acted as though they were afraid of an old lion who was clearly toothless. To the west, and within walking distance, was Charlie Chaplin's studio. On our block lived Chuck

Riesner,[13] Charlie's assistant director, his wife, Miriam, and their eighteen-month-old son, Dean,[14] whom everyone called "Dinky."

We had been settled and enjoying our new home on De Longpre Avenue for several months when my friend Merna Kennedy[15] came to call and spend the weekend with me. I had known Merna since 1916 when, as eight-year-old girls, we had attended a dancing class together. Grandfather, who was so opposed to having any member of his family associated with theatrical people, did not know that Merna and her brother, Merle, had been doing a dancing act in vaudeville. Merle had recently broken his leg and was still fitted with a cast. This provided Merna the opportunity to become a frequent visitor to the house, where we would chortle over the silly things we had done in our dance class days. We thought it was particularly funny that I had sung a song at a dance review entitled "I Want to Be a Janitor's Child." Merna was naturally graceful and had a talent for dance. I was not so agile. However, this silly song that I sang brought me a favorable critique in the school newspaper: "Lillita Parker is a petite Sophie Tucker."[16]

13. Charles Francis Riesner (1887–1962) had much stage and film experience before joining Chaplin in January 1918. A collaborator on most of the Chaplin First National films, he appeared as an actor in *A Dog's Life* (1918), *The Kid* (1921), and *The Pilgrim* (1923). Riesner was associate director on *The Gold Rush* (1925) and went on to direct films of Charles Chaplin's half-brother, Sydney Chaplin: *The Man on the Box* (1925), *Oh, What a Nurse!* (1926), *The Better 'Ole* (1926), and *The Missing Link* (1927).

14. Dean Franklin ("Dinky Dean") Riesner (b. 1918) enjoyed a short career as a child actor. In *The Pilgrim* (1923), he plays the brat kid. Riesner went on to become a successful screenwriter, writing such Clint Eastwood films as *Coogan's Bluff* (1968), *Play Misty for Me* (1971), *Dirty Harry* (1971), and *The Enforcer* (1976). His best-known television credit is the miniseries *Rich Man, Poor Man* (1976). *Bill and Coo* (1947), which received a special Academy Award, is Riesner's sole director's credit.

15. Merna Kennedy (Maude Kahler) (1908–1944) was recommended for the role of the equestrienne in *The Circus* (1928) by Lita, her childhood friend. Kennedy had no previous film experience, but she had toured with her elder brother Melvin Kennedy (called Merle, his middle name, and Bud at various times) in a dancing act on the Orpheum and Pantages vaudeville circuits. She had an indifferent film career; her other notable film appearances are *Broadway* (1929) and *The King of Jazz* (1930). Kennedy married choreographer-designer Busby Berkeley in 1934. The couple divorced in 1936. Kennedy died of a heart attack shortly after her second marriage to Forrest Brayton.

16. Sophie Tucker (Sophie Kalish Abuza) (1884–1966), known as "The Last of the Red Hot Mamas," was the great vaudeville and burlesque entertainer whose signature song was "Some of These Days."

Proud of the notice, I took it home with me but soon thought better of that, as Grandfather might find it. I quietly took it to our backyard, lit a match to it, and reduced it to ashes. "Can you imagine?" I said to Merna. "My first notice in ashes, at the age of seven."

On one particular day in the spring of 1920, I was on our front porch doing my homework with Merna, when I looked up and saw Chuck Riesner walking along in front of our flat. He was motioning to me to come and join him. He was with a man I did not know. Leaving Merna, I ran across our lawn to join the two men. "Lillita," said Chuck, "I want you to meet Charlie Chaplin." This Mr. Chaplin did not look anything like the Charlie Chaplin I had seen before. I understood from Hal Parker that real people were used for the movie screens and that makeup and costume altered one's appearance, but this man did not look anything like Charlie Chaplin.

Chuck Riesner evidently could see the incredulity on my face. "This is Mr. Charlie Chaplin, Lillita. I've been telling Mr. Chaplin about you and thought you might like to be in a movie. We're using some young people, and I think you'll photograph well."

Charlie spoke. "Would you like to be in a movie?"

"I'd love to be in your movie," I said. "But I'll have to ask my mother."

"Oh, certainly," said Chuck.

Chuck Riesner was fond of me. I was spending a lot of time at his house playing with Dinky; I have always loved babies. Chuck wanted to do something kind for me by having Charlie use me in one of his films.

"You go and get your mother," said Chuck. "I'm sure she'll let you be in a movie."

"All right!" I said. "I'll go get her." I raced across our lawn, stopped on the porch to tell Merna that I would be right back, and dashed up the stairs to our flat on the second floor. Finding Mama in the kitchen ironing one of my dresses, I yelled, "Mama! Mr. Riesner is downstairs with Charlie Chaplin! They want me to be in a movie. Can I? Oh, please can I?"

My mother put her iron down on the metal plate and turned to look at me. Calmly, she said to me, "Why, you're covered with perspiration. Go wash your face."

"But Mama, they want to see you! Will you go downstairs and talk to them?"

My mother was not about to be rushed.

When I passed her inspection, my mother and I went downstairs and met with Chuck Riesner and Charlie.

Mother and Chuck did all the talking. Charlie and I just looked at each other. He was striking in appearance—with coal black hair, which was greying at the temples, and marvelous blue eyes. He wore a grey business suit with a shirt open at the neck and buttoned shoes. He had beautiful eyes, I thought. When he smiled, I recognized the toothy smile of the Tramp I had seen before.

Mama told Chuck that I could be in the movie as long as my education was not neglected and that I was given a chaperone.

"Oh, that's no problem," assured Chuck. "The board of education will make certain Lillita has a tutor for her lessons, and as far as a chaperone is concerned, I don't know anyone better suited for that role than you, Mrs. Parker." Mama was pleased.

And so it was arranged. We were to be at Charlie's studio at ten in the morning. We would be introduced to Alf Reeves,[17] who was the general manager of the studio, and then meet with Rollie Totheroh,[18] Charlie's cameraman. Photographic tests would be made to determine whether I was suitable for films. If all went well, I would be put under contract as an actress for the Charlie Chaplin Film Company, with my mother also hired as actress and chaperone. The film I was to work on was called *The Kid*, and it would be one of Charlie's finest achievements.

When I related the news to Merna, she was enthusiastic and full of questions. "You'll be working for the famous Charlie Chaplin," she exclaimed. "Some say he's a genius." I really did not know

17. Alfred Reeves (1876–1946) managed Karno's Speechless Comedians on their visits to the United States, where he first knew Chaplin from his 1910 and 1912 tours. Reeves was the general manager of the Chaplin Studio from 1918 until his death in 1946.

18. Roland Herbert Totheroh (1890–1967) began his film career at the Essanay Film Manufacturing Company in Niles, California, where he first met Chaplin in 1915. Hired by Chaplin as second cameraman at Mutual, he soon became Chaplin's head cameraman and photographed all the Chaplin films from 1916 to 1947 and remained an indispensable employee until 1954, the year he brought the Chaplin film archives to London.

what a genius was; I just took Merna's word for it. All this was too much for me. I was excited and a little overwhelmed.

Mama and I were punctual for our appointment at Charlie's studio the next day. We met Alf Reeves, who had known Charlie from his days in England with Fred Karno's Speechless Comedians, an organization of comedy players who performed pantomime sketches in music halls. He was a quiet, refined man who made us feel welcome at the studio. We were disappointed, however, to learn from Alf Reeves that we would not be seeing Charlie. He had some pressing business to attend to but had left detailed instructions as to what was to be done with me.

First and foremost was the signing of the contract. Charlie decided that my employment at the studio was not contingent on my screen test. Regardless of whether I could be made to appear older or not, there would be work for me in the film. My mother read and signed the contract. I was to have a chaperone, and my education was not to be neglected as a result of my employment. The contract was for five years. It was understood that the end of each year was option time; if the studio desired, my contract could be canceled at the end of any given year. Mama and I were to receive the combined salary of $50 per week. I thought it to be a considerable sum at the time, for I would have gladly worked for Charlie Chaplin for free. However, $50 per week for the work of two people was a small wage in 1920. Although we did not work every day, we had to be on call for the six-day workweek, and they were ten-hour days.

After the contract was signed, Alf took us over to meet Rollie Totheroh, the head cameraman of the studio. I was made to dress in some of my mother's clothes. My hair was arranged and makeup applied in such a way that I appeared in my screen test to look several years older than I actually was, which is what Charlie had wanted. I was tall for my age, and the makeup and wardrobe enabled me to look old enough to play the role of the flirting angel who tempts the Tramp in the film's dream sequence. It was a role that Charlie had created just for me.

After the test was completed, Rollie had some still photographs taken, as well as a special photograph Charlie had requested. Following Charlie's instructions, I was posed like the girl in Sir

Joshua Reynolds's[19] famous portrait *The Age of Innocence,* for I had reminded him of the little girl in the oil painting. He thought it would make a memorable photograph.

When we had finished with Rollie Totheroh and the wardrobe department, Alf gave Mama a copy of the contract. We thanked him, received our timetable for the following days, and left the studio.

We were not required at the studio for some time. We received information, filtered through the studio grapevine, that Charlie was having marital problems. He had married Mildred Harris,[20] a popular Hollywood actress, in October 1918. A son, Norman Spencer Chaplin,[21] was born in July 1919 and lived for just three days. Norman Chaplin's death proved to be the end of their marriage. It was believed, however, that the baby's tragic death inspired Charlie to make *The Kid.* Further complicating the production of the film was his longtime leading lady, Edna Purviance,[22] who was getting bloated from excessive drinking. For a time, Charlie seriously considered replacing Edna in the film, as

---

19. Sir Joshua Reynolds (1723–1792), the English painter and writer, was the foremost portrait painter in England in the eighteenth century. His painting *The Age of Innocence* (1788) is held by the Tate Gallery, London.

20. Mildred Harris (1901–1944) had been an actress in films since childhood, beginning in 1910. Harris had achieved her greatest success in films under the direction of Lois Weber before she married Charles Chaplin on 23 October 1918 upon informing him that she was pregnant. After the death of their son, Norman Spencer Chaplin, on 10 July 1919, the marriage quickly deteriorated. Harris was granted a divorce on 13 November 1920. Her film career declined after her marriage to Chaplin, and she would later appear in vaudeville and nightclubs.

21. Norman Spencer Chaplin (7 July 1919–10 July 1919), the only child of Chaplin and his first wife, Mildred Harris, was born malformed and lived only three days. The infant was buried with the simple marker "Norman Spencer Chaplin, The Little Mouse."

22. Edna Olga Purviance (1894–1958) was Chaplin's leading lady from 1915 to 1923 and appeared in the majority of Chaplin's Essanay, Mutual, and all of his First National films. Chaplin attempted to launch an independent career for her as a dramatic actress with *A Woman of Paris* (1923), but the film failed to meet Chaplin's expectations. Another film, *A Woman of the Sea*, produced by Chaplin and directed by Josef von Sternberg, was never released. Purviance made one last film in France, *L'Education du Prince* (1927), directed by Henri Diamant-Berger, then retired from the screen. She did, however, remain on Chaplin's payroll until her death in 1958.

she had the key role of the mother of Jackie Coogan[23], the five-year-old star of the picture.

Edna Purviance was a very important woman in Charlie's life, and more needs to be said of her than to chronicle the decline of their relationship, which I saw firsthand. On 15 February 1915, a friend introduced Charlie Chaplin to a very pretty teenage blonde by the name of Edna Purviance. She lived in San Francisco, and Charlie brought her to the Essanay Film Manufacturing Company studio in Niles (east of San Francisco) to work for him. There was no written contract, but it was understood that she would work for him exclusively.

Edna appeared with Charlie in thirty-five films during the next eight years and was, for most of them, his leading lady both on and off screen. However, it was not always a happy time for her. Charlie had married Mildred Harris when he should have married Edna. She was forever loyal to Charlie and endured, at his insistence, two abortions and a ligature tie to prevent further pregnancies.

By 1920, when I came into the picture, Edna had a serious drinking problem. Charlie had to call off shooting several times because Edna was so drunk—literally staggering—that he could not use her in the scene. He had changed his mind about replacing her and thought that if he could get her to tone down her drinking and lose some weight, he could put up with her until he had the time and inclination to make a film starring Edna. This might compensate her for the many years of devotion, patience, and loyalty she had shown him. The idea of such a vehicle for Edna, *A Woman of Paris*, was in his mind a long time before he would make it.

Edna had the best dressing room in the studio, with wicker furniture, carpeting, a tasteful decor of her own selection, and her own bathroom. She was spending a lot of time lately in her dress-

---

23. Jackie Coogan (1914–1984) was performing in his father's vaudeville act at the Orpheum in Los Angeles when Chaplin discovered him in 1919. His performance opposite Chaplin in *The Kid* (1921) began a career that made him the most popular child actor of the 1920s. He also appears in Chaplin's *A Day's Pleasure* (1919) and *Nice and Friendly* (1922), an unreleased film. As an adult actor, Coogan is best known for his portrayal of Uncle Fester in the television series *The Addams Family* (1964–1966).

ing room entertaining men friends like Carl Miller,[24] who played the role of the artist-father in *The Kid*. Charlie did not pay much attention to her meetings as they came and went, but when he started to show some real concern over her condition and the friends she was entertaining, she mistook this for a possible rekindling of some romantic interest. She cooperated with him, and over a three-year period she accomplished a miracle.

In 1923, Charlie's first United Artists release was *A Woman of Paris*, which was a dramatic film he had written and directed but one of only two films he would make in which he did not appear as an actor in any significant role. Instead it starred Edna Purviance, and I remember Mama reading to me at the time some of the excellent notices she received when I came home from school.

In March 1924, I was hired as the leading lady in Charlie's second United Artists picture, *The Gold Rush*. Edna had been enjoying her status as a dramatic screen star. *A Woman of Paris* had relieved her insecurity, but this did not last very long. When I was hired, Charlie had given orders that his new leading lady was to have the star's dressing room. Edna was heartbroken. She had thinned down, curbed her drinking, and given a good performance in *A Woman of Paris*—and now this. An argument between Charlie and Edna ensued, and he eventually appeased her with another film project. But Edna never again occupied rooms at the studio. The film project, which was produced by Charlie and directed by Josef von Sternberg,[25] was never released. She made a film in France and, soon after, retired from the screen.

Mama and I were not sure how we would handle Grandfather's emotional outburst when we finally told him that we had signed a contract with the Charlie Chaplin Film Company. He took it much better than we thought. He was still difficult, as he always could be, reminding me that the dancing lessons he had paid for were to give me poise and a ladylike attitude; it was not the initial groom-

---

24. Carl Miller (Charlton Miller) (1893–1979) acted the roles of the Man in *The Kid* (1921) and Jean Millet in *A Woman of Paris* (1923).

25. Josef von Sternberg (Jonas Sternberg) (1894–1969) had directed *The Salvation Hunters* (1925), for which Chaplin expressed great enthusiasm. Chaplin would hire Georgia Hale to replace Lita as the dance hall girl in *The Gold Rush* (1925) based on her performance in the Sternberg film. Chaplin would later produce *A Woman of the Sea*, a vehicle for Edna Purviance, which was written and directed by Sternberg but never released.

ing for a theatrical career. However, Grandfather acknowledged that working with Charlie Chaplin on a film was an entirely different matter. Grandfather believed Charlie Chaplin to be one of the world's great artists. Also, Charlie, like my grandfather, happened to be English, which was, I believe, the reason that Grandfather did not react in a hostile manner when we broke the news to him of the contract. My grandfather was born in England and had shipped off on a frigate to come to America. Although he had become an American citizen in 1885, he remained surprisingly pro-British.

I was relieved. "Thank goodness for that," I said to myself. "Now at least he might not start on his favorite subject—condemning show people."

Grandfather examined our contract and was pleased with the arrangements. He also told us, based on an interview he had recently read, what a horrible childhood Charlie must have had in the East End of London. He noted that Charlie Chaplin was now a remarkable luminary, not just in America but in Great Britain as well.

Our employment at the Charlie Chaplin Film Company, and Grandfather's supportive attitude, had a terrific effect on Mama. A noticeable change took place. She decided to join a class that met two evenings a week which taught the rudiments of musical instruction. Through all her years growing up, Mama was frustrated by her father not allowing her to pursue a musical career. She had a real gift. Now she would learn to teach music to others.

We had always been a musical family. Many an evening in our family was spent at the piano with Mama playing, Grandfather singing with his mellow bass voice, and me chiming in with my girlish contralto.

Our lives seemed on track now, and Mama looked forward to the time we would be by ourselves. Mama had always worked, ever since Hal Parker's death. In Westlake, she worked as a part-time bookkeeper for a small market in our neighborhood. In Hollywood, she was employed as a filing clerk for a printing establishment. She never had to pay rent as long as we lived with my grandparents, so she had saved her money. Now that she worked for the Charlie Chaplin Film Company, she felt that we should have a car. Mama shopped around and found a Model T Ford for $200 and bought it on the installment plan.

A friend looked over Mama's new acquisition and gave the opinion that the car was in good working order but that we should not drive it faster than twenty-five miles per hour or we would get a good shaking up from the vibration. We now had to live with the fun poked at us when we drove anywhere. The Model T was good transportation, but it was not elegant. Some people called the Model T "Tin Lizzy."

Mama decided to call Alf Reeves at the studio to find out whether we could take a trip, not knowing when Charlie Chaplin would be back to work. He was very pleasant and said that there would be no problem in our going away for a week, and he asked about our travel plans. Mama said that she thought it would be nice to go to San Francisco. "Lillita's father's family lives there," Mama explained. We were on especially good terms with Edwin T. McMurray,[26] my uncle, who was a prominent attorney. Alf bade us to have a good time, and Mama, Grandmother, and I were soon off for a road trip to San Francisco.

Grandmother had packed a simple lunch of sandwiches, cookies, salad, and iced tea for the trip. We were having a heat wave and were wearing cotton clothing to keep cool. Not only the heat but also the car made the trip difficult. We soon found that our friend's advice about our car was painfully true. Mama once had the car at thirty miles per hour and we had a lot of vibration. We had been driving all day with just short stops for gasoline and refreshments, and we had only reached Paso Robles, a little more than halfway between Los Angeles and San Francisco. The temperature was taking its toll on Grandmother. She told us to stop at the nearest inn or hotel. She just had to cool off. We checked into a moderately priced inn that advertised rooms for $6 a night. As soon as we checked in, Grandmother stripped off her wet clothes and ran a bath of cold water. She remained in the bathtub for most of the evening. At dawn the temperature was quite cool. After a modest breakfast we were on our way.

It was evening on our second day of driving when we finally arrived in San Francisco. The ride of some five hundred miles had

---

26. Inexplicably, members of the MacMurray family would cavalierly change the spelling of their surname from MacMurray to McMurray and back again. Lita maintained that her name and the name of her father was spelled MacMurray, the original family surname, and recognized that her Uncle Edwin preferred to spell his surname McMurray.

exhausted us completely. To make matters worse, we had to do all our traveling in the city on foot; the streets were too steep for a novice driver like Mama to negotiate. The car was left at the hotel garage, and we did all of our sightseeing via foot or trolley car. The most memorable part of our stay in the city was when we took the trolley to Golden Gate Park. The breeze from the sea was refreshing, and the city at night looked like a spray of diamonds.

We called on my uncle Edwin McMurray and had a nice visit with him while in town, and we were soon on the road headed back to Hollywood. After two days of vibration—despite the fact that the temperature had cooled down a bit—we were very happy when we pulled into the driveway of our flat. Grandfather greeted us with the news that the studio had telephoned. Mr. Chaplin was expected back at work the next day and we would soon be needed. Mama and I were to come to the studio to watch the rehearsals of a street scene. I could hardly sleep that night in anticipation of the next day. It was to be my first opportunity to watch Charlie Chaplin at work.

The Kid was Charlie's first feature-length picture.[27] In it he pioneered a new type of comedy film with dramatic scenes. It was a big production, and Charlie still had no firm story. Despite these pressures—along with the pressures that Mildred Harris, Edna Purviance, and the film's distributor, First National Exhibitors' Circuit, were placing on him—it was a very happy time at the studio. *The Kid* tells the story of an abandoned baby rescued by the Tramp who raises the child as his own. The five-year-old star of the film was Jackie Coogan, who became the most famous child actor of his time as a result of his performance in *The Kid.*

When I arrived to watch rehearsals, Charlie was beginning work on the newly decorated Heaven set. It was to be a rehearsal in costume, except for Charlie who was wearing his street clothes. Although he was not dressed as the Tramp, he was going through the motions as if he were. Artificial flowers lined the gutter, and all the actors were dressed as angels, wearing white smocks over their costumes on which were sewn papier-mâché wings. Charlie was wearing a harness around his waist. A mechanism had been

27. Chaplin appeared in the first feature-length comedy film, *Tillie's Punctured Romance* (1914), directed by Mack Sennett. *The Kid* (1921) was the first Chaplin-directed feature film.

put together with pulleys so constructed that the wiring, function-
ing with the aid of the property boys, would give the appearance
of flight—a smooth glide from a ten-foot wall with no mishaps.
The key was that the property boys had to give just the right
amount of slack or tautness.

Charlie was ready for the first rehearsal. "Now pay attention,
boys," he said. "I'll give the signal. When I count 'three,' give me
just enough slack to let me get off the wall and enough tautness to
ensure a slow ride down to the street." Charlie climbed the ladder
to the top of the wall and counted out to three. Down came Charlie
with a thud, landing flat on his stomach. He groaned, got up rub-
bing his midsection, and exclaimed, "Who in hell was in charge
of that fiasco? I could have broken my neck!"

The company braced themselves. A quick review of what was
required of the property boys was given, and Charlie was soon
climbing the ladder again. The property boys were ready but nervous. "One. Two. Three!" yelled Charlie. Down came Charlie in
a graceful, birdlike flight, and he landed directly in a group of
simulated angels. He was pleased. "Now that you've got the hang
of it, let's do a take." He called a short break and quickly departed
for his dressing room to get into the Tramp costume. He was gone
about a half hour.

Returning to the set dressed as the Tramp, Charlie climbed the
ladder and called for the cameras. Rollie Totheroh and his assistant, Jack Wilson, began cranking the cameras, and soon we saw
the Tramp leaving the wall in a slow flight to the street. When the
cameras stopped grinding, the onlookers applauded and breathed
a sigh of relief. Charlie proudly exclaimed, "Wrap it up. We'll
use it."

This was, perhaps, the first time Charlie had been pleased with
a first take.

"Go home now," Charlie told the cast and crew. "We've had a
long day," he said, looking quite satisfied.

The story of *The Kid* had caused Charlie much dissatisfaction.
Earlier in the production, before I had arrived, he had stopped
work on the film and completed a two-reeler called *A Day's Pleasure*. Later, he again stopped work on *The Kid* and began a two-
reeler, *The Professor*, which was never released. Charlie did not
know how to end *The Kid*. He had recently been doing a lot of
rethinking about it, and he told me that I had played an important

role in his decision to include the elaborate angel dream sequence. Chuck Riesner had introduced me to Charlie believing he would hire me as just one of several children needed as extras. However, as soon as he saw me, Charlie had other plans—making a screen test and having his wardrobe department dress me to appear older than my twelve years. The role of the flirting angel was created for me, Charlie had told me. He was counting on me not to disappoint him by working hard and taking his exact direction.

Several days later, on 9 June 1920, I was on the set and ready for work on the flirting angel section of the dream sequence. Charlie first explained the scene to me. "Lillita, the Tramp has fallen asleep on the doorstep after looking for the boy—Jackie has been taken away from him—and he dreams that the street is Heaven. You are the little angel who flirts with the Tramp." He then choreographed the movement I was to do as the flirting angel—a sort of balletic dance that lures the Tramp into pursuit.

"Lillita," he said, "I want you to stick your leg out from behind the corner of this set. Slowly count four, then relax. On camera this will be the long shot, then we'll shoot an insert of your pretty face and dark eyes—not a leering look, mind you." I giggled with embarrassment. "Do you think you have that all in your mind?"

"I think so," I said.

"However," he continued, "we'll do it a few times as rehearsal until we get it right."

Charlie had a way of making actors feel comfortable. He would gently coach them from behind the camera as they were performing, telling them what to do. Moreover, he did not care how much film, time, or money was spent on a sequence to get it as perfect as he could make it. The rest of the flirting angel sequence took several more days of rehearsals and takes; it was not a difficult scene, but Charlie would look at the rushes the next day and want to refine and perfect the previous day's work. For me, each day was a pleasure, and I acted not only with Charlie but with Chuck Riesner as well.

Some sections of the dream sequence were filmed but never used in the final cut of the film. One scene involved the Tramp's conception of a lunch counter in Heaven, where the price of a meal was love. This was a common practice for Charlie, who never used a script for his silent pictures. He would try out his ideas on film and either improve on or discard them after looking at the rushes the next day. Some of the most interesting Chaplin moments, in my opinion, were from scenes that were never used.

The flirting angel scene is only a small part of the film's Heaven sequence. I also worked with the other players as background action for other parts of this sequence, and the shooting lasted two months. Esther Ralston,[28] who became a popular film actress a few years later, also appears as one of the angels in the background.

Whether I was needed or not, Mama and I would come to the studio during the last weeks of the film's production that summer. It gave me an opportunity to become familiar with the one-man operation that was the Charlie Chaplin Film Company.

Charlie Chaplin's studio was located at 1416 North La Brea Avenue, Hollywood, at the corner of De Longpre and La Brea Avenues, and covered five acres. The back part, facing east, was an orange grove. The front of the property, on La Brea, had a long line of offices—the reception area, bookkeeping, Mr. Reeves's office, and Charlie's dressing room. Also on the La Brea side was the auto gate, at which sat an elderly man in a boxlike room who would inspect incoming traffic. The auto gate opened onto a driveway that led back to a garage where Charlie's car, a Locomobile, would be parked when Charlie was at work. He was always driven to work by his valet-chauffeur Toraichi Kono.[29]

A large ten-bedroom house that faced Sunset Boulevard was used by Charlie's half-brother Sydney[30] and his wife, Minnie. A small house behind it was the Toraichi family home.

---

28. Esther Ralston (1903–1994) was known for a time as "the American Venus" for her starring role in the 1926 film of that name. She was an extra in *The Kid* (1921) before becoming a popular silent film actress in the 1920s, appearing in such films as *Peter Pan* (1924) and *Old Ironsides* (1926). (See *Some Day We'll Laugh: An Autobiography,* by Esther Raiston [Scarecrow Press, 1985])

29. Toraichi Kono (b. 1888) began as Charles Chaplin's chauffeur and eventually became his personal assistant, valet, and confidant. Kono was employed by Chaplin from 1916 to 1934. He can be briefly seen playing a chauffeur in the Chaplin films *The Adventurer* (1917), *How to Make Movies* (an unreleased short of 1918), and *A Day's Pleasure* (1919).

30. Sydney Chaplin (Sidney John Hill) (1885–1965) was the elder half-brother of Charles Chaplin. His reputed father was called Sidney Hawkes, but Sydney adopted the name Chaplin early in life. He joined Karno's Speechless Comedians in 1906. Sydney Chaplin later managed the business interests of his famous half-brother. His film appearances include the Charlie Chaplin comedies *A Dog's Life* (1918), *The Bond* (1918), *Shoulder Arms* (1918), *Pay Day* (1922), and *The Pilgrim* (1923), as well as *Charley's Aunt* (1925) and *The Better 'Ole* (1926). Sydney Chaplin later retired to the south of France with his second wife, Gypsy.

Beside the auto gate driveway, on a second level, were the film developing and editing rooms. Across the way, down on the south side facing De Longpre, was a stage, and above it were the wardrobe and makeup departments. On De Longpre there was a door from Charlie's dressing room to give him an exit if he wished to use it.

The entire studio was protected with wire fencing. Along the south side of the auto gate driveway was a row of dressing rooms; the first and largest was for Edna Purviance, with four additional rooms for the other actors in the Chaplin company.

The very center of the studio had a well-kept green lawn and a small swimming pool. There were times during the making of *The Kid* when Charlie would join the other actors, including Jackie Coogan and myself, for a swim in the pool. Jackie and I used to have fun not only in the swimming pool but also playing in and around the sets. Hide-and-seek was a favorite game of ours. We often had to be cleaned up, as Jackie and I got very dirty playing in the studio.

Despite my very limited previous experience visiting motion picture studios, I could nevertheless see that Charlie's studio was unique. It was a very happy place, and the employees were like a family. Rollie Totheroh, Edna Purviance, Henry Bergman,[31] and Alf Reeves were among the people who made up this family. A charming ritual was practiced with Charlie's arrival at the studio each day. As soon as his limousine arrived in the morning, Alf Reeves or Rollie Totheroh would yell, "He's here!" That was all that was said. It was enough. All of us understood by it that it was time to present ourselves as ready to begin work. As soon as Charlie was in costume or had attended to his morning business, he would be ready to start work with the actors or his crew on one of his two open-air stages.

Charlie was a very private man. Few people, outside of Alf Reeves, his secretary Nellie Bly Baker,[32] or very special guests,

---

31. Henry Bergman (1868–1946), the rotund actor, began his long association with Chaplin in the Mutual Film Corporation comedy *The Pawnshop* (1916). Bergman worked in the capacity of actor and assistant until *The Great Dictator* (1940). Bergman's delicatessen, Henry's, was a popular Hollywood Boulevard establishment in the 1920s.

32. Nellie Bly Baker (b. 1894) was originally employed as a secretary at the Chaplin Studio but soon found herself doing double duty, performing as herself in Chaplin's *How to Make Movies* (an unreleased short of 1918), a slum woman in *The Kid* (1921), and the masseuse in *A Woman of Paris* (1923). She went on to become a character actress in the 1920s, most notably in Josef von Sternberg's *The Salvation Hunters* (1925).

were allowed access to his dressing room. I guess I was very special on the day I asked if I could see Charlie's collection of autographed photos that adorned his dressing room walls. Charlie welcomed me to come and look at them. "I've not had such a request from someone as young as you, Lillita," he said. "Of course you may see them. If you like, you may also watch me put on the Tramp's makeup." I was thrilled and waited for Mama to be busy so I would not be thwarted in my visit to his dressing room.

A short time later I knocked at Charlie's dressing room. Kono opened the door and invited me inside. The first thing I noticed upon entering the inner sanctum was the aroma of Guerlain's *Mitsouko*.[33] It permeated every place where Charlie had been. When I mentioned the fragrance to Charlie, he acknowledged that he had Kono buy it in large bottles. "I love it," he said with a smile.

An entire wall in Charlie's dressing room was devoted to autographed photos of such famous personages as Anna Pavlova,[34] Jascha Heifetz,[35] Amelita Galli-Curci,[36] Vaslav Nijinsky,[37] and Enrico Caruso.[38] All were inscribed to Charlie. After carefully examining the photos, Charlie invited me to sit down. Kono offered me a chair. "You can now watch me as I make the transformation into the Tramp," said Charlie with childlike glee.

Though it was obvious that this room had no pretensions of being anything other than a large dressing room, the furnishings

33. Guerlain, a Paris-based company, still manufactures *Mitsouko*, which is a woman's fragrance.

34. Anna Pavlova (1881–1931) was a Russian ballerina who enjoyed international fame for her performance work, particularly the solo *Le cygne* (1905), frequently referred to as *The Dying Swan*, which was created for her by choreographer Michel Fokine.

35. Jascha Heifetz (1901–1987) was a Russian-born American violin virtuoso, whom Chaplin had known since 1920.

36. Amelita Galli-Curci (1889–1963) was an Italian coloratura soprano who was a star of the New York Metropolitan Opera in the 1920s.

37. Vaslav Nijinsky (1889–1950) was a great Russian ballet dancer and choreographer best known for his work as the lead dancer in Sergei Diaghilev's Ballets Russes. Nijinsky was appearing in Los Angeles when he first met Chaplin, who was then filming *Easy Street* (1917). Chaplin's comic ballet in *Sunnyside* (1919) was a tribute to Nijinsky's legendary performance in *L'Apres-midi d'un Faune* (1912).

38. Enrico Caruso (1873–1921) was a great Italian opera tenor whom Chaplin had met in New York in 1916.

looked expensive. An impressive three-piece sectional sofa graced one corner of the room, and a large cabinet occupied a nearby wall. On the north wall an open door led to a white-tiled bathroom laden with lotions and monogrammed towels. In one corner was a special setup for makeup and clothes changes. Above where Charlie sat was a curtain on a metal ring that was pulled around to hide anyone changing clothes.

Charlie took a tube containing the base makeup used in films called greasepaint. Smearing it on his face and smoothing it out evenly was the first step in making up. He then used a dark eyebrow pencil to blacken his eyebrows and ring his eyes. He used a giant powder puff to powder all this, then cut a small mustache from a sheet of crêpe hair with a pair of scissors. He applied spirit gum to his upper lip then pressed on the mustache, trimming it as needed with the scissors. "I never comb or brush my hair in the morning when I get up if I'm going to make up as the Tramp," he said as he frizzed up his hair with his hands. "I like the Tramp's hair to look unkempt under his bowler."

Kono pulled the curtain around and Charlie stood behind it, with only the Tramp's head exposed. He looked at me and winked, pulled on his baggy trousers, and put on the oversized shoes and the tattered vest. "Voilà!" he said. Stepping out from behind the curtain, he emerged as the world-famous Tramp. Putting on the derby hat and grasping the bamboo cane, he began to waddle around the room and assumed some of the character's familiar stances. The transformation made a terrific impression on me, because he became a totally different person when he was in costume. It was as if he was in a different world.

I applauded this wonderful performance, and Charlie took a bow. Our revelry was soon interrupted by a knock at the door. It was my mother.

"Well, here you are!" she said. "I wouldn't have known where you were if one of the property men hadn't seen you come down this way. I was worried."

"Well, your daughter's all right, Mrs. Parker," Charlie said. "She's been admiring my photograph collection and watching me make up. Won't you have a cup of tea? Kono has some steeping."

"Oh, no, thank you," Mama said curtly. "We must go now. I've promised Lillita's grandmother we'd take her to lunch."

"Thank you," I said to Charlie, and I followed Mama out the door.

The Kid was released in February 1921 and was a tremendous critical and popular success. Grandfather, Grandmother, Mama, and I all went to see the film at a Hollywood movie theater and were very enthusiastic about the picture. It was subtitled "A picture with a smile—and perhaps, a tear," and we certainly laughed and cried with the rest of the audience. Grandfather appeared proud of my work in the film, and it was a tremendous thrill to see myself joining Charlie Chaplin as a comic shadow on the silver screen. I made Grandmother take me back to see the film several more times that week. Grandmother and I were counted among the many who believed that it was the best film Charlie had made.

It was also in February 1921 that I reported back to work at the studio. Mama and I were to appear as French maids, outfitted with tailored suits and old-fashioned bonnets that tied under the chin, in a two-reel short that was released as *The Idle Class*. We had very little to do in the picture, but it was great to be working with Charlie again.

One day at the studio I met Charlie coming out of his Locomobile town car. He was coming to work and was in a hurry. "I'm glad to see you," he said. "I've been meaning to ask you if you'd like to come to a birthday party I'm giving for May Collins,[39] a friend of mine. It will be at seven o'clock on Friday, and my chauffeur can pick you up."

"I would love to come," I said.

Charlie gave his familiar lupine smile and said, "I've been watching you when you haven't been looking. You have very pretty eyes, my dear." As I blushed, Charlie gave me a playful wink as his exit line and hurried off to his dressing room.

Friday night came, and Mama and I were dressed for the occasion. The doorbell rang and it was a Japanese chauffeur I had not seen before. He spoke little English. "I come for Missy Lillita," he said, and I was surprised he pronounced my name so well.

"That's my daughter," said my mother. "You mean Missy and Mrs."

---

39. May Collins (1906–1955) was a New York stage actress who was sexually involved with Chaplin in the summer of 1920. Her friendship with Chaplin, along with her beauty, provided her the opportunity to appear in several Hollywood films in the early 1920s.

"No, just Missy," he said. "That's my order."

Mama became upset. She asked the chauffeur to wait and closed the door. "What was Mr. Chaplin thinking? He knew that we had an agreement. Lillita would go nowhere without a chaperone. I'll have to find out about this."

She opened the door and told the chauffeur to go home. He had a look of wonderment on his face. "OK," he said. "I tell Mr. Chaplin I couldn't get just Missy," and he left.

The following work day Mama met Charlie in the studio yard. "I'm sorry about the other night," she said.

Charlie was angry. "And well you should be, Mrs. Parker. What possible harm could come to your daughter at a birthday party? I didn't think you'd apply this contract to social events and to me."

When option time came at the end of the year, Alf Reeves notified us that Charlie was not picking up the option. Mama did not know what to think. Had she been wrong about her insistence on a chaperone?

2

The Gold Rush and Marriage to Chaplin

When my option was not picked up by the Charlie Chaplin Film Company, I returned to school at the Cummnoch School of Elocution and also took courses at the Hollywood Secretarial School. I was always an indifferent student. I enjoyed reading and had read many of the great English novels under Grandfather's tutelage, but I was only willing to learn at my own pace and on my own terms.

Mama had married again during the time we had worked for Charlie Chaplin. Her husband's name was Robert Spicer, a nice, handsome man from Alabama who worked as an engineer. There was soon a marital rift over Bob's desire to change his profession and enter the motion picture industry. They separated in November 1923, divorcing five years later. Mama's failed marriage only brought the two of us closer together. We even slept in the same bed.

Merna Kennedy and I were still the very best of friends. We were talking one day about Charlie Chaplin and his work. Merna wanted to meet him. She said, "Why don't we go to his studio? I'll bet he's already forgotten about that misunderstanding with your mother. Just think about it."

During the next few days I did think about it and told Merna the next time I saw her, which was on a Friday when she was spending the weekend with me, that I would stop feeling embarrassed about what happened between Mama and Charlie. "What do you say we go to his studio tomorrow?"

"Good," she said. "I'm glad I brought a nice dress."

I decided against telling Mama where we were going; instead I told her that Merle, Merna's brother, would be driving us to the malt shop for a soda. Merle showed up about eleven in the morning, and we girls were ready.

Merna and I arrived for a visit at Charlie's studio on Saturday, 3 February 1924. We were lucky. Charlie was in the studio's foyer talking to Alf Reeves. He was normally not found in that part of the studio.

He was astonished and full of enthusiasm when he saw me. "Why, it's my 'Age of Innocence' girl!" he said as he motioned to me to come near him. "You have grown to be quite the lady. Come here and stand next to me. I believe you're just my height." I was. We both stood five feet six-and-a-half inches tall. I noticed that his eyes were going up and down my body.

"You're just in time. I've been testing," he said. "I'm looking for a brunette to play the leading lady in this picture I'm making. I can't seem to find the right girl. Would you like to test for it?" he asked me.

"Oh, that would be wonderful," I said.

Charlie had apparently forgot about the incident of almost three years ago, or he preferred not to remember it. "Well," he said, "you're a pretty girl and you're old enough. How old are you, Lillita? Sixteen? Seventeen?"

"Not really," I said. "I'm fifteen."

"Well, that doesn't matter. You look much older than your years. Remember?"

I knew then that Charlie remembered everything but preferred not to make a point of it.

I introduced Merna Kennedy, who asked Charlie what kind of film he was going to make.

"I'm making a film about the great gold rush of Alaska," he said. "Do you remember your history?"

"Oh, sure," said Merna, blushing.

Charlie looked at me and smiled. "Well, what do you say, Lillita? Do you have time to make a test?"

Alf Reeves, who had been busy talking to a bookkeeper, joined us. "Alf," said Charlie, "tell Rollie I want to make a test of Lillita. It might just be that she's the one I've been looking for."

Charlie then excused himself. "I must go now, ladies. I have to look over some work being done on the cabin set."

Alf called Rollie Totheroh on the studio intercom, and I soon found myself being tested once again for a role in a Charlie Chaplin film.

On the way home, Merna Kennedy was full of excitement. "You see?" she said, "You never know what can happen if you're not afraid to take a chance. I told you that you had nothing to lose if you came by to see Mr. Chaplin, and now look what you have gained. You may be working for him again."

Several days went by before Kathleen Prior, Alf's secretary, called the house. Fortunately, I was home to answer the telephone. The secretary said, "Mr. Chaplin would like to see you and discuss your screen test. Could you come to the studio this afternoon?"

"Yes," I said. "I could come with my mother. About four o'clock?"

"That will be fine," she said and hung up.

I decided that Mama had to know about the test, and the sooner the better. I had to take the chance that a meeting with my mother would not change anything at the studio.

Now there was another problem to overcome, I thought. What will happen when Charlie and Mama see each other again? I confessed to Mama that I had not gone for a soda with Merna on Saturday—we had gone to Charlie's studio and that I had made a test for a part in his film. I asked her whether she would come with me to the studio.

"Does he know I'm going to be with you?" she asked.

"Yes," I fibbed to Mama. "He knows I don't go anywhere without you."

At four o'clock we were at the studio. The first person Mama and I saw was Rollie Totheroh, rolling his Bull Durham cigarettes, waiting for Charlie. The three of us reminisced until Charlie entered.

"Hello, Mrs. Spicer," Charlie said to my mother. "I hadn't expected you today, but I'm glad you came. Lillita's test is not bad, not bad at all."

Mama realized I'd been fibbing to her, that she had not been expected. However, she thought better of making an issue of that with me at this moment, particularly since it appeared as if Charlie were planning to hire us again.

"Now let's see Lillita's test. Shall we go into the projection room where Rollie will run it for us?"

The projection room was already dark when we entered. It was not a conventional projection room, but it was where Charlie watched all his rushes and ran his old pictures. We sat down, and Rollie ran the film test for us. When it ended, Rollie turned on the room's overhead ceiling lights.

"You see," said Charlie, "Lillita has the right coloring and looks I want for the girl in this picture. Her age is OK. She looks mature enough. She's always looked older than her years." We then remembered my work in *The Kid* and how the wardrobe department had put my hair up, and with the right makeup and aided by my mother's clothes and high heels, I had looked more like sixteen than twelve.

Charlie finally posed the question: "Well, Lillita, would you like to be a leading lady?"

I was thrilled. "Yes," I said quickly.

"Alf will take care of all the details. I'm afraid I must leave you now. I've got to go see how the prop men are doing with their problems."

Charlie left us, and I had a good feeling that all was going to be well between Mama and him. My immediate problem was going to be coping with the lecturing I would get for fibbing, when Mama and I were alone. Mama had always abhorred deception. I did not like doing it, but I blamed it all on Merna. I told Mama it was all her idea, which was not entirely false. Merna was not supersensitive; I knew she could handle the blame. "Besides," I reminded Mama, "look what came of it. We're going to work for Mr. Chaplin again."

Mama was easier to pacify than Grandfather, who was not pleased with my motion picture ambitions. He told Mama and me, "You two are going to have a bad end dealing with these film people."

It was a few days later that Charlie requested a meeting, and Mama and I found ourselves inside his dressing room once again. The subject of the discussion we knew in advance: a possible name change for me.

"Mrs. Spicer, I'd like to call you Lillian—it's much more friendly. You may call me Charlie. I believe that Lillita MacMurray-Parker is a long, awkward name for such a pretty girl, and what if she should become famous? A shorter name would be better for a theater marquee. What do you think of 'Lita'?"

"That's pretty," said my mother.

"And what do you think about 'Grey' as a last name? I've always thought it to be a fine name."

"Lita Grey," I said. "That sounds nice."

"That settles it," said Charlie. "It's Lita Grey from now on. It will take a while for people to get used to, but name changing is quite common in the theater and in pictures."

A few days later, Alf Reeves and Mama got together and a contract was negotiated. I was signed as Charlie Chaplin's new leading lady at the salary of $75 per week. The day of the signing I remember quite well: 2 March 1924. It was the happiest day of my life. I was to be photographed, so I wore my best dress, which was of black satin and trimmed with marabou. Eddie Manson, one of Charlie's publicity men,[1] had arranged for photographs to be taken to be used for publicity purposes.[2] In addition to the photographs, the studio publicity department had also given out my age—as nineteen.

I was actually not quite sixteen years old, with a new name and a career.

For several weeks after the signing of my contract, I was not needed to work. Nevertheless, I would come to the studio to watch the day's shooting. I was fortunate to watch the majority of scenes of Charlie and Mack Swain[3] in the cabin. Vivid in my memory are the three days spent shooting the celebrated sequence of the Tramp boiling and eating his shoe. The shoe that Charlie and Mack ate was actually made out of licorice. They had many such candy boots prepared, as Charlie kept retaking and refining the sequence. The result of such perfectionism was that Charlie and Mack became sick from eating the shoes and shooting had to be

---

1. During this period, Chaplin's publicity team also comprised Carlyle Robinson and Jim Tully.

2. Two cans of unknown length of Chaplin and Lita, most likely made at the signing of her contract, existed in the Chaplin Studio until 1954. No such footage is now believed to exist.

3. Mack Swain (1876–1935) was the comic heavy in many Chaplin films, who began his film career at Keystone Film Company in 1913. Swain played in twelve Chaplin Keystone comedies and later appeared in the Chaplin First National films *The Idle Class* (1921), *Pay Day* (1922), and *The Pilgrim* (1923). Swain was blacklisted for a time after incurring the wrath of a movie mogul, but Chaplin revived his career by engaging him as Big Jim McKay in *The Gold Rush* at a salary of $250 per week.

called off. Consuming large amounts of black licorice apparently
has the effect of a laxative.

Sometimes shooting would be called off simply because Charlie
did not want to work. Everyone would be at the studio waiting for
his arrival when Alf Reeves would get a call from Charlie saying,
"I don't feel funny today." Sometimes we were sent home, but
most of the time we remained at the studio, as no one knew
whether Charlie would suddenly become inspired and come to
work expecting everyone to be ready for him. The silent Chaplin
films were made without a script. As a result, the day's shooting
depended on whether Charlie was inspired.

Inspiration also determined his temperament on the set. If he
had an idea, he was happy and greeted everyone with laughter. If
he was without an idea—and therefore could not create—he could
be sullen and impatient. If friends visited Charlie at the studio on
a day when he was without an idea, he would avoid them or tell
Alf, "I don't want any visitors," and ask him to send them away.

My first assignment as Lita Grey, Charlie Chaplin's new leading lady for his forthcoming comedy production, was not what
any of his leading ladies had to endure before—an extensive location expedition, which was most unusual for Charlie. We were
to go to Truckee, in northern California. The weather is mild in
Hollywood, but it can be quite cold and the snow very deep in
the northern part of the state. Charlie needed snow for key shots,
primarily the opening shots, which would consist of a long line of
prospectors trudging up a mountainside called the Chilkoot Pass.
The Truckee location had been scouted and approved a couple of
months prior to the journey. A crew had already left to make
things ready for the arrival of the main party, which was to consist
of the film's principal players. We left in mid-April. I remember
that as a birthday present Mama had given me some new clothes
suitable for the trip north.

Sid Grauman,[4] the well-known Hollywood theater owner, was
at Union Station to see our company off to Truckee. Standing in
the private drawing room, Sid and Charlie were talking about the

---

4. Sidney Patrick Grauman (1879–1950) was the film exhibitor known for his
two Hollywood cinemas: Grauman's Egyptian Theatre, which opened in 1922, and
Grauman's Chinese Theatre (now Mann's Chinese Theatre), which opened in
1927. Grauman had participated in the Klondike gold rush of 1898 and acted as an
unofficial adviser on *The Gold Rush*, which premiered at the Egyptian.

plans for shooting the scenes in Truckee. The trainman called, "All aboard!" and Sid made a move to leave. Charlie grabbed him by his coat lapels and said, "Oh, no, you don't. You're coming with us!" He and Sid were good friends and often played practical jokes on one another.

"But Charlie," said Sid, "I don't have a clean shirt, not even a toothbrush."

"Oh, that's all right," said Charlie. "You can wear mine. We're the same size. And I'll buy you a toothbrush."

"Oh, come on Charlie, be a sport, let me go," said Sid. But it was too late. The train had pulled out of Union Station and was already on its way. Sid Grauman sat down and resigned himself to the fact that he was going to take an unscheduled vacation, whether he liked it or not.

I had lived my entire life in mild weather and had never really seen snow before. When I was under contract to Charlie for the films *The Kid* and *The Idle Class*, Hollywood experienced a rare light dusting of snow that did not last long. I did not consider that a true snow encounter. So when our train got into snow covered areas on our trip of nearly four hundred miles, I became excited. "Look, Mama!" I said, "Look out the window. Isn't it beautiful? The sun setting on all that snow looks like a picture postcard." This trip is going to be fun, I imagined—sleighs and fur coats.

We arrived in Truckee just as the sun had gone down, and we were met by four sleighs. There were, however, more people in the Chaplin Studio entourage than could comfortably be accommodated in the four sleighs. Among those in our party were Charlie, Kono, Mack Swain, Tom Murray,[5] Jim Tully,[6] Henri d'Abbadie d'Arrast[7] (everyone simply called him Harry), the

---

5. Tom Murray (1874–1935) acted the role of Sheriff Bryan in *The Pilgrim* (1923) before his engagement as the villain Black Larsen in *The Gold Rush* (1925).

6. Jim Tully (1891–1947) was known professionally as the "hobo" author who wrote the novel *Beggars of Life* (1924). Tully was an employee of the Chaplin Studio for eighteen months during the production of *The Gold Rush*. He later wrote a four-part profile of his former employer published by *Pictorial Review* in 1927 under the title "Charlie Chaplin: His Real-Life Story." Chaplin brought an unsuccessful suit against Tully's *Pictorial Review* articles in 1927 on the grounds that they were unauthorized.

7. Henri d'Abbadie d'Arrast (1897–1968) was a technical adviser to Chaplin on *A Woman of Paris* (1923) and an assistant director on *The Gold Rush* (1925). D'Arrast would later direct two of Adolphe Menjou's best silent films, *Service for Ladies* (1927) and *A Gentleman of Paris* (1927).

studio secretary Della Steele, Mama, and me. Nevertheless, we crammed into the sleighs, together with our luggage, and were deposited in the lobby of a wooden edifice that was meant to be a hotel. Its main room served as dining room, sitting room, and card room. A log fire crackled in the grate, but the heat from it scarcely warmed the large room. Upstairs, we were told, were the guest rooms. They opened out on a hallway that looked over a railing so that you could see the room below. A couple of clerks assigned us to our rooms, and somebody in the company inquired whether dinner had been ordered. We were all cold and tired, but mostly hungry.

"Yes," said the desk clerk. "But it won't be ready for about an hour. That will give you plenty of time to get settled and to freshen up."

This was a typical small-time mountain hotel, but it looked like they were going to give us their best service. Mama inspected our twin beds. There were plenty of blankets—there was even a large, comfortable-looking quilt. A potbellied stove stood over in a corner. It was filled with a small amount of fuel and kindling. "It's a cinch we won't be cold," Mama said. "I guess the management figures on about an hour's heat from this thing to warm up the room." The room was also equipped with a chamber pot and a cuspidor.

There was a knock at the door. It was one of the clerks from downstairs. "I'm ready to light your stove," he said. "It won't take a minute, and this will last just long enough to warm the room when you're ready to retire." He fired up the stove and informed us that dinner would be ready downstairs in fifteen minutes. After he left, Mama said, "Pretty good service for an old rattletrap like this. I'm sure our stay is going to be pleasant." The meal turned out to be nothing you would write home about, but it was not bad. Surprisingly enough, the dessert was delicious and the coffee was excellent. At dinner, we were told by Eddie Sutherland,[8] Charlie's assistant director, what tomorrow's work conditions would be like.

---

8. Albert Edward Sutherland (1895–1974) was an assistant director on *A Woman of Paris* (1923) and *The Gold Rush* (1925). Impatient with delays, Sutherland left *The Gold Rush* after eighteen months to accept a directing post at Paramount Pictures.

The next day found us re-creating the prospectors of the great gold rush of 1898. We were out on the snow for many days, with time out only for lunch breaks back at the hotel and occasional trips to nearby rest rooms. The extras, about six hundred of them, had been recruited from Sacramento. The important opening shots for Charlie's film were to consist of a long line of gold prospectors trudging single file up a steep snow-covered mountain, called Summit Mountain. The Truckee ski club had made a path up the mountain, and we were to re-create the miners crossing the Chilkoot Pass. This scene was to be photographed primarily in long shots and would require many takes, knowing Charlie. Another scene would be of a bear following the Tramp around a curved, narrow, precipitous pathway. The bear was named John Brown. Though trained and tame, John Brown was not behaving properly. The bear's handler, Bud White, thought it best that this scene be done back at the studio where the atmosphere was more controlled and there would be a minimum of distractions. Bud was with the company, so he caged the bear and joined us as a prospector in the opening shots.

I quickly began to dislike the snow. It must be very cold, I discovered, to have lots of snow, and working with Charlie on the exterior scenes required the company to be in the freezing conditions for extended periods. We were not long in Truckee before Della Steele and Eddie Manson came down with bad colds, and Charlie was complaining about feeling feverish. A local doctor was called who took Charlie's temperature. It was 102 degrees. Bed rest was ordered, as Charlie had a bad case of the flu.

Charlie's illness lasted not quite two days before his temperature returned to normal. Still in bed, but accepting visitors, Charlie permitted members of the company to pay him a call, including me. It was good for company morale for the cast and crew to have an audience with him, as it was desolate in Truckee, and many of us were losing our enthusiasm.

Charlie greeted me warmly. "Please sit down here," he directed, patting the side of his bed. "There's no chair in this room."

I sat down on the bed near his feet. Before I could say anything, he bent forward and clasped my hand. I pulled away from him when I noticed a look of unmistakable passion registering in his expressive blue eyes.

Suddenly, he surprised me. He leapt out of bed, shoved me to the wall, and pushed his body against mine. I slid along the wall and managed to get away from him.

"I have to go now," I said. "Mama will be wondering where I am."

"Please, Lita. I can't help myself," he said. "You're so desirable."

Reaching the door, I grasped the doorknob. Turning it, I opened the door and let myself out. What would I do now? I wondered. He is my boss and I respect him. With all the beautiful women, in Hollywood and elsewhere, who would give anything to be pursued by the famous Charles Chaplin, why me? What have I done or said that would make him act this way toward me, and now, how can I be comfortable in his presence? I felt guilty and frightened but somehow flattered that he would want to make love to me.

I did not tell Mama, who was in bed fighting off a cold, what had happened in Charlie's room. I was afraid she would confront him and create an embarrassing scene. I was happy being a part of his film. I did not want to spoil it in any way.

Back at work, Charlie was explaining to me what I had to do in the opening scene. "You're just part of the line," he said, and I did not sense that he thought anything unusual had happened between us. Mama and I joined the trail of prospectors climbing the re-creation of Chilkoot Pass.

Work in Truckee was finished after two weeks. All of us were exhausted and half-frozen. We were to leave in the morning by train bound for Hollywood. We had a last evening playing cards, singing, and telling stories. We even coaxed Charlie to entertain us with a few tunes on his violin.

We returned from Truckee in early May 1924. Charlie was working out problems in the film's story and the possibilities of doing some of the film's exterior shots within the confines of the studio. He was not shooting for the next two months and would not be needing me for work until he got to the dance hall scenes.

When shooting resumed that summer, I watched Charlie and Mack Swain in the scenes involving the cabin teetering at the edge of a precipice. The cabin was a set inside the studio. The floor of the cabin set was on top of a pivot. The set was given further malleability by the hinges built into the walls and roof, and the swaying effect was made complete by the crew pushing the cabin back and forth outside camera range. In the sequence where the cabin is actually slipping off the cliff, the cabin set was suspended in the air by an elaborate system of cables and pulleys. The crew would make the house slip a bit each time the Tramp would cough or sneeze. These scenes, which took many days of shooting, were hilariously funny to watch being filmed. Each take sent the crew and onlookers like me into a frenzy of laughter.

Besides experiments with hair and costume tests, I had very little to do except watch the day's shooting. However, Charlie had a brainstorm to keep me occupied. He would find someone who would accompany him and me as chaperone but would not know she was a chaperone. She would think she was Charlie's date, and I would just happen to tag along for publicity purposes—that way he would not have to include Mama. He could drop the "date" off at the end of the evening, and we would be free to be alone. I went along with the plan, for I had such hero worship for Charles Chaplin I could not resist.

He found the chaperone in Thelma Morgan Converse,[9] the twin sister of Gloria Vanderbilt. Thelma was ideal for this part—she was smitten with Charles Chaplin and convinced that he was enamored with her. Thelma was a very nice woman whom I thought very exotic, as she wore red nail polish on her finger- and toenails, which was uncommon in 1924. Charlie had explained to Thelma that he was proud of me and wanted to show off his new leading lady.

The first evening of the plan was tried out at a dinner at the home of Sam Goldwyn.[10] It was a small party: Sam and Frances Goldwyn,[11] Charlie, me, Thelma, Louella Parsons,[12] and her future husband, "Docky."[13]

---

9. Thelma Morgan Converse (1904–1965) was the twin sister of Gloria Morgan Vanderbilt. At a later time, as Lady Furness, she would introduce Edward, Prince of Wales (Duke of Windsor), to the American divorcee Wallis Warfield Simpson.

10. Samuel Goldwyn (Schmuel Gelbfisz) (1882–1974) became an independent producer in 1925, releasing his films through United Artists Corporation. Goldwyn would later be named as a defendant in Lita's divorce complaint as "Doe Two" for the $150,000 loan Chaplin had given him in exchange for profits of the two Goldwyn-produced films, *Stella Dallas* (1925) and *The Winning of Barbara Worth* (1926).

11. Frances Howard Goldwyn (1903–1976) was the wife of Samuel Goldwyn.

12. Louella Oettinger Parsons (1893–1972) was the notorious Hollywood gossip columnist, syndicated through the Hearst newspapers. Chaplin had first met Parsons in Chicago in 1915, where she worked in the scenario department of the Essanay Film Manufacturing Company.

13. "Docky," Dr. Harry Watson Martin (1890–1951), was a film industry physician who specialized in urology. Martin married Parsons in 1930.

It turned out to be a short evening. Everyone begged off early claiming they had commitments the next morning, but I suspect it was owing entirely to the heated argument that Louella Parsons got into with Charlie. It had embarrassed everybody. The argument had been over the art of the motion picture and the possibility of synchronized dialogue and what effect that might have on films. Charlie had said that when films with synchronized dialogue came into practice, the art of the motion picture would be dead. He liked the idea of synchronized music to film, but sound for speech was abhorrent to him. "In all forms of art—whether it be dance, painting, or sculpture—a great deal is left to the imagination," Charlie said. Louella Parsons had taken the opposite point of view, and the argument went on and on for quite some time between the two of them. One could sense that Louella and Charlie disliked each other, and I never felt comfortable around her. I did, however, like Sam Goldwyn from the start. Charlie respected Sam and enjoyed his company.

On the way back home, Charlie dropped off Thelma at her house, then continued on down Sunset Boulevard toward Beverly Hills. At one point he turned off to drive up Cove Way, where his house was located.[14] "I'd like you to see my home," he said. "I have an interesting jade collection, and I think you'll enjoy seeing the house. I'm very proud of it."

Charlie's fourteen-room house sat on six-and-a-half acres overlooking Beverly Hills. The house was on a hill, just below Pickfair, the home of Mary Pickford and Douglas Fairbanks. We drove up his steep driveway that curved around to the front entrance. Frank Kawa,[15] one of several Japanese servants in a white jacket, met us at the front door. He took my wrap as he ushered us inside. The entry hall, which extended the length of the house, was carpeted with black-and-white checked carpeting. To the right was a large room with a cathedral ceiling that at one end had an organ

---

14. The residence that Chaplin considered home for nearly thirty years is located at the intersection of Cove Way and Summit Drive. During Lita's marriage to Chaplin, the mansion had the street address of 1103 Cove Way. The address later became 1085 Summit Drive, the result of a reassignment in the rapidly developing Beverly Hills.

15. Frank Kawa was employed by Charles Chaplin as houseboy and chauffeur. Kawa would replace Toraichi Kono as majordomo when Kono left Chaplin's employment in 1934.

console. At the other end and up a few steps was a window, behind which was the projection booth from which motion pictures were screened. Frank had disappeared. Charlie opened the door to the left that led to a large kitchen with a long pastry and salad table down the middle. The house appeared to be empty except for the two of us, but Charlie explained that the servants' quarters were in the basement.

We walked along the checkered hallway. On the left was the dining room, all wood paneling. On the right was the living room, which was cluttered with books, a piano, and his jade collection. Sectional furniture faced the fireplace. The room was comfortable, but it lacked a woman's touch. It was essentially an English home in character, despite the outward "California Gothic"[16] appearance, with eclectic color schemes and objects that filled the rooms.

We stepped out onto the veranda, and beyond the expanse of lawns before us we could see the lights of the downtown Los Angeles skyline. The house also enjoyed a distant view of the Pacific Ocean, which was about four miles away. The fresh air on the veranda was most welcome, as the entire house reeked of Guerlain's *Mitsouko*.

"Let me show you a unique feature of the house," Charlie said to me, guiding me up the stairs to a landing. We turned left, and he opened the doors to two bedrooms.

"There don't seem to be enough bedrooms for a house of this size," I said.

"Well, it suits me," Charlie responded. "Besides, I rarely have company who stays overnight."

Down the upper hallway and to our right was the master bedroom. Windows were on the south and west sides of the room—another great view of the lights of the city below.

"Let me show you a wonderful feature of my bath," he said. His bathroom was between his room and one of the guest bedrooms. The bath was attractively designed and featured a steam room, which was uncommon at the time.

"Did you ever have a steam bath?" Charlie asked.

---

16. This is in reference to Chaplin's own humorous description of the architectural style of his home, which he had designed himself and called "California Gothic." Built by studio carpenters in 1922, the house was dubbed "Breakaway House" as it began to fall apart over the years.

I responded through nervous laughter that I had not.

"It might be fun to try it. What do you say? Here's a towel. Take off your clothes and step in. I'll wait for you outside."

I waited until I heard the door of the bathroom close behind him before I removed my clothes and stepped into the steam bath. The steam was gushing out of a vent at a very fast rate. It was only a few minutes until I could not see my hand before my face. I decided to lie down on the marble slab and enjoy the feeling of warmth permeating the air.

Suddenly, I heard the door of the steam bath quietly open and could feel Charlie's hand gently going up and down my body. He was silent for a very long time. I thought to myself that I had asked for this, that I had secretly hoped this would happen, but I was quite timid. Charlie sensed my hesitation.

"Don't be ashamed," he said. "This is an ideal way to make love. We can't see each other."

I relaxed and allowed him to make love to me. It was a warming feeling, and I did not feel much pain. Charlie eventually left the room, and the steam began to disappear.

Out of the steam room I took a shower and then dressed. I was more than a little alarmed to see the blood-stained towels I had left in the steam room. However, I was feeling fine and experienced no discomfort in Charlie's company.

"Do you feel all right?" was his greeting to me as I entered his bedroom.

"It was a wonderful experience," I said. "Do the servants know what we've been doing in the steam room?"

"Perhaps," he said, "but it doesn't matter. They're close-mouthed. That's the way the Japanese are." He escorted me downstairs, and his chauffeur drove me home.

As soon as I arrived home, I got out of the car and dashed upstairs. The driver left, and I found Mama talking to our next door neighbor. Mama and our neighbor were making plans to meet the next day for a sewing session.

When Mama saw me, she said, "Oh, you're home early. Did you have a good time?"

I told her I did and mentioned the heated discussion that took place at Sam Goldwyn's dinner party.

"How was Thelma?" Mama asked.

"Fine, just fine. She's a nice lady" I said.

Mama never suspected a thing. My naïveté was rivaled only by hers.

Charlie's chaperone subterfuge was working well, and the three of us regularly enjoyed evenings at the Montmartre Cafe or the Ambassador Hotel.[17] Sometimes we went to dinners at the homes of King Vidor[18] and Ernst Lubitsch.[19] Occasionally we went swimming at the Santa Monica Swimming Club. No matter where we went, the evening would always conclude with our dropping Thelma off early at her home, and then the two of us would spend some time alone at his Beverly Hills house. It was during this period that I came to understand Charles Chaplin the man. His mind was always active, and he was never far from his work. He began to share with me his ideas about what he was planning to film the next day. I was always enthusiastic about his film ideas. Yet although he would tell me an idea that he thought would be hilariously funny, it almost always never did sound funny to me. I soon realized that his film ideas were not nearly as funny explained as when they were seen performed the next day at the studio, for Charlie was essentially a pantomimist.

However, Charlie enjoyed discussing topics besides motion pictures. Favorite topics of his included politics, of which he was an advocate of socialism, and music. He also relished discussing

---

17. Chaplin was not only pursuing Lita and Thelma Morgan Converse in early 1924 but also novelist and critic Rebecca West (Cicely Isabel Fairfield Andrews) (1892–1983). West declined Chaplin's advances, and when they met again in 1927, Chaplin told West that her rejection of him caused him to regress sexually and pursue the young Lita. He also told West that his sexual relations with Lita caused him to become impotent with mature women for six months. See West's 3 April 1927 letter to her elder sister Letitia Fairfield in Victoria Glendinning, *Rebecca West: A Life* (London: Weidenfeld and Nicolson, 1987), p. 94.

18. King Vidor (1894–1982) was the director of such silent films as *The Big Parade* (1925), *The Crowd* (1928), and *Show People* (1928). Chaplin and Vidor were particularly close in the early 1930s, and the two remained friends throughout the years.

19. Ernst Lubitsch (1892–1947) was the German-born film director who came to Hollywood to direct Mary Pickford in *Rosita* (1923). Lubitsch's important silent films include *The Marriage Circle* (1924) and *Lady Windermere's Fan* (1925). Lubitsch was said to be influenced by Chaplin's *A Woman of Paris* (1923), yet he had made sophisticated, comedy-of-manners films like *A Woman of Paris*prior to Chaplin's film, as did Mauritz Stiller and Cecil B. DeMille.

things that can only be described as macabre—violent crime, disease, murder. The Leopold and Loeb case[20] fascinated him, and he would often bring it up for discussion. He read *The Police Gazette* and *True Crime* and gave me issues to read so I could become current on such cases.

The story of Napoleon had fascinated Charlie since he was a boy, and he often told me he wanted to make a film of Napoleon and Josephine.[21] He felt that I would make the perfect Josephine, and sometimes he called me in private "My Empress Josephine." Occasionally, when his enthusiasm for *The Gold Rush* was waning, he would lift his spirits by telling me his plans for the film about Napoleon.

Charlie accused me on several occasions of being the cause of his film work suffering. He said he now found it difficult to concentrate on *The Gold Rush*, as he was always planning where we would go in the evenings and how soon we could get rid of Thelma Morgan Converse without her becoming suspicious. I too spent most of my days thinking about those evenings, mainly because I loved being with the great Charlie Chaplin, but partly because there was so little for me to do at the studio during the day.

We would invariably end the evenings in his bedroom; he al-

20. The trial of two teenage youths, Nathan Leopold Jr. and Richard Loeb, for murder was one of the notorious criminal cases of the 1920s. On 22 May 1924, Bobby Franks, aged fourteen years, was found murdered near his home outside Chicago, Illinois. Leopold and Loeb, university educated and of wealthy families, later confessed to the killing; their motive was the excitement of committing a perfect murder that would be incapable of detection. At their trial in July 1924, Clarence Darrow as defense counsel saved them from execution, but they were given life sentences for murder and sentenced to ninety-nine years for kidnapping. Chaplin retained a lifetime fascination of the personalities of the killers. He read Meyer Levin's book *Compulsion* (1956), which was based on the case, and discussed it with Richard Meryman ten years later in Meryman's extended 1966 interview with Chaplin. Chaplin's interest in the macabre was given artistic expression in his film *Monsieur Verdoux* (1947), subtitled "A Comedy of Murders."

21. Napoleon Bonaparte had intrigued Chaplin since early childhood, when his mother told him that his father resembled the emperor. In 1922, when searching for a dramatic vehicle for Edna Purviance, Chaplin first entertained the notion of a film about Napoleon and Josephine. As Lita suggests in her text, Chaplin promised many women the role of Josephine over the years—Merna Kennedy, Raquel Meller, and Paulette Goddard among them. Chaplin had still photographs made of himself in the role in the early 1930s. In 1936, after much work in finding a suitable script, Chaplin abandoned his efforts to bring his interpretation of the Little Corporal to the screen.

ways wanted to make love to me. Contraceptives were never used; Charlie believed that there was no danger of my becoming pregnant. I was young and totally inexperienced—I had never even been on a date before—and I had such complete hero worship for Charlie Chaplin that I trusted him implicitly. As I look back on those evenings, it astounds me that Charlie was never troubled by the possibility of my becoming pregnant. I can only attribute this to the childlike nature of the man.

After a short while, Thelma Morgan Converse became aware of her true role in our frequent nights out. In the middle of dinner at Musso & Frank Grill one evening, she walked out and refused to have anything further to do with Charlie. I was now without a chaperone.

Charlie, however, was becoming overconfident. He arranged for a swimming party at his home, to which Mama and I were invited. Alf Reeves telephoned and extended the invitation. Mama accepted and was excited at the possibility of visiting Charlie's home. I understood immediately why he was having a party—it was a means to provide us an opportunity to be alone together.

Sunday proved to be a hot day. It was the end of August and without a cloud in the sky, a perfect day for a swimming party. We arrived at Charlie's house at 1103 Cove Way at about two in the afternoon in our new car. Mama had traded our Tin Lizzy for a Studebaker. She felt the old Ford car had seen better days and was not fitting for a leading lady at the Charlie Chaplin Film Company.

Frank Kawa, the houseboy, opened the door for us, and I was a bit apprehensive when I realized that he could ruin the subterfuge if he showed any sign indicating that I was a frequent visitor to the Chaplin home. I had to pretend to Mama that I had never been in the house before. I need not have worried, for Frank did not change expression. He greeted us with a deadpan face, then disappeared.

Charlie came into the foyer to greet us. "You brought your swimsuits?" he inquired. "The change rooms are down next to the pool, but I'd like to introduce you to some of my guests who have arrived early." Charlie escorted us through the glass doors in the living room, down across a path that led to a lower level where the swimming pool and change rooms were located. Around the pool had been set tables, chairs, and place settings for the buffet.

Mama and I were introduced to Dr. Cecil Reynolds,[22] the prominent English brain surgeon, who had aspirations of becoming a
professional actor. Someone had told me about the good doctor
when I saw him from a distance visiting Charlie one day at the
studio. He was a tall, skeletal man with piercing eyes. Alf Reeves
and his wife Amy were also in attendance, as well as King Vidor
and Eleanor Boardman.[23] Everyone had their bathing suits on, so
Mama and I went in to the change rooms to get dressed.

At four o'clock, Frank and a kitchen helper began preparing the
cold buffet. By this time other guests had arrived, and rounds of
iced drinks had been served. Mama and I settled down at one of
the tables with King Vidor and Eleanor Boardman. The conversation was mostly related to motion pictures, although the subject of
spiritualism—then a topic in vogue—was also discussed. I enjoyed King Vidor's dry wit and Eleanor's charm. King was, at the
time, making what would become one of his greatest successes,
The Big Parade.

The party started thinning out at about six o'clock, and Charlie
took Mama aside. "Why don't you stay over, Lillian? I haven't
seen much of you and Lita lately. I'd like your company. You
don't have anything of importance to do tonight or tomorrow, do
you? I was thinking I'd take tomorrow off. I'm tired!" An odd
request, I thought.

"All right, Charlie, I can't resist an opportunity to be waited
on," Mama laughed. "You're spoiling us!"

"So enjoy it," he responded.

The last guests to leave were Dr. Reynolds and his wife. Charlie
saw them to the front door and came back to join Mama and me
in the living room. Mama was admiring Charlie's jade collection.

Frank entered the room and raised the dark shades that had been
down during the day to keep the afternoon sun from heating the
room. "Great thing about California," Charlie said as he entered

22. Dr. Cecil Edward Reynolds (1880–1947) was a friend and neighbor of
Charles Chaplin in Beverly Hills. His medical insight, passion for acting, and
obsessive-compulsive disorders were to provide Chaplin with an amusing and fas-
cinating friendship until Reynolds's suicide in 1947. Reynolds appears briefly as
the minister in *Modern Times* (1936).

23. Eleanor Boardman (1898–1991) was the silent film actress best remembered
for her performance in King Vidor's *The Crowd* (1928). Boardman and Vidor were
married from 1926 to 1934.

the room, watching Frank intently all the while. "In summer the days may be hot, but it cools down by evening—wonderful climate here."

The three of us walked out onto the veranda. The lights of the city had not yet come on. The sun was on the horizon. It was beginning to become quite cool.

Frank soon called out from inside, "Mr. and Mrs. Fairbanks."

"That's Mary and Douglas," said Charlie. "They're stopping by for a short visit. I wanted them to meet the two of you."

Douglas Fairbanks[24] and Mary Pickford,[25] sometimes referred to as the King and Queen of Hollywood, came into the living room, and Charlie, Mama, and I came into the house to welcome them. I was so thrilled to finally meet these great film stars. I had always been a Mary Pickford fan, seeing her films with my grandmother at the little cinema on Alvarado Street. I was equally impressed to meet the dashing Douglas Fairbanks, whom I had seen at a distance at the Chaplin Studio when he came to visit.

Mary had her hair done up this night—probably because of the weather—it was too hot for her famous long curls. Douglas was in a light-colored suit, his face tanned to the point of being almost swarthy in appearance. They had a previous engagement and stayed only a short time. They both complimented their friend on his selection of a leading lady, chatted briefly about matters concerning their mutual business concern, United Artists, and quickly made their good-byes to Mama and me.

"It's nice meeting you, Lita. I look forward to seeing more of you," said Mary. Douglas, in a gesture typical of his screen per-

---

24. Douglas Fairbanks (Douglas Elton Thomas Ulman) (1883–1939), the American actor and producer, was a successful stage actor before he made his film debut in 1915. His early films portrayed him as the athletic and resourceful all-American youth, but the films for which he is best remembered are the costume dramas he made for United Artists, the organization he helped found with Chaplin, D. W. Griffith, and Mary Pickford in 1919. Fairbanks and Pickford were married in 1920 and divorced in 1936. Chaplin was to comment late in his life that Fairbanks was the only close friend he had ever had.

25. Mary Pickford (Gladys Louise Smith) (1892–1979) was the great international film star of the 1910s and 1920s, affectionately known as "America's Sweetheart," the girl with the golden curls. Pickford was also one of the film industry's most influential producers. She formed United Artists with Chaplin, D. W. Griffith, and Douglas Fairbanks in 1919 and married Fairbanks the following year after divorcing actor Owen Moore.

sona, made a graceful sweeping bow. They then left us to be on their way to their appointment.

When they had left, I said to Charlie, "I think Mary Pickford has the prettiest face I've ever seen."

Mama interjected, "A typical Irish beauty—blond hair, long eyelashes, clear skin. And Fairbanks—always smiling and full of energy!"

Charlie was amused by our star-struck reactions to his friends. "We've been friends, particularly good friends, ever since we formed United Artists," he said by way of dismissing them as a topic of conversation.

The topic of books came into the conversation, and Mama asked if she might look through his book collection. She had heard that he kept a wonderful library. "By all means, help yourself," said Charlie. "I'm afraid you'll find very little fiction. I like realism— biographies, history, and the like."

I thought this a strange response from a man who made his living creating fictitious exploits for the screen.

"You may find a volume of H. G. Wells[26] interesting. Three years ago I spent a lovely weekend with Mr. Wells and his family in England. He's quite a man!" said Charlie.

We talked about favorite books. He was impressed that my grandfather had made me read a large amount of Dickens. Charles Dickens was Charlie's favorite author, and he acted out scenes for us from *Oliver Twist* and *The Old Curiosity Shop*. We also talked of the history books he had read that discussed the Donner party;[27] it was his research for *The Gold Rush*.

In a short time Frank appeared and asked Charlie when he would like dinner to be served. "Well, I'm not really hungry yet," he said. "I suppose we'll have to eat sometime soon, we can't keep the help waiting." Charlie winked at Frank, but Frank did not change expression. His face was a blank.

---

26. Herbert George Wells (1866–1946), the English novelist and journalist, had met Chaplin in England in 1921. Chaplin enjoyed his nonfiction work *Outline of History* (1920) and the compressed version, *A Short History of the World* (1922). Chaplin would later encourage Lita to familiarize herself with these volumes.

27. In 1846, George Donner and his group became snowbound in the Sierra Nevadas on the trail to California. The privations among the survivors were such that they resorted to eating the corpses, cowhides, and moccasins of their fallen comrades.

It was eight o'clock. Charlie arranged to have dinner at nine. Frank briskly went into the kitchen.

At nine o'clock, dinner was served in front of the fireplace. It was a thrill for Mama and me to have Charlie's undivided attention. We had a delicious dinner—it was plain food, very much in the English taste.

After dinner, Charlie got out his violin and played us some of his favorite tunes. Although he liked classical music, what he played on the violin were mostly his own compositions or the music hall tunes from his youth. I confess I was not too thrilled with what he played, but I was impressed with the way he handled the violin. Charlie was naturally left-handed and had the instrument restrung to accommodate him.

After the recital, Mama and I praised Charlie's talent. He acted embarrassed and did not seem to think his musical talent was extraordinary. He looked at the time. It was very late, and arrangements were made for Mama and me in the guest bedroom.

Frank had made up the twin beds in the guest bedroom, which was adjacent to the master bedroom. As for sleepwear, we were given some of Charlie's pajamas, which were a little big on Mama but were just right for me, as Charlie and I were the same height at that time. "You'll find new guest toothbrushes in the cabinet," said Charlie with the ease of one who was accustomed to many overnight guests. "Hope you have a good night's rest. Good night to you both."

"This is such an unusual experience," said Mama.

"Oh, but it's fun!" I said as I climbed into bed.

An hour passed and I was sure that Mama was asleep. I pulled my bedclothes back. The bed springs creaked a bit as I got up. Tiptoeing across the room and through Charlie's connecting bathroom, I went into the master bedroom and into his bed. He had been waiting for me and clasped me in his arms.

What I did not know was that the creaking springs of the bed had awakened Mama, and she got up and followed me into Charlie's room.

Charlie and I were startled when she entered his bedroom.

"Lillita!" she gasped. "What are you doing? How long has this been going on?" Great tears welled up in her eyes, and she began to shake.

"Please, Lillian," said Charlie. "Don't cry. I love Lita. We've

been together several times when you didn't know about it." He
was already in his dressing gown and comforting Mama. "If Lita
gets pregnant, we'll get married," he told Mama in an effort to
console her.

Mama tried to control her emotions, but she was still shaking.

"Go back to bed, the two of you," said Charlie. "We'll talk
about this in the morning."

Back in bed in the guest room, I stared at the ceiling. I heard
Mama crying for a long time. It was to be the first of many sleep-
less nights for me.

In the morning, Charlie met us downstairs. "Come, Lillian," he
said, "have some breakfast. It isn't the end of the world."

"It's the end of my world," said Mama. "She's my baby. I've
always tried to protect her from any harm." Mama began to cry
again. Charlie sent us home in his limousine.

I did not hear from Charlie for about two weeks, and at the end
of that time it was discovered that I was pregnant. Mama called
Charlie. "I'm taking Lita to our family doctor," she said. "I'll let
you know what he says."

Our family doctor was an Irish-Catholic named Dr. James F.
Holleran. He was head of the Queen of Angels Hospital. After
some questions and an examination, it was confirmed that I was
truly pregnant. Mama brought up the idea of an abortion. Dr. Holleran was emphatic. "No, Lillian, I certainly wouldn't consider an
abortion. You go back and tell the father he has to marry her."

On the way home, Mama said she would talk to Charlie about
the pregnancy. "He has to marry you," Mama said. "That's all
there is to it."

I felt terrible about the whole affair. I felt very much like a
thief—somehow I had stolen something from Mama. I went home
and cried on our bed.

Mama telephoned Charlie at home. I was with her when she
made the call. Charlie told her not to get excited but to keep calm.
He would come by and pick her up tomorrow to discuss the matter. I was happy to have Mama deal with my problem. I was not
emotionally capable of dealing with the consequences of my own
actions.

At one o'clock the next day, Charlie picked Mama up at home,
and the two drove off. According to Mama, Charlie was not
pleased with Dr. Holleran's professional opinion. "Easy for him

to say," Charlie told Mama. "He isn't making a picture with millions of dollars at stake. My career could be ruined with the wrong kind of publicity."

Mama and Charlie were not able to resolve anything in the car. She told Charlie that her great concern at the moment was my grandfather; if he found out what was happening, all hell would break loose. Until some arrangement could be made, Mama told Charlie that he needed to find some place for the two of us to stay. I was already suffering from morning sickness, and it was only a matter of days before my grandparents figured out what had happened to me.

According to Mama, Charlie looked perturbed. "I can't do all this in one day" was his refrain to Mama's suggestions. Charlie told Mama that he would have Kono arrange the rental of a little bungalow somewhere, and that all this would then be worked out. Mama and I could tell, however, that Charlie was looking for a way out of marrying me.

Mama made up a story to tell Grandfather, and Kono found a bungalow where we could stay. By now I was deathly sick—could keep no food down—as I kept to a bed at the bungalow wondering what was going to happen to me.

Several weeks passed, but Charlie seemed unwilling to discuss the possibility of marriage. What Charlie wanted was to arrange for an abortion as soon as possible. If I was unwilling to do that, his other offer was to pay me $20,000 to marry someone else.

Weeks went by and nothing was being resolved. I suppose to precipitate some sort of action, I told Grandfather the truth of what was going on between Charlie and me. Grandfather flew into a rage. "That son of a bitch," he said. "He'll marry you or I'll kill him!" We returned back home. I was still sick, and Grandmother and Mama watched Grandfather day and night, hoping he would not do something drastic like using his shotgun.

Several telephone calls were made. I was not made aware of what was going on with my own future, which, as I confessed earlier, I was emotionally ill equipped to handle even if I wanted to—which I did not. I know that my mother was at a loss, having gotten nowhere trying to handle matters on her own. I am not certain, however, that it was entirely Grandfather and his notifying my Uncle Edwin in San Francisco that forced Charlie to action, for events on the Hearst yacht in November 1924 lead me to be-

lieve that the death of Thomas Ince[28] might also have prompted
Charlie to go through with the marriage.

As I understand the events, W. R. Hearst[29] and a party of friends,
which included his mistress Marion Davies,[30] Thomas Ince,
Louella Parsons, Elinor Glyn,[31] and Charlie, set off on a short trip
on Hearst's yacht, the *Oneida*. On the second day of the trip, Ince
was carried off the boat mortally wounded, and he died a day later.
It is one of the great unsolved Hollywood mysteries. The "official" story is that Ince died of heart failure. The general belief is
that Hearst shot Ince in the back of the head, believing he was
Charlie. Prior to the trip, it was known that Charlie and Marion
Davies were more than just friends. Charlie, Marion Davies, and
Elinor Glyn would never mention the incident, and it was a forbidden topic in the presence of Hearst, which makes the official version all the more improbable. I do not believe it was merely a
coincidence that after months of stalling on marriage, Charlie finally decided to go ahead with our marriage less than a week after
the Ince tragedy. It is merely conjecture on my part, but I believe
that by marrying me, Charlie was also pacifying Hearst. It was a
gesture that implied that in the future Charlie would confine his
attentions to me and not Marion Davies.

Whatever the reason that prompted him to action—whether it

---

28. Thomas Harper Ince (1882–1924) was the pioneer American motion picture
director and producer whose accomplishments include the Triangle Corporation,
which he formed with D. W. Griffith and Mack Sennett, and the development of
the matrix of what would later be known as the "studio system" at Inceville, his
motion picture studio.

29. William Randolph Hearst (1863–1951) was the publisher of a vast newspaper and magazine empire whose very name became synonymous with "yellow
journalism." Hearst formed Cosmopolitan Productions to produce films for his
mistress, Marion Davies. Chaplin had known Hearst and his wife, Millicent, since
1916. Orson Welles's masterpiece *Citizen Kane* (1941) is loosely based on Hearst
and his exploits.

30. Marion Davies (Marion Cecilia Douras) (1897–1961) had been an actress in
films since 1917. Chaplin met Davies during the production of *The Gold Rush*,
when Davies was filming *Zander the Great* (1924). The mistress of William Randolph Hearst, Davies and Chaplin were romantically involved for several years.
Chaplin appears in the Marion Davies vehicle *Show People* (1928) in a cameo role
as himself.

31. Elinor Glyn (1864–1943) was the popular English novelist and Hollywood
celebrity who wrote the romantic *Three Weeks* (1907) and *It* (1927), which were
considered daring at the time of their publication.

was the Ince tragedy, a telephone call from my Uncle Edwin, who reminded Charlie that his having intercourse with a fifteen-year-old girl was seen by the law as statutory rape, or a combination of circumstances—Kono had arrived with some news. We were to go to Mexico for the marriage ceremony in an elaborate cover to avoid the press. He instructed us to tell no one but pack and be ready by tomorrow night. Mama was relieved but Grandfather was furious.

Mama, Grandmother, Uncle Edwin, and I were taken to Union Station and boarded the train to Mexico without incident. However, Harrison Carroll, a reporter for the *Los Angeles Times*, had been sneaking about trying to get a scoop on what the *Times* had suspected all along, knowing Charlie's history with the ladies. We were in a state of fear of being found out by Harrison Carroll.

In Guaymas, Mexico, accommodations were arranged at a small inn, called the Albin, where we waited for Charlie to arrive. When Charlie finally did arrive, Harrison Carroll had somehow gained information about where Charlie and I were marrying. Therefore, the wedding, which was originally to take place in Guaymas, was changed to Empalme, another town, at the last minute for the sole purpose of putting Carroll off our tracks. We were successful; nevertheless, Charlie sent his cameraman, Rollie Totheroh, and a small crew out on a fishing boat to photograph outdoor scenes to confuse any spying reporter or curious Guaymas residents.[32]

Charlie had not spoken to me since the day Mama and he had taken a drive to talk over what they could do about this problem. He now seemed harried and completely humorless. It was a side of Charlie I had never seen before.

The marriage ceremony was performed in the depressing little railroad town of Empalme, a suburb of Guaymas, in the early morning of 25 November 1924. We had to awaken the aged and sole justice of the peace of Empalme, Judge Haro, who spoke no English, to perform the ceremony. The marriage took place in his dusty little parlor. Those in attendance included Kono, Nathan Burkan,[33] Charlie's attorney, Mama, Grandmother, Uncle Edwin,

---

32. One can of scenes in Mexico, 1,600 feet in length, exists in the Chaplin Archives.

33. Nathan Burkan (1878–1936) was the prominent New York–based entertainment lawyer and copyright expert who represented the legal interests of Charles Chaplin as well as many other prominent individuals and companies of the motion picture industry in the 1920s and 1930s.

Eddie Manson, and Chuck Riesner, who had tears in his eyes as he watched the ceremony.

Words cannot describe how grim the wedding actually was. Charlie really outdid himself in arranging the most depressing marriage possible. To make matters worse, I was suffering from morning sickness on the day of the wedding.

After the brief ceremony, we convened for a wedding breakfast. It felt as if we had gathered for a wake instead of a wedding. Charlie was not in attendance. A few hours after the marriage, a morose Charlie went fishing with members of his crew. I did not see him again until late that night, when he joined me in the drawing room of the train headed back toward Los Angeles. I had heard him outside the drawing room saying to his entourage, "Well, boys, this is better than the penitentiary but it won't last long."

In our stateroom, Charlie said to me, "Don't expect me to be a husband to you, for I won't be. I'll do certain things for appearances' sake. Beyond that, nothing."

My throat was dry and I felt nauseated. "Please, would you get me a drink of water."

"Get it yourself. You might later claim I tried to poison you." I staggered to my feet and got the water.

After watching me for several minutes, Charlie said, "Come on, I'll take you outside. The air will do you good." Standing on the platform of the observation car, I stared at the couplings of the train below, breathing deeply the cold night air. Charlie broke his aggressive silence and said to me, "We could put an end to this misery if you'd just jump."

I pulled back closer to the entrance of the sleeping car. I could not believe what I was hearing. If there ever was a Jekyll and Hyde, it was Charlie Chaplin. It was the same Charlie Chaplin who had, only a short time ago, pledged his love for me. It was too much for me to understand. I went back to our stateroom, hoping he had just meant that remark as a joke.

Early the next morning, I was awakened with a pot of hot coffee and the announcement that we would be getting off the train outside Los Angeles to avoid reporters; the press already knew that Charlie and I were married. At Shorb, a deserted station near Los Angeles, Charlie and I left the train and moved with haste to the awaiting limousine. We had failed to dodge Carroll, and we briskly went to the car without answering any of the questions posed to us. A car chase began.

We thought we had lost Harrison Carroll, but we had not. If there had not been a security gate at the bottom of the steep drive-way leading up to the Cove Way house, which responded only to the chauffeur's signal, Carroll would have been able to follow us up to the house. As it happened, only one car at a time could pass the gate.

After arriving at the house, we each went our separate ways— Charlie to take a bath and I to collect myself in the guest bedroom, which was to be my bedroom. We then had lunch together down-stairs. It was just the two of us—no one but his servants were in the house—so Charlie took this opportunity to be verbally abu-sive.

"This marriage won't last long. I'll make you so damn sick of me that you won't want to live with me." He then labeled me a "blackmailer" and a "gold digger" and said that I was "a whore who should have gotten rid of the baby" but instead was going to try and "get money out of him." He disavowed his paternity of the baby I was carrying and insisted he would somehow get the marriage annulled. Such verbal tirades would come out regularly during the course of our marriage. I never fought back; I was ill equipped to spar verbally with him. I usually listened to as much as I could, until I cried and was then allowed to leave.

As the days went on, Charlie's resentment of my very presence never wavered. I found living in the Chaplin home quite depress-ing, isolated as I was in such a large home, and never seeing any-one but the servants who controlled the house. I saw more of Kono than Charlie, who gave me an allowance and established a charge account for me at a drugstore. When Charlie and I saw each other, one of his tirades was usually the result. We only went out once or twice "for appearances' sake," as he called it, while I was preg-nant.

One evening early in our marriage, Charlie came into my room in the middle of the night, woke me up, and commenced on a verbal tirade that lasted until early in the morning. He blamed all his problems on me; Charlie had the ability to make himself be-lieve that everyone was to blame for his problems and that he was faultless. It was during this time that Charlie and I were both becoming nervous wrecks as a result of the hostility he had gener-ated between the two of us. I was just miserable and cried easily. Charlie suffered from insomnia and was becoming paranoid about the possibility that someone from the press was watching him. He had a .38-caliber automatic hand gun and began creeping around the house with it. He even threatened me with it one night. He began to spend most of his time in the bathtub or steam room, taking as many as a dozen steam baths a day.

Despite the fact that Charlie was furious with me and resented my very presence in his home, he still wanted to have sex with me. I could not understand this in the beginning. At first, I thought it was a sign that he was breaking down his resentment and that he would soon be nice to me again, as he was before I became pregnant. I was wrong. A night's intimacy meant nothing in the morning, and his tirades against me would begin again.

My health was beginning to suffer as a result of my surroundings. My chief concern was for my baby. Moreover, Charlie was not working on *The Gold Rush*; production was suspended. It was the opinion not only of my doctor but of Charlie's friend, Dr. Reynolds, that I should be moved into a less hostile environment with Mama for the health of the child.

It was understood between Charlie and me that this would not be seen as grounds on his part for desertion. A document signed by both our doctors stated that I needed a peaceful retreat for health reasons. This pleased Charlie, as he could have me out of the house and resume work on his film.

Since it was clear that Harrison Carroll would be a permanent fixture near the house, moving to a new location would require careful planning so as not to be detected. It was during the middle of the night in early February 1925 that Mama and I were moved to a one-story, two-bedroom house with a double garage Kono had rented in Hollywood. By an odd coincidence the house was located in Whitley Heights, on the very property where I had been born sixteen years before.

The house was a charming cottage, comfortably furnished, with a nice kitchen. We needed help to take care of us, for it was important that we were not seen. Kono then advertised for a couple who would care for a lady and her daughter.

A couple showed up, answering Kono's advertisement. Mama interviewed them. Their names were Tomi and Todah, a married couple. Todah had studied under the chef who had cooked for Kaiser Wilhelm II before the First World War. Tomi was a registered nurse and had taken courses in cosmetics and hairdressing.

Mama was very pleased with them and told Kono that we wanted them hired. Kono approved and made the arrangements for their salaries.

My nausea had dissipated somewhat, and I was feeling much more my old self. I was four months pregnant and could now feel the slightest of movements in my body.

After we had been settled about a week, Todah came to make an announcement: Mr. Chaplin was here. Charlie's chauffeur had driven up and announced his arrival, parked the car in the garage, and told Tomi to tell her husband that Charlie was at the front door. I did not know what to expect.

Mama answered the door. Charlie was in his "charmer mode," all smiles and armed with props—a bouquet of flowers in one hand and a box of candy in the other.

"Come in," said Mama. "I'll get Lillita." Mama left him standing at the door while she hurried to find me.

Charlie appeared rested, kindly, and at ease when I came down to see him. I was not impressed. "Well, you're the last person I ever expected to see here" was my greeting to him.

"Oh, I know," said Charlie. "I know I've said some unkind things, but I didn't really mean them." He then paused. "What kind of behavior would you expect from a man forced to marry a girl and not at his own time? I was frightened of the newspapers. I was afraid it would mean the end of my career. Can you understand that?"

"I guess I could—in time," I answered. He handed me the flowers and candy. I asked him to come and sit down. We started to have our first conversation in many weeks.

"I guess I'll call you Charlie now. After all, I'm carrying your baby." Charlie looked as if he was going to wither away in embarrassment.

"Good thing Kono thought about a two-car garage when he was looking for a house," he said, groping for some way to begin a conversation.

"Yes, that was clever of him," I said.

"Oh, he's smart," Charlie continued. "I can trust him and his judgment anytime."

"I want to tell you about a plan Kono and I have devised," he said. "I want you to live here until you're ready to deliver the baby, then we'll move you back into my house. I've talked things over with your doctor, and he said he can equip the guest room with everything one could possibly need to deliver a baby. We'll keep the birth a secret for eight weeks and then make a formal announcement so the press will think it's the ninth month. That way they'll have nothing to write about."

I had Mama join us to see how she felt about Charlie's plan, as she would have to be in seclusion with me during the next several months. Mama thought it would be fine, so we accepted the idea. Charlie was pleased. In a generous mood, Charlie added, "Lillian, I would like you to consider moving in with us. I'm very busy and often get home late. Lita will be lonesome in that big house with nobody but the help. You could care for the baby and be company for Lita. You wouldn't interfere with my life at all."

Mama said she would think it over. There was plenty of time to make such a decision.

After the initial visit, Charlie's visits became rather regular, at least once a week. He always brought something—flowers, a bottle of perfume, a trinket. He always wanted to make love to me. Mama and the help always gave us privacy. There was the second bedroom, and the help did not live in. I would try to discourage him, but he always promised to be gentle.

An announcement from the studio was soon made to the press that the role of the dance hall girl—the leading lady for Charles Chaplin's forthcoming production—was to be given to Georgia Hale.[34] It was reported that I had given up the part, for I was much too occupied in my new role of Mrs. Charles Chaplin.

Despite the odd circumstances under which we were now living, Mama and I decided to have a good Christmas that year. Kono had provided enough money for our needs to see us through for the months it was estimated that we would be spending in the cottage before going back to the Cove Way house. Charlie said he would come on Christmas morning, and Grandfather and Grandmother planned to join us for Christmas dinner. I was assured by Grandfather that if, by any chance, he and Charlie would meet, he would be civil, for my sake.

---

34. Georgia Hale (1900–1985) is best remembered for playing the dance hall girl in *The Gold Rush* (1925). Chaplin had seen her in Josef von Sternberg's *The Salvation Hunters* (1925), her other notable screen credit. Chaplin and Hale were to become constant companions for several years after his divorce from Lita.

Todah had brought a small tree and ordered a small turkey. Tomi, Mama, and I were trimming the tree when the postman pushed the doorbell and delivered a parcel addressed to Todah. We opened it and the enclosed card read, "Have a Nice Christmas." It was signed "Charlie." Sadly, Charlie never came over to see us Christmas Day.

The weeks and months went by quickly. It was in the early hours of 5 May 1925 that I went into labor.

Mama called Charlie and Dr. Holleran. Dr. Holleran left for the Chaplin house in Beverly Hills. Kono seemed the most prepared of all of us. He had devised a careful surveillance of the area surrounding the Chaplin house to make certain where any newspaper people might be located. There evidently not being any sightings of Harrison Carroll or his associates that could threaten our exposure, Kono made arrangements to transport Todah, Tomi, Mama, and me, together with our belongings, to the Cove Way house.

When we arrived, Frank, the houseboy, helped Todah and the chauffeur unload the two cars used in the trip over to the house, and I was hustled upstairs to the guest suite and put into bed. The suite had been made over into a state-of-the-art delivery room, complete with a pullmotor and a bassinet.

The nurse, who was sent by Dr. Holleran, busied herself with tying some sheets to the lower posts of the bed for me to pull on and unpacking instruments to be sterilized. Charlie was standing at the guest room door. Dr. Holleran examined me and concluded that we were going to have a long wait. The pains were still far apart, and there was very little dilation.

It was nearly twelve noon. The doctor was at our disposal until the baby arrived; Charlie arranged for him to take time off from his hospital duties. As there was nothing he could do at the moment, Charlie took him downstairs for lunch.

As time went on, hour after hour, I pulled on the sheets, perspired heavily, and cried out as the pains grew closer together. By the time night fell, the pains were excruciating.

At this point, Dr. Holleran, Charlie, and Mama alternated in keeping me company. Charlie, to his credit, was nearby for most of the time I was in labor. I remember him in the background, pacing, timing the labor pains with a pocket watch. Dr. Holleran said it would be very soon now. He had Tomi prepare a tub of hot water and a tub of cold water. Instruments had been sterilized. Mama was mopping my brow and trying to console me.

A few more pains and the baby came, ashen colored and not breathing. The doctor cleaned out the baby's mouth, doused him headfirst into hot water, then cold water. He then gave the baby a slap on the buttocks. There was a faint gurgle. The baby took his first breath.

While the doctor had been working on the baby to get him to breathe, I had been up on my elbows waiting for the first sign of life. When it came, I fell back and slept for seven hours.

When I awoke, the baby was in my arms, feeding at my breast. Mama and Tomi were standing over me at the bedside. A boy! I thought to myself. "Isn't he cute?" I said to Mama and Tomi. Wet ringlets of hair covered the infant's head. He looked contented. "How many hours did it take?" I asked Mama.

"Eighteen, I believe," she answered.

Charlie came into the room to see me. He thought the baby's head and ears looked like his. He appeared to be very pleased. We had previously discussed possible names for the baby. If it were a boy, I wanted to name the child Charles Chaplin Jr. Charlie thought the name would be a handicap. I said that the name could only be an asset. We had quite an argument about it—however, I won. The child was named Charles Spencer Chaplin Jr.[35]

To avoid Harrison Carroll's prying eyes, we left for Dr. Holleran's cabin in the middle of the night. The doctor was leading the way, and in our car, with the chauffeur driving, was Mama, Kono, Charlie Jr., and me.

It was a good hour's ride up into the San Bernardino Mountains, and it was good planning on Dr. Holleran's part to bring along Kono, for he said Kono's help would be needed. There would be groceries to purchase, and once we got there he would need to find some extra bedding at the town store. Fortunately for us, they had a good stock of everything we needed.

---

35. Charles Spencer Chaplin Jr. (1925–1968) appeared in the small role of the policeman in the ballet sequence of his father's film *Limelight* (1952), as well as some minor stage and film productions. Chaplin had two short-lived marriages. His only child, Susan Maree Chaplin (b. 1959), was his father's first grandchild. His early life is recounted in *My Father, Charlie Chaplin* (New York: Random House, 1960), which was written with N. and M. Rau. Chaplin's death in 1968 was a result of many years of alcohol abuse.

There was plenty of firewood for the potbellied stove, but we would have to manage without a telephone, electricity, or hot water—there was none. It was a good thing I was nursing the baby.

Shelves above the wash basin held a good supply of canned goods. "You don't have to worry," said Dr. Holleran. "You'll only be here for a short time. Kono will have to get you moved to a better location where you will be more comfortable."

The main idea behind the move to the cabin was to get me out of the house where Carroll and his associates might catch me coming and going. However, as Dr. Holleran warned us, smoke from the cabin would invite visitors to call on us. "As soon as a neighbor sees smoke coming out of the chimney, they'll think I'm here and be knocking at the door welcoming me to an early vacation. I'm never here at this time of year," Dr. Holleran said.

We were in the cabin for about a week when a knock came at the door from a man inquiring about the doctor. "Oh, we're just here for a couple of days," said Mama, not identifying herself. "I'll tell the doctor when he comes. He'll be here tomorrow."

After the man left, Mama went to the town store where there was a telephone. She called Charlie and told him what had happened. Charlie told her to pack our things; Kono and Frank would come for us that day.

We were then moved to a large house in Redondo Beach, and Amy Reeves, Alf Reeves's wife and a delightful woman, came to oversee things. Now we could relax. No one in the area would know who we were.

After two weeks I developed a caked breast, caused by an overproduction of milk, and I started hemorrhaging. Mama took my temperature. It was 104 degrees. Amy called the Cove Way house and got Charlie on the telephone. "Charlie, Lita is very ill with a 104 degree fever. Come with the doctor at once!"

Charlie and Dr. Holleran arrived about three hours later. The doctor immediately went to work massaging my breast. He told Amy to get olive oil from the kitchen. The pain of massaging the lump out was excruciating, and I was screaming with pain. In time, however, Dr. Holleran managed to stop the hemorrhaging.

I slept most of the next day. When I awakened I still felt feverish and sick, but I was glad that Charlie had come to me immediately. It renewed my hope that he did care and that he loved me. He seemed rather perturbed, and an awful thought flashed through my mind. Did this mean that he thought I might die? And was he disappointed that I had not? I remembered his words on the train coming from Mexico: "We could put an end to this misery if you'd just jump." I thought, no, I must think positively.

It was a long two months spent in seclusion in Redondo Beach. The afternoons were warm enough, but the evenings were very cold with the wind from the Pacific Ocean. However, I knew I was much better off at the beach than confined to the Chaplin house— the "cabin fever" would have been maddening.

We were finally instructed to come back to Cove Way. Charlie had finished editing *The Gold Rush* and was now prepared to deal with me. Two days after the premiere of *The Gold Rush*, Charlie's publicity department announced that a son, Charles Chaplin Jr., was born 28 June 1925. Charlie had paid Dr. Holleran $25,000 to falsify the birth certificate.

I guess Charlie felt greatly relieved. Since the birth announcement, he had been in a good mood. He was especially charming to Mama, who had moved into the nursery. I was beginning to hope that, with the arrival of Charlie Jr., he would change and spend more time with me at home. We were intimate with one another once again, and he began to act like the Charlie I had known before our marriage. He was trying to make the best of the situation, I believe, and also trying to educate me. Charlie enjoyed playing the role of teacher.

Charlie gave me books to read during the day, from H. G. Wells's *A Short History of the World* to a well-thumbed copy of *Memoirs of a Woman of Pleasure*.[36] I was particularly intrigued with a biography of Napoleon Bonaparte that Charlie had me read. My interest in educating myself was growing during this period, and Charlie kept a wonderful library. The Los Angeles school authorities had insisted that I continue my schooling after I married Charlie, and a private tutor, Miss Hilden Petersen, was engaged and came to the house for a while. Now I was learning on my own. Not all of my education was academic. When Charlie

---

36. *Memoirs of a Woman of Pleasure* is a sexually explicit eighteenth-century English novel by John Cleland that was first published in London by G. Fenton (a cover for Fenton Griffiths) in two volumes, the first volume in 1748 and the second volume in 1749. Considered obscene in its original form, an expurgated abridgment was prepared by Cleland and published in 1750 as *Memoirs of Fanny Hill*.

returned home from the studio, he would give me lessons in love-
making. He wanted me to learn what pleased him. He told me that
Pola Negri[37] was the most satisfying sexual partner he had ever
had, and he wanted me to equal Pola. I had no interest in sex until
this time, for it was only after the birth of Charlie Jr. that I was
sexually awakened. Charlie's continual sexual instruction produced the inevitable results. Although I could hardly believe it, I
discovered early that summer that I was pregnant again. It had
been two months since 5 May 1925, the real date of Charlie Jr.'s
birth.

Charlie was not pleased with the news. He wanted me to have
an abortion, which I refused. He did not fly into a rage, but he did
say, "What do you want to do, populate Los Angeles?"

During the short period after the official birth of Charlie Jr., and
before Charlie's trip to New York, Charlie had been taking me to
dinners and parties. Mama had expressed her firm belief that
Charlie would continue to change and that he would eventually be
a good husband.

In late July 1925, Charlie, along with Kono, left for New York
for the premiere of *The Gold Rush* at the Strand Theatre. His intention, as he had explained to me before he left, was that he
would be gone for two weeks. As it turned out, he did not return
until mid-October. Charlie was keeping his word that he had no
intention of behaving like a husband.[38]

Charlie's absence gave Mama a little more freedom in the
house, although she scarcely needed it, except for occasional
lunches downstairs in the dining room, she was spending all her
time in the nursery, which was the guest bedroom that faced east-
ward. She had her meals brought up by Tomi. Charlie had said he

37. Pola Negri (Barbara Apollonia Chalupiec) (1897–1987) was the Polish-born
silent film actress who was, at various times, sexually involved with Charles
Chaplin. They had first met in 1921 when Chaplin visited Berlin. When Negri
arrived in Hollywood in September 1922, the two soon became inseparable. The
ensuing public romance was unusual for the private Chaplin; most of their short
relationship was spent announcing and retracting their supposed engagement.
38. Unbeknownst to Lita at the time, Chaplin had an affair with Louise Brooks
(1906–1985) while in New York in the summer of 1925. Brooks was then a performer in the Ziegfeld Follies. She would later gain fame for the two German silent
films in which she acted under the direction of G. W. Pabst, *Pandora's Box* (1928)
and *A Diary of a Lost Girl* (1929).

was sure if she lived with us she would not interfere with our lives, and she intended to live up to that understanding.

Charlie Jr. was taking up all our time, of course. He was a happy baby. Tomi, Mama, and I gave him constant attention. I was feeling pretty well during this period. I did not have the morning sickness I had had carrying Charlie Jr. I had many visitors to the house during Charlie's absence, among them Charlie's friends Mary Pickford and Douglas Fairbanks, Alf and Amy Reeves, and Dr. Reynolds and his wife, Nora.

Charlie was received in New York with great adulation. *The Gold Rush* was considered by many critics to be his greatest work. I know that this was a great relief to him, for *The Gold Rush* had worried him. It was the most expensive film he had ever made, costing nearly one million dollars. Moreover, at nine reels, it was the longest comedy he had ever made, and he was unsure whether the public would accept him in such a long picture. He spent a long time—over two months—editing the film and cut a whole reel from it after the premiere. He told me that "a film is made or broken in the editing." He wanted *The Gold Rush* to be as perfect as he could make it.

The film's reception satisfied him, and he on one occasion remarked to me, "I'm better known than Jesus Christ," which I thought was an immodest thing to say. However, over the years I have found that he was right. There have been more people that have laughed at his humor than have ever heard of Jesus Christ. Even today, the Charlie Chaplin films—particularly *The Gold Rush*—are seen in cinemas and on television throughout the world whereas most of the period's films and books have been forgotten.

While in New York, Charlie had promised that he would bring me a bauble of some sort, as I had complained that I was embarrassed to be in the company of his rich and famous friends without even a fur coat or a diamond ring. To my delight, he brought home a three-carat diamond ring. On the evening of his return home, we had dinner on a bridge table in front of the fireplace. We did not need the fire, but this was a good change from formal dining. He told me after dinner that he had had a nervous collapse in New York and thought he was going to die. As a result of that experience, he seemed a much kinder man and expressed his desire for the two of us to live more amicably. Maybe Mama was right. "Give him time," she would say, "give him time."

With Charlie's return, things were going all right between us. Charlie liked going to only a few select restaurants, Musso & Frank Grill being one of them. We went there one evening not long after his return from New York, and he became intimidated by the waiter while trying to order dinner. He became very embarrassed. I could not quite understand that, but he tried to explain that he felt intimidated by people quite often.

Music seemed to be a form of therapy for Charlie. As a result, he enjoyed attending film premieres (where an orchestra accompanied the silent film) and going to the Hollywood Bowl for concerts, two of our most frequent evening activities. We both enjoyed music, but our musical tastes were not the same. I enjoyed the popular songs and dance music of the day, whereas Charlie enjoyed classical music, particularly music that was somber and melancholy. It somehow stimulated him and helped him conjure up his cinematic ideas. It was one of the things that made me unhappy while I was married to Charlie. His great need for classical music—particularly Wagner—to me was deeply sad and made me feel uneasy.

There were also happy times. In particular was the gala given by William Randolph Hearst and Marion Davies at the Ambassador Hotel in Los Angeles. Anyone who was famous in the film industry was in attendance, not to mention many of the business elite of Los Angeles. The whole room was aglow with special lighting that somehow managed to make the assembled constellation of film stars even more luminous. Hollywood parties of this kind were filled with fun and laughter as well as the gossip, backbiting, and embarrassing scenes one finds in today's Hollywood social events. This party is dated by modern standards in that it was a costume party, and the music was provided by Earl Burtnett's orchestra.

Mr. Hearst, our host, stood dressed in white tie and tails at one of the bars talking to some of the guests who approached him. I could also see Irving Thalberg,[39] Mary Pickford, and Douglas Fairbanks nearby. Some other people I recognized despite their costumes were Marion Davies, King Vidor, Eleanor Boardman,

---

39. Irving Grant Thalberg (1899–1936) was vice president and joint head of production, along with Louis B. Mayer, of Metro-Goldwyn-Mayer, where he personally produced the quality films of that studio from 1924 to his death in 1936.

John Gilbert,[40] John Barrymore,[41] and Rudolph Valentino.[42] Charlie was dressed as Napoleon, and I was dressed as Josephine, an Empire-waistline velvet gown concealing my pregnancy.

Charlie had left me to my own devices, to join the people whom he wished to impress with his Napoleon impersonation. He had left me—perhaps purposely, I suspected—to get away from John Barrymore, who was now quite drunk, even slurring his words, and coming my way. Grabbing my arm he said to me, "There you are, my pretty—what are you doing with that old comic Charlie?" He was dressed as Hamlet and wearing a pair of tights that modesty should have prevented him from wearing. I had a time breaking away from him and retreated to a chair at one of the more peaceful tables near the wall. I enjoyed watching the people interact with each other. I felt very much the outsider. I was the type of romantic teenage kid for whom these people made movies, but since I thought I looked appealing in my Josephine costume, it boosted my confidence somewhat. I kept remembering Charlie's line before we were married: "You're so attractive Lita, and with so much charm, you would make a wonderful Josephine. I'm going to make that film one day soon."

Marion Davies came over to see me. I had met her previously at a film premiere. She was a charming woman with reddish blonde hair and a fine sense of humor. "You look simply radiant in that gown Lita," she said. "What do you think of me as Little Bo Peep?" She whirled around in her costume. "Let's get together sometime soon. I'd like to get to know you, Lita." She was trying to say something else. Marion was known for not always being very articulate, as she had a stuttering problem.

We were interrupted. It was John Barrymore again. Barrymore

---

40. John Gilbert (1895–1936) was one of the leading romantic actors in the 1920s. He is best known for his performances in *The Big Parade* (1925), one of the most successful films of the decade, and *Flesh and the Devil* (1926), with Greta Garbo.

41. John Barrymore (John Blythe) (1882–1942), the American stage and motion picture actor known as "The Great Profile," played a wide range of roles in silent films, the last of which were released through United Artists.

42. Rudolph Valentino (Rodolfo Pietro Filiberto Raffaele Guglielmi) (1895–1926), the Italian silent screen actor, became a sensation with the films *The Four Horseman of the Apocalypse* (1921) and *The Sheik* (1921). Valentino's last two films, *The Eagle* (1925) and *The Son of the Sheik* (1926), were produced by Joseph M. Schenck and released through United Artists.

almost turned over the empty chair next to me, reciting lines from Shakespeare. Marion had the presence of mind to take me by the arm and quickly usher me out of what would have been another difficult moment with Barrymore. She was then interrupted by a guest who wanted her undivided attention, and I found company with Eleanor Boardman and a friend she was talking to in another quiet part of the room.

I then had the pleasure of meeting a couple who, like me, did not need to mingle with a lot of people to have a good time at a party, Rudolph Valentino and his wife, Natacha Rambova.[43] We introduced ourselves and had a nice conversation. Valentino was now a star under the United Artists banner, and he and Rambova seemed happy. I was thrilled when the great Valentino asked if I would care to dance with him. I happily accepted and was gracefully whirled around in his arms. This did not escape the eyes of Charlie, who felt inferior to the exotic screen lover. Shortly after my dance with Valentino, Charlie told me it was time for us to go home.

The whole evening was an unforgettable experience, and I had a wonderful time. Unfortunately, it was to end on a decidedly sour note. Once we were home and had shed our costumes, Charlie announced that he had an appointment. It was now eleven o'clock and I was wondering what kind of appointment he could possibly have at this late hour.

I asked him where he was going. Charlie flew into a rage. He then proceeded to tell me he had a date. There had been numerous late-night rendezvous I did not know about, he asserted. He then proceeded to list several women with whom he regularly kept company. I remained silent. He abruptly left.

I stood at the window as I watched Charlie's car go to Marion Davies's nearby house. For the next couple of hours I went back and forth from the window to see whether the car had returned. Lying in bed I thought of the rumor that had recently reached

---

43. Natacha Rambova (Winifred Shaunessy Hudnut) (1897–1966), a dancer and stage designer, was also the stepdaughter of Richard Hudnut, the millionaire perfume manufacturer. Rambova went to Hollywood to work with Alla Nazimova on her film *Camille* (1921), in which Nazimova starred opposite Rudolph Valentino. Rambova became Valentino's second wife in 1923, divorcing shortly before his death in 1926.

my ears—Marion Davies and Charlie Chaplin were seen dancing together at Eddie Brandstatter's Montmartre Cafe. I did not get to sleep until about one o'clock in the morning. I was awakened at about three when I heard Charlie enter his bedroom.

3

Pickfair and San Simeon

Kono brought me a piece of mail one morning. It was addressed to Mr. and Mrs. Charles Chaplin. It was an invitation from Mary Pickford and Douglas Fairbanks. A dinner party was to be given at Pickfair for Lord and Lady Mountbatten.[1] I had never been to Pickfair or met Lord and Lady Mountbatten. It sounded wonderful to me.

My immediate concern was, What will I wear? I knew I did not own anything elegant enough for an occasion such as this, much less something that would somehow hide my bulging figure. I would have to have something made, and Charlie could be so frugal. Charlie was home, sleeping late, and I did not dare disturb him, but I was anxious to know whether we were going to accept this invitation.

When Charlie awoke, I showed him the invitation. He was having his usual breakfast—bacon, soft-boiled eggs, toast with marmalade, and coffee—which he liked having served in bed. "This should be an interesting evening," he said. "Lord and Lady Mountbatten are very charming."

I wanted to get to the business of what I was going to wear. I mentioned my concern to Charlie. "Oh, I wouldn't worry about that," Charlie said. "There's a designer named Bess Schlank who has dressed some well-known people. Her name comes up all the

---

1. Lord (Louis) Mountbatten (1900–1979) and Lady (Edwina) Mountbatten (1901–1960) had first visited Hollywood in the autumn of 1922, a few months after their marriage. They were guests at Pickfair, where Chaplin was their host in Pickford and Fairbanks's absence. As a wedding present for the young couple, Chaplin made an unreleased one-reel film called *Nice and Friendly* (1922), in which they appear with Chaplin and Jackie Coogan.

time among film actresses. Kono will take you to her salon, and she'll dream up something for you."

"She's probably expensive," I said.

"I suppose so," Charlie said, "but then, for an occasion such as this, I don't think we should try and save money, do you? It's going to take some doing to camouflage that bulging tummy of yours, and if anyone can do it, Bess Schlank can."

The following morning Kono took me to the Schlank salon. Miss Schlank went to work immediately, selecting fabric, texture, and color to suit me. "We don't want you to look *garish*, do we?" Miss Schlank said. "After all, you're a very young lady. I think something soft and pastel, a wide sheath—no waistline of course—maybe chiffon and not cut too low."

It all sounded good to me. Miss Schlank looked at her assistant. "Oh, by all means," said the assistant, "chiffon and pastel."

The date of the Pickfair dinner was soon upon us, and Charlie and I stood before the full-length mirror in my bedroom looking at Bess Schlank's creation.

"She did a fine job," said Charlie, inspecting me in the mirror. "The dress is very becoming, and you don't show your condition much."

Charlie was also pleased with the new suit he was wearing. As was his custom, Charlie would buy four or five identical suits at the same time. He did not care for change when it came to his wardrobe. In addition to the sameness of his suits, his choice of shoes seldom altered. His offscreen footwear was nearly as famous in Hollywood circles as the Tramp's boots. Charlie almost always wore his high button-top shoes of patent leather with grey suede tops, which gave the appearance of spats. They were very much out of date in 1925, but that did not stop Charlie from wearing them. He had them custom made, several pairs at a time. I would open his closet door sometimes and see a row of these shoes, all identical.

Pickfair was just at the top of the hill above us, a couple of blocks from Charlie's house. A steep brick driveway led us to Pickfair's front door. I was very nervous.

Pickfair was formerly a hunting lodge, which Douglas Fairbanks has bought and remodeled as a wedding present for Mary Pickford. It had the appearance of an English country house, situated on eighteen acres.

A houseboy greeted us, opened our limousine door, ushered us in, and took our light wraps. Mary Pickford met us outside the living room. "Hello," she said, motioning us to follow her. "I'll introduce you to some people you don't know." Although I was still nervous, Mary somehow managed to put me at ease.

Charlie knew the Ernst Lubitsches and the Mountbattens, and he had met previously "Puffin" Asquith[2] and his sister Elizabeth, who were the children of England's Liberal Prime Minister Herbert Henry Asquith. I was introduced to all these people, and then Charlie and I were introduced to a tall, blond man with a strange dialect, who had been standing quietly in a corner talking to his date. "He's from Wales," Mary said when we were alone, "and he's here on a special mission for the British government. I've placed you next to him at dinner."

The Mountbattens waved to Charlie from across the room and a squeal came from Puffin Asquith when he saw Charlie. Puffin was introduced to me. He had red curly hair that appeared to have a life of its own. Puffin's voice, gestures, and behavior were very effeminate. That was about all I was able to really absorb about Puffin, as I could only think of my predicament of being seated next to the man from Wales whom I could barely understand. I knew Mary was counting on me to make dinner conversation with him.

I appealed quietly to Puffin Asquith. I felt that he would know something about Wales. "Would you pardon me if I ask you some questions about Wales?"

"Oh, I wouldn't mind a bit," said Puffin. He cleared his throat as though he were going to make some wondrous remarks.

I thought I would clarify my request before Puffin began to make a speech. Puffin was the type of person who did not converse with people—he lectured at them. "You see," I explained, "I'm sitting next to the Welsh guest at dinner, and it's going to be pretty

2. "Puffin" Asquith was the childhood name of Anthony Asquith (1902–1968), who was to become a noted English motion picture director. Asquith was the son of Herbert Henry Asquith and the former Margot Tennant, the Earl and Countess of Oxford and Asquith. Asquith, who was one of the original twenty-nine founder/members of London's Film Society in 1925, came to California that year with his sister Elizabeth (Princess Antoine Bibesco) (1897–1945) and studied filmmaking for six months in Hollywood.

embarrassing if I don't know anything about his country. Wales is a part of England, isn't it?"

Puffin said, "Well, yes, in a way. You see, sometime in the sixthteenth century there were four rivers. These four rivers lie in Wales, and the eastern boundary drawn at that time united England and Wales politically but disregarded cultural and linguistic distribution. Millions of Wales's inhabitants still speak Celtic Welsh, and some use English as a second language."

Puffin was still talking, but my eyes had already glazed over. I was confused. At age seventeen, in 1925, I could hardly be expected to digest the relationship between England and Wales, and what did he mean by a boundary?

"Well, thank you, Puffin," I interrupted. "I'm not sure I understand all of what you said, but at least I know now that Wales is a part of England. I'm sorry if my question led you into such a lengthy explanation."

"Oh, not at all," said Puffin, "glad to oblige."

Charlie and Douglas Fairbanks were enjoying one another's company, so I had a chance to look about at the lovely decor of Pickfair. I did not know much about period furniture, but I guessed this was French. On the main level, the foyer was a room of simple elegance, with a highly polished parquet floor and some attractive chairs and couches from the eighteenth century. The living room, where the guests were enjoying conversation and drinks before dinner, had a light green and gold color scheme, and the lighting was very soft. The decorator evidently understood that side lighting was much more flattering to ladies than overhead lighting, which tended to make one look older. The wall sconces, with their light shining straight on, made the eyes sparkle. The home was comfortable and welcoming—the opposite of Charlie's house. Mary promised me a complete tour. I was delighted at the invitation.

I was in the middle of this reverie when one of the servants announced dinner, and at that very moment John Barrymore, accompanied by a pretty young lady, appeared. Barrymore was without doubt intoxicated, half leaning on the arm of his date. He lifted a cocktail from the butler's tray, swinging it back and forth in the air, exclaiming, "Viva Mary and Douglas—may they live forever—may they forever reign."

Standing next to me, Mary half-whispered in my ear, "He's

drunk. We're going to have a time with him tonight. Douglas shouldn't have invited him."

The party moved slowly to the dining room. Barrymore had gulped three cocktails and was waving an empty glass as he walked. Barrymore and his date were the last to enter the opulent dining room. Douglas managed to get Barrymore and his date seated in their chairs next to Lady Mountbatten. At that moment, Barrymore stopped all conversation. "I'm going to show all of you how Doug gained his fame," he declared in his large, theatrical voice. He then began to fence an imaginary foe, which climaxed with him turning his chair around and attempting to leap over it. His girlfriend caught him by the elbow, just in time, or he would have fallen to the floor. "He's an athlete!" declared Barrymore.

Mary's eyes blazed with her displeasure, but Douglas laughed heartily. "Oh, that's all right," he said. "I'm used to him teasing me." I looked at Charlie, who was enjoying the situation. To Charlie, all life was seen as though through a film frame. This was his perspective on life. Indeed, a lot of times when I was with Charlie, he would be looking at me, but I was never sure if he was seeing me. I knew then he was actually creating something for his films. I have spoken to others about this and am not alone in sensing this in Charlie. It was as if he were very often in another world. At the dinner table at Pickfair, however, it was easy for me to see why he found the situation a potentially amusing film sequence. He did all that he could to keep from laughing out loud.

I looked at the beautifully set table in front of me. A large cluster of lilies graced the center of the table. Place settings with several forks and knives lay on either side of gold-rimmed dinner plates; three silver, odd-shaped forks and spoons lay crosswise above the dinner plates. The tablecloth was an elegantly embroidered damask in a pale yellow, with napkins at the left with the initial P (for Pickfair). How was I going to know which fork, knife, or spoon I should use with each course? I would have to watch Mary to get my clues.

Finger food on a small plate was the first course. Following that was a fingerbowl with a floating slice of lemon. Watching Mary, who sat at the head of the table, I dipped my fingertips in the cool water and then wiped my hands with my napkin. A servant came around collecting the fingerbowls. Then came a small soup bowl with a clear broth. That spoon I could recognize. Red wine was poured, which indicated that the main course was going to be beef. I knew that much from hearing my grandfather talk about which wines you should serve with which foods.

I got through all the courses with no mishaps—until the dessert course. The dessert was a whipped-cream-topped sweet, served on a silver platter with a large spoon and fork. I moved my bread and butter plate, with its fancy doily, to a place in front of me, and when the big platter came by me I used the large spoon and fork to help myself to a good portion of the gooey mixture. I failed to realize that I had a dessert plate and placed my dessert on my bread plate, with the linen tatted doily still on it. When I realized what I had done, I looked at Lord Mountbatten, who was seated to my left, and then at the Welshman on my right. They had not noticed my faux pas, so I could relax.

The Welsh gentleman began a conversation with me, which turned into a monologue on his part, for I was finding it impossible to understand a word he was saying. Besides his dialect, he managed to swallow the words that were not mumbled.

I could see Charlie sitting across from me trying to hold back his laughter. He saw the comedy of a dumb kid thrust into the awkward position of trying to make conversation with a Welshman at an elegant dinner party.

I had another dilemma. Should I address Lord Mountbatten as "Sir" or "Your Lordship?" I settled for "Your Lordship," and I guess it was all right, for no eyebrows were raised.

The party broke up at about eleven o'clock. Getting our light wraps, Mrs. Lubitsch approached me. "It was *vunderful* seeing you. Have *Sharlee* bring you to our house sometime, eh?"

Charlotte Pickford, Mary's mother, entered from outdoors. "Nice to see you, Lita. How are you feeling? And when do you expect the baby?"

I hedged. "Well, I don't know exactly," I said. "We think we gave the doctor the wrong month for conception."

"That's too bad," she said. "It makes it hard for your plans." She did not know the half of it.

On the way home, I told Charlie how I had handled that situation. "You had a few situations to handle tonight, didn't you?" he teased. "I was watching you all evening. What bothered you so much about Leni Lubitsch?"[3]

"Well, she gave us a left-handed invitation," I said. "She said, 'Have *Sharlee* bring you to our house sometime, eh?' 'Sometime'—what kind of an invitation is that?"

"You have to remember that she has only been in this country a short time. She's still learning the language," Charlie said. "Speaking of language barriers, couldn't you have done a little better with the Welshman?" Charlie started to laugh. "I saw you struggling to understand him." He knew he was getting me riled. "Oh, come on now," he said. "All this dinner party nonsense isn't something to worry about. You're too sensitive. I'm sensitive too, but about things that are important. None of it means anything. How about that sot John Barrymore? Wasn't that a terrible scene to inflict on poor Mary and Douglas? He's a bore.

"Let me tell you about Mary," he continued. "She's a wonderful woman in a lot of ways, but she's a snob. She doesn't remember her shanty Irish background. It's the mark of a truly great individual who never forgets where they came from. One of these days I'm going to equip a Biltmore Hotel waiter with expensive luggage and wardrobe, introduce him to Mary as some person of title and privilege, and she'll have him for a house guest for a fortnight!"

"You wouldn't," I said to Charlie.

"I just might," said Charlie, laughing at the scene, a situation he alone could conjure in that mind of his, continually playing scenes for pictures that the public never got to see.

In November 1925, Charlie began preparing his next film, *The Circus*. He said he had the nucleus of an idea for a film about the circus for some time. He soon began testing girls for the role of the circus equestrienne.

At home one evening, exhausted from testing, interviewing, and looking at rushes, Charlie seemed discouraged and told me so. "I can't find the right girl for this part," he said. "She has to look, physically, like an athlete, but has to be pretty and take direction well. It's not easy to find someone who has all these things."

---

3. Helene ("Leni") Sonnet Lubitsch (1898–1960) was the first wife of Ernst Lubitsch.

My old friend Merna Kennedy came to mind. I knew Charlie did not appreciate suggestions on his work from anybody, particularly those close to him, unless he asked for an opinion. However, I thought I would risk having my opinion ridiculed. "Charlie, do you remember the girl who was with me the day I visited you at the studio when you were going to test me for the part in *The Gold Rush*?"

"I remember vaguely a girl with red hair," Charlie said.

"Merna Kennedy is her name. I've known her since dancing school when we were eight. She has theatrical experience. She's been touring one of the vaudeville circuits in a dancing act with her brother. She has not only the developed legs of a dancer but a pretty face. Would you consider testing her?"

Charlie did not seem impressed. "Oh, I don't know," he said. "I have a few more girls to interview and test tomorrow. We'll see."

Well, I thought to myself, that was half a consideration—I'll keep after him. I was so confident Merna would be right for the role that I became persistent.

The next day of testing found Charlie no better. That night he was disappointed.

"Please, Charlie," I said, "why don't you give Merna a chance? I believe she's really right for that type of part."

"Well, all right," said Charlie, rather irritated. "If it's only to get you to stop pestering me, I'll make a test of her. Tell her to come to the studio at about ten o'clock in the morning."

The next evening Charlie seemed in a good mood. "Rollie made a test on your friend, and it's good. I think maybe you were right about her."

"I can't wait to tell her," I said.

"Just a minute!" said Charlie. "I haven't interviewed her."

"Oh, well," I said. "Let me know."

Within a few days, Merna was signed to a contract. Charlie was very pleased with his decision, but I did have the satisfaction of hearing Charlie compliment me with "You were right. I think she'll do for the part."

I was very happy at the news. Merna and I had been the best of friends for as long as I could remember. I was anxious to talk to her to see how she felt about the good news. Strangely enough, with Charlie signing Merna, I felt my marriage had a good chance of working. His decision somehow bolstered my confidence in myself. Maybe Mama was right, I thought—perhaps he will change.

Merna came to visit me, and she could not thank me enough. "I know this is the beginning of something wonderful," she said. "I can't begin to thank you. You're a real friend, Lillita—I mean Lita."

Many weeks passed, and Merna called me several times on the telephone, but I did not see her. She was too busy. "I'd like to come over," she would say over the telephone, "but I've so much to do now. Charlie is showing me the test and advising me about wardrobe fittings, a hair cut, and what will be required of me in this part. Maybe later on we can get together like old times, eh? Call me and let me know."

In Merna's absence, I had been seeing Marion Davies more and more frequently. She had instigated the friendship out of curiosity, which was mutual. She came to the house on Cove Way a couple times for lunch, but usually I would go and see her at her home. She appeared isolated and lonely, much like I felt, despite the fact that she had a career in films. She enjoyed talking about W. R. Hearst and Charlie—particularly Charlie—with a glass of champagne always nearby. She confessed to me early on that she was surprised to find me such a nice and refined girl, for Charlie had told her that I was a crude, uneducated person who was out to get his money.

I had the courage finally to ask Marion one afternoon, after she was feeling particularly uninhibited by several glasses of champagne, whether she was still intimate with Charlie. She vehemently denied this. She conceded that they had once been intimate but that it had ended when I married Charlie. Marion was such a charming companion, and I was so young and naive, that I believed her when she swore her affair with Charlie was over and professed to be my friend. It was only later that I discovered that Marion was not being honest with me.

Our second Christmas as husband and wife was as disappointing as our first. Mama, Grandfather, Grandmother, Charlie Jr., and I were to have a nice Christmas dinner with Charlie. However, before Grandfather and Grandmother arrived, Charlie left without explanation and did not return until late that night. It was like a scene out of *The Gold Rush*, as we were reluctant to begin without him, waiting for the arrival of the guest who never came.

Kono informed me one afternoon that Charlie and I were invited to stay for a long weekend at the Hearst Castle—San Simeon, in northern California—and that Charlie had already accepted the invitation.

I knew very little about W. R. Hearst, only that he owned a vast newspaper and magazine empire and that my grandfather referred to the Hearst press as "yellow journalism." I did not know what to expect upon meeting him. A rumor had persisted, since 1914, that his influence was so great that he was responsible for the First World War, when he had flattered Kaiser Wilhelm II of Germany by telling him he had an army powerful enough to conquer the world.

A nine-passenger limousine pulled up to our front door, and the houseboy, Frank, announced its arrival. Mr. Hearst, as was his way, had ordered the car to take us up the coast of California to San Simeon, where we would be met by a shuttle bus that would take us the rest of the way up the steep hill to Hearst Castle. Charlie and I came down our front steps just in time to see Elinor Glyn get out of the middle seat to make room for us. Instead of joining Norma Talmadge[4] and Gilbert Roland,[5] who were in the backseat, Elinor came over to us, standing in the driveway. She said hello to Charlie, then looking at me she said, "Lita, haven't I always told you to stand up straight and hold your tummy in?" and with this, she poked a gloved finger into my abdomen.

"Oh, please don't, Miss Glyn. You might hurt the baby!"

"Oh, I'm sorry," she said. "I haven't seen you in a while. I had no idea that you were pregnant." She shrugged, turned around, walked to the car, and got in. Norma Talmadge and Gilbert Roland did not pay much attention. They were interested mainly in each other.

---

4. Norma Talmadge (1895–1957) was a silent screen actress who began her career with the Vitagraph Corporation and by 1915 was being billed as "The International Darling." The eldest of the three Talmadge sisters (the others being Natalie Talmadge, the first wife of Buster Keaton, and film actress Constance Talmadge), Norma was married to Joseph M. Schenck from 1917 to 1929. Schenck was the president of United Artists from 1924 to 1935.

5. Gilbert Roland (Luis Antonio Dámaso de Alonso) (1905–1994) was a Mexican motion picture actor who began his career in silent films. His first featured role was in *The Plastic Age* (1925), starring Clara Bow, but his best role of the 1920s was as Armand in *Camille* (1927), starring Norma Talmadge.

I had known Elinor Glyn ever since my marriage and had always found her to be flashy and sometimes rude. She was in her early sixties, wore white makeup, gloves, and a hat, and usually had a young man on her arm. She was famous for her novel *Three Weeks*, which was considered daring and a bit scandalous in its day. She amused Hearst, and he often invited her to his gatherings or dinners.

Charlie and I got into the center seat of the car. I had never met Norma Talmadge or Gilbert Roland, so Charlie introduced me to them. Despite the assemblage of celebrity personages in this limousine headed up the California coast, the trip was uneventful. Norma Talmadge and Gilbert Roland were cooing and only had eyes for each other. Charlie and I had little in common with Miss Glyn so there was little conversation the whole trip.

At San Simeon, another one of Hearst's limousines appeared, and Charlie said to me, "That's Donald Ogden Stewart[6]—a nice enough fellow, a little pushy." Stewart waved to us and then came over. Several people got out of his limousine, but they were too far away for me to tell who they were.

"Haven't seen you for quite a while," said Stewart. "You busy making a film?" If there was any one thing Charlie hated most, it was a discussion about his work while it was in progress. Charlie bit his lip and looked uncomfortable. He relented some. "The subject matter is about a circus."

"Oh, jolly," said Stewart. "I can just see your Tramp character in that environment." Stewart was starting to ask Charlie another question about the film when Charlie interrupted.

"Oh, look, I believe that's our shuttle bus now," Charlie said. He was so glad to be free from any more talk about his work.

The shuttle bus took us up a long, winding, unpaved road past grazing zebras, horses, and goats. Near the castle, on the slope of the hill, was an aviary with numerous colorful screeching birds.

---

6. Donald Ogden Stewart (1894–1980) was a screenwriter, playwright, and author best known for his film scripts for director George Cukor. In the 1920s, Stewart was a regular humorist in *Vanity Fair* and member of New York's Algonquin Round Table, and he had written several books and novels that proved popular. Stewart would later become a political exile, settling in London with his wife Ella Winter and remaining friends with Chaplin, who was in exile in Corsier-sur-Vevey, Switzerland.

At last we pulled up to the front door of "La Casa Grande," the main house of the estate.

W. R. Hearst loved Mediterranean art and architecture. As a result, San Simeon was a great Renaissance villa combining Spanish and Italian designs. La Casa Grande had over a hundred rooms. It looked like a cathedral. There were three guest houses, numerous fountains, gardens, swimming pools, tennis courts, and perhaps the largest private collection of animals in the world. Hearst was very fond of animals, and most of the creatures roamed free; bears, lions, and tigers were kept in a zoo on the estate.

The views from this magnificent estate were extraordinary. The property was set on some 250,000 acres, with fifty miles of ocean-front. I was told that all the food—meats and vegetables—came from the property.

A man came running out to greet us. "Welcome to Mr. Hearst's ranch. I'm to show you your quarters and give you some information you'll need. I'll get the tram to take you and your luggage to your quarters. The shuttle driver will help load everything on. I'll be right back."

Charlie had been to Hearst Castle previously, but he never grew accustomed to the lavish splendor. He enjoyed my reaction to the surroundings and explained to me what he had learned of the ranch from W. R. Hearst and Marion Davies. When I looked up at the ceiling, for example, Charlie immediately said, "That's gold leaf, and all the plumbing fixtures are solid gold."

Our guide came back with a tram that would carry at least ten people. "We have to wait for the next shuttle. I'm told there are twelve guests this time." Just then the second shuttle pulled up with John Gilbert, Greta Garbo,[7] Louella Parsons, and her date Docky Martin.

We were the last to be delivered to our rooms. Our guide stood by our door and said, "There's only one really fast rule here, and that is that dinner, in the dining hall, is served at eight o'clock sharp. Other than that, all the facilities are at your disposal—the swimming pools, the tennis courts, viewing a movie, horseback

---

7. Greta Garbo (Greta Louisa Gustafsson) (1905–1990) was the protégée of film director Mauritz Stiller. Leaving Sweden for America in 1925 to work in films at Metro-Goldwyn-Mayer, Garbo was developed into a major international film star. She remained friendly with Chaplin through the years, occasionally visiting his Beverly Hills home for tennis.

riding. For any of your needs here in your apartment—a valet, food, and drinks—just press the button, it's over there near the door. Have a pleasant stay."

When the guide left, I said, "Wow, talk about service! This beats anything I've ever heard of."

We had rung for something cold to drink, showered, and spent a lot of time talking about Marion Davies, the amazing W. R. Hearst, and this fairyland-like place. Charlie told me that Mr. Hearst slept in Cardinal Richelieu's old bed, which delighted Charlie. It brought to my mind Hearst's living arrangements. I was hesitant to ask the inevitable question; nevertheless, I naively asked Charlie, "Does Mr. Hearst sleep with Marion?" I had no need to be bashful, for the whole world—except me—knew that Marion Davies was Hearst's mistress. Charlie had to explain their relationship to me.

Before we realized it, it was nearly 7:30 P.M. Our doorbell rang. It was our guide. "I'm a bit early," he said, "but better to be early than late." He took us through beautiful gardens and past the other guest houses until we finally reached the assembly hall, the largest room on the estate. Two of Donald Ogden Stewart's shuttle bus companions were there waiting, Louella Parsons and Docky Martin. Joining us at last, and waiting at the door, were John Gilbert and Greta Garbo. Others in the party were already inside. The heavily carved wooden doors were closed, but suddenly they swung open, and there stood Hearst beaming and welcoming us to join him.

Inside the dining hall we met up with the rest of the party, including Marion Davies, who was with one of Hearst's newspaper employees. There were place cards at the table settings, and we all quickly found our names and sat down. Louella Parsons was on Hearst's right, which normally would be the "guest of honor" spot, but whether that meant anything I am uncertain, for Hearst was seated in the center of the table. At the far end of the table was Donald Ogden Stewart, and he fitted that position very well, for he immediately acted like a toastmaster, telling jokes and keeping everybody laughing.

Marion was seated directly across from W. R. Hearst. To my mind, she would always have to occupy a central position at the table as well as at the estate—her vibrant presence brought much to the estate and prevented us from feeling we were in some sort of museum. Next to Marion was Charlie, and down the line I was next to Gilbert Roland.

Everybody was fascinated by the beautiful and strange Greta Garbo, who was aloof even at this early stage of her career. No one except John Gilbert knew her well, and he was happy to have been placed next to her. There was talk at this time that Gilbert and Garbo were offscreen as well as on-screen lovers. What I was able to tell for certain was that he could not keep his eyes off her—he adored her.

W. R. Hearst started to speak, and I fully expected a mellow tone in a man of his size and distinction, but instead he addressed us in a high-pitched voice. "You know there are only thirteen of us, but we've set up for fourteen—for the benefit of the superstitious!" He laughed, enjoying the situation.

The massive wooden dining table and chairs were the only pieces of furniture in the huge room. Everything else in way of decor was on the walls in the form of various banners and flags from an ancient time. In one corner stood suits of mail with swords protruding as if ready for warfare. A mammoth fireplace decorated one wall, the open grate large enough to hold a standing man who would not reach the flue above him. A long box was on the wide hearth containing some logs. In this room, until dinner was served, one had the feeling of being in medieval Europe.

When dinner came, we were figuratively brought back to America. Down the center of the dining table was a row of condiments: steak sauce, mustard, catsup, pickles, salt and pepper grinders, and paper napkins. Dinner consisted of steak, mashed potatoes, garden-grown green vegetables, peach pie, coffee, and liqueurs.

It was a diverse group despite the fact we were all connected in some way with motion pictures—as guests we had little in common with one another. Yet in spite of the differences, this assemblage provided lively conversation and seemed to be having a good time. Many subjects were discussed at length—art, music, filmmaking, even food recipes. Hearst had requested that politics not be discussed. "It makes for better harmony," he said. He talked a lot about his collections. Time passed quickly, and before we knew it, it was eleven o'clock.

Hearst stood up and moved away from the table. "Now, we have strange hours here," he said. "It's not too late to enjoy tennis—the courts are lighted—the water in the pools is warm, and there's the movie. We have a good one tonight—one of King Vidor's directorial accomplishments I believe—or you can simply enjoy the night. The stars are out, and the view is exceptional from your balconies.

"But all this is not for you my pet," Hearst said to Marion. "Give me your glass—you've had enough champagne. Get your wrap and I'll escort you to your quarters."

No one was surprised, for they all knew that Mr. Hearst could take on a grandfatherly manner with Marion when she had imbibed too much and had not eaten much dinner. Marion was famous for her champagne consumption. She got her shawl and dutifully followed Mr. Hearst out the door.

The guests dispersed. Norma Talmadge and Gilbert Roland found a place in the garden where they could be alone, Greta Garbo and John Gilbert were going to take a swim, and Charlie and I decided to go to bed early so we could get up early for a horseback ride to enjoy the countryside. Louella Parsons and Docky said they had been up since early in the morning, and they were worn out—they would go to their quarters, read, and go to bed. The rest decided to see the movie.

Back at our quarters, I went out on the veranda. The sight below was extraordinary. On the hillside a great pile of crates lay in seeming disarray. "Is that more of Mr. Hearst's collections?" I said.

"Yes, and if we're invited again we'll probably know what they contain," said Charlie as he was changing to go to bed.

"I noticed that Marion and Mr. Hearst kept referring to the castle as a 'ranch.' I've always thought ranches had cattle, cowhands, and a barn."

"A castle by any other name . . . ," said Charlie. He was very pleased with himself. He thought he'd said something very witty.

The following day Hearst caught up with us just as we were mounting our horses for a ride at the paddock. "I've been waiting to get you two alone for a few minutes so I could talk to you. I've been planning a trip to Mexico to look over some property I'm considering buying, and I thought I would make a party out of it. It'll be a small group, maybe eight or ten. We'll lunch at the Hotel del Coronado on the way down, and there is a halfway house down there where we can have dinner and stay the night if we care to.

It's pretty rough country—nothing but sagebrush, tumbleweed, and unpaved roads, but I was wondering if you and Lita would like to come along—that is, if you think Lita would be all right in her condition. What do you think, Charlie?"

Charlie thought it over. "It's up to you, Lita. What do you say?"

"I say let's go!" I replied without hesitation.

"It's settled then," said Hearst. "You'll join us. There will be two carloads of us."

Charlie and I mounted our horses, and we took off down a path that would lead us to some beautiful country. The two of us were not great riders—I was pregnant, and Charlie was not fond of horses in general. We were riding at a slow trot, enjoying the scenery.

We spent the next four days cramming everything in—not to miss anything—we swam, rode horseback, saw movies. By the end of our stay we were exhausted and would be glad to get home.

We packed, ready to leave, and the tram picked us up to take us to the shuttle bus. Along came our guide. He had some of our party with him. Hearst and Marion Davies were going back with us to their Beverly Hills home, which was not far from Charlie's house on Cove Way.

Not long after our return from San Simeon, Charlie and I, along with Hearst and his entourage, started from Beverly Hills, bound for Mexico. The weather was nice, but it was going to be hot in Mexico. I was wondering how Elinor Glyn would fare with her calcimine-like makeup, hat, and gloves south of the border. Charlie must have read my mind. He said, "I trust Mr. Hearst instructed his drivers to take a coastal route to San Diego; that way at least we'll be comfortable for much of the trip south."

The automobiles used were nine-passenger limousines. There were many people in this entourage, and the cars were pretty crowded. We were sure to be very uncomfortable when we got down into Mexico. Lunch at the Hotel del Coronado, the famous Victorian-style hotel across the bay from San Diego, was very pleasant. We sat on the hotel's veranda while the management fixed up a table. Hearst handled all the arrangements. He even ordered our lunch.

As we left the hotel, a sea breeze sprang up, and it was very refreshing. The trip down from the San Diego area was a rough one—for a while we were on unpaved roads, rocks of various sizes cluttering our path. An occasional boulder caused our chauffeur to stop the car, get out, and remove the big rock. A couple of times the terrain was so bumpy Charlie held me in the air so I would not feel the jolting. He was afraid I might miscarry.

It was dusk when we arrived at the halfway house Hearst's friend had described. Hearst stepped out of the car. "My God," he said. "This can't be it! This shanty-like wooden structure isn't at all like my friend described."

A Mexican man came out of its door. "Can I help you?" he said.

Hearst said, "We'd planned on dinner and maybe staying over one night." He looked past the Mexican at the dilapidated wooden building. "Can you arrange that?"

"I have food," said the Mexican, "and some sleeping quarters out back."

"I see," said Hearst. "And how far away is the next town from here?"

"Oh, about fifty miles."

"What do you have for food?"

"I have chicken. Also potatoes, canned green vegetables, and candy for dessert," he laughed, revealing some jagged front teeth.

"All right, show me your sleeping quarters," said Hearst, and he followed the Mexican out back to some boxlike buildings with no windows, a double bed, and a couch in each.

"Well," said the proprietor, "I can put up all of you if some of your party are willing to sleep on cots."

Mr. Hearst came back from looking at the shacks. He talked to Charlie. Charlie said, "If Louella Parsons could see us now—how the famous people of motion pictures spend a holiday!"

Everyone within earshot of Charlie's remark laughed, all but Elinor Glyn. She saw nothing funny about anything that removed her from elegant surroundings. Charlie was finding humor in our present situation.

"All we need now," said Charlie to me, "is a picture of Mr. Hearst—all six-foot-three of him—lying lengthwise across a cot with his feet sticking out a few inches."

"All right," said Hearst. "We'll put up here for one night."

The party drew straws to determine who would get the beds, the couches, or the cots. Fortunately, with me being pregnant, Charlie and I got one of the iron beds.

The proprietor said, "I have washrooms and a lavatory. You can take turns using them while I get dinner ready." In a few minutes we heard the squawking of chickens—the proprietor was chasing them around the yard. Several of us lost our appetites and settled for potatoes, canned green vegetables, and coffee.

One could feast themselves in the surroundings. It was a beautiful evening, the moon was full, and only the sounds of tiny wild creatures clicking and scratching could be heard. Everyone was exhausted and decided to bed down in the iron beds, the couches, and the cots. Elinor Glyn had drawn the couch in our shack. She had always worn a stiff corset, and it was comical to see her stretched out on the couch with her arms folded over her chest, her white makeup still on, and wearing her hat. "I won't even take off my hat in this dreadful place," she said.

Charlie and I laughed so hard and so long at Miss Glyn's remark it seemed like it took us forever to fall asleep.

The next morning we all decided to skip breakfast and drive fifty miles to the next town for the meal. In that vicinity was the property Hearst had been told about. He drove over and looked at it, came back, and said, "I think I've had enough of Mexico for a while."

I had three marvelous visits to Hearst Castle at San Simeon during my marriage to Charlie, and as a result of these trips, a clique had formed. Everywhere Charlie and I were invited, with a few exceptions, we found ourselves in the company of the same people—Norma Talmadge and her swain Gilbert Roland, Elinor Glyn, John Gilbert, Sam and Frances Goldwyn, King Vidor and Eleanor Boardman. The strange aspect of this clique was that none of these people, at this time, were particular friends of Charlie's or mine.

Charlie's friends—and they came to be mine—were not motion picture celebrities but people like "Big Bill" Tilden, the tennis champion;[8] Dr. Cecil Reynolds, the brain surgeon, and his wife, Nora; and Sid Grauman. As to Charlie's relationship with Douglas Fairbanks and Mary Pickford, they were business partners, and their friendship has been exaggerated over the years. Charlie was very fond of Douglas, but I do not believe he approved of his

---

8. William Tatem Tilden (1893–1953) won seven U. S. tennis singles titles in the 1920s and the British singles title three times (1920, 1921, 1930). Chaplin and "Big Bill" Tilden were to remain lifelong friends.

films. After watching one Fairbanks film together, Charlie said to me that Douglas was just a "jumper," albeit one with great personality. As for Mary, Charlie and Mary did not get along very well. Perhaps they were too much alike in many ways. Charlie would have admired Mary's business sense had she been a man, but because she was a woman it was somehow unseemly to him. Charlie had a rather English view toward women.

Charlie and I would separately visit Marion Davies at her house frequently. Charlie and I went together only a few times. One visit I recall was before the birth of my second boy, not long before I left Charlie.

At Marion's for an informal gathering, Charlie and I were in the company of the King Vidors, Norma Talmadge, and Gilbert Roland. John Gilbert was to join us later. Gilbert was shooting *Flesh and the Devil* and had to remain at the studio for some additional shots. He said he would be late. Mr. Hearst was away in New York on business. Marion was ecstatic to be free of Mr. Hearst's overprotectiveness, and it was certain that she would make the most of the time she had.

For the average person, entertaining eight guests at dinner would be quite an undertaking, but for Marion it was a breeze. She was used to assisting "W. R.," as she always called him, at San Simeon where there might be as many as forty or fifty guests. This particular evening she had given her butler instructions not to announce dinner until there had been at least two rounds of champagne, and when I saw the second round come into the living room on a tray, I became apprehensive. Charlie was not a drinker, and after the second glass he began to dance about the room. I was praying that dinner would be served soon, for I knew that food would be the only thing to sober him up. Fortunately, dinner was soon announced, and I held Charlie's arm all the way to the dining room for fear he might trip over something.

During the course of the evening, John Gilbert arrived dressed in studio wardrobe—a decorated soldier's uniform. He was still in makeup and looked strikingly handsome, but he was obviously distressed. He called Marion from the gathering so that he might speak to her in private. In Marion's bedroom he flung himself across the bed saying, "She won't marry me, she won't marry me!" Great tears rolled down his cheeks. "She turned me down again today," he said between sobs. He was talking about Greta Garbo.

I witnessed this scene from the doorway of Marion's bathroom, where I had gone after excusing myself from the dining table. Gilbert stood up and wiped away the tears. He refused to be consoled.

Back in the dining room, Marion brought John and sat him down in the chair that had been reserved for him. A pall had fallen over the festivities. "Get Mr. Gilbert a drink," said Marion to one of her servants.

Adjourning to the living room, Charlie had recovered from his dizziness. John Gilbert had managed to sober everyone up from the earlier frivolity, except Marion. Everyone looked for Marion so they could say good night, but the butler said, "Miss Davies is sorry—she begs to be excused." Marion was upstairs, where she had passed out as a result of her overdrinking.

When we left Marion's house, I said to Charlie, "Mr. Hearst is so right about controlling Marion's drinking."

"Yes," said Charlie. "She shouldn't have served dinner so late. All that champagne just about knocked everybody out. For a while there I was seeing double."

"Well, no harm done," I said. "But you looked pretty silly acting like you thought you were a ballerina."

Charlie and I laughed.

4

The Beginning of the End

Charlie had been taking me out lately; however, I had begged off finally, for I was getting very uncomfortable now. I was far along in my pregnancy, and it was a strain for me to sit for long periods at the dinner table or a film premiere.

And I was right. I turned down our next invitation, and sure enough I went into labor. The birth, like the birth of Charlie Jr., took place at the Cove Way house attended by Dr. Holleran. I delivered the baby in my bedroom, which was the middle bedroom of the house. It was much easier than the birth of Charlie Jr., three pains and Sydney Earl Chaplin,[1] as he was named, was cleaned and in my arms before Charlie came home on 30 March 1926. Despite the fact that Sydney arrived five weeks premature, reporters with calculating minds could find no fault in the matter. The children were officially born nine months and two days apart. Charlie had wanted a girl, but he was not disappointed at having another healthy boy. In fact, from Sydney's infancy, Charlie seemed to favor him over Charlie Jr.

I received a note of congratulations from Merna when Sydney was born. I would rarely hear from her over the next eight months.

Mama was devoting all her time to the care of baby Charlie. In many ways she was more his mother than I was. We hired a nurse for Sydney. The nurse so spoiled Sydney by rocking his bassinet

---

1. Sydney Earl Chaplin (b. 1926) appeared in two of his father's films, as Neville in *Limelight* (1952) and as Harvey Crothers in *A Countess from Hong Kong* (1967). His stage credits include the original Broadway productions of *Bells Are Ringing* (1956), for which he received a Tony Award for best featured actor in a musical, and *Funny Girl* (1964). Sydney Chaplin later became a restaurateur and is now retired. His marriage to dancer Noelle Adam (marriage dissolved) produced a son, Stephan Chaplin (b. 1960). He lives in Palm Springs, California.

back and forth that on her day off little Sydney would yell all day
to be rocked. Charlie was very pleased with the situation, for it
gave him all the freedom he wanted. I was busy with the children
and had Mama for company. Charlie was working on his film *The
Circus*.

One morning on his way to work at the studio, Charlie stopped
in the guest bedroom where Charlie Jr. was lying, completely
naked. Charlie, in a fatherly mood, bent over near the baby only
to have Charlie Jr. urinate all over his white shirt and suit. Charlie
refused to change clothes. He went to the studio wearing the
stained clothing and proudly announced what his son had done
to him.

Despite this story of paternal pride, Charlie had no real emotional attachment to the children and seldom held them. The only
times he showed any interest was in their naming, as well as making sure that they were not circumcised. Charlie was not circumcised and he did not believe in circumcision. He also did not
believe in baptizing the children. He felt that they should be free
to choose their own religious beliefs in adulthood. It was only in
January 1928, long after I had left Charlie, that I finally had the
boys christened at the Church of the Good Shepherd in Beverly
Hills.

In the spring of 1926, I persuaded Charlie to take the children
and me to meet his mother, Hannah,[2] who lived in a small rented
home in the San Fernando Valley.[3] She was under the constant
care of a very nice couple, Mr. and Mrs. Carey. Hannah had been
mentally ill since Charlie was a little boy.

Charlie was reluctant to make the visit to see his mother. He
rarely visited her, because it made him incredibly depressed to see
her in her present condition. A visit with her could make him

---

2. Hannah Harriett Pedlingham Hill Chaplin (1865–1928) appeared in music
halls under the stage name Lily Harley. She spent much of her adult life in asylums
owing to mental instability. She came to America on 26 March 1921, where
Chaplin provided her with a modest home and the care she needed. She died at the
Glendale Hospital on 28 August 1928.

3. Contrary to most published accounts, including Chaplin's *My Autobiography*
(London: Bodley Head, 1964), p. 271, a document in the Chaplin Archives states
that Hannah Chaplin did not live in a bungalow by the sea in Santa Monica but
rather in the rented home of Mr. and Mrs. William Carey at 4217 Arch Drive,
North Hollywood (present-day Studio City), California, for virtually all the time
she was in California.

unable to work at the studio for days, and he would stay home and shut himself in the library and brood. He believed that insanity ran in the family, and he was worried he might end up like his mother. Charlie told me once that he was afraid of two things: insanity and poverty.

During this first visit, Hannah's mind was back some thirty years, and she thought my little Charlie and Sydney were her little Charlie and Sydney. Charlie remained passive during the visit, deferring to his mother and her whims. At one point, she abruptly started dancing around the room. She was once a delightful woman, Charlie told me, but she was completely gone when I met her. I did not think Charlie looked much like his mother. I was told she was a Spanish Gypsy. Charlie, however, had an obvious Jewish look about him, which I attributed to his father, whom I had only seen in pictures and who was thought to be half-Jewish. Charlie himself did not believe himself to be Jewish, and, of course, according to the Jewish faith, one is Jewish only if the mother is Jewish. Perhaps that is why Charlie, in private at least, denied that he was a Jew.

Charlie's elder half-brother, Sydney, also looked very Jewish. It is not certain who Sydney's father was. I did not get to know Sydney well, owing entirely to an unpleasant experience I had with him in the summer of 1925 when Charlie was in New York promoting *The Gold Rush*. I had left to spend a few days on Catalina Island with Mama. Alone on the beach, I encountered Sydney Chaplin. I do not know whether this was a matter of coincidence or design on Sydney's part. I was surprised to see him and even more surprised when he made a pass at me. I was completely shocked by his behavior and said, "Sydney, your brother is my husband. How could you suggest such a thing?"

"What's the difference?" was his response.

I quickly left the beach, and that was my only impression of Sydney Chaplin. This partially explains why my son Sydney was called "Tommy" in my home for many years after my divorce from Charlie. I had originally wanted to name Sydney after my paternal grandfather, Thomas Edward, but after some discussion, I bowed to Charlie's wish and named him after Charlie's elder half-brother.

The more I learned about Charlie's traumatic early life—and there was no more tangible reminder of those early years than visits with his mother—the more understanding I became of his behavior. I do not believe, for example, that Charlie was particularly cheap; his films were made under conditions that were far from cost-efficient, and he maintained people like Edna Purviance on payroll even when she was no longer working for him. His tightness with money was born out of his fear that if he was not careful with his money, he was going to end up poor. It was ridiculous, sometimes, when I would have an argument with Charlie or Kono over an $85 bill from the drugstore when I knew perfectly well that Charlie was worth millions of dollars. However, I understood early in our marriage that there was nothing I could do to change this insecurity, which was no doubt formed in the poverty of his early childhood.

For my birthday, I asked Charlie if I could have a party with people who were my own age. I was always around Charlie's friends, who were older, distinguished people. I wanted to act my age and be with some of my old Cummnoch School friends. He consented to a small party.

Kono arranged for me to have a party of friends at the Biltmore Hotel. We had a lovely dinner, and I was so happy and proud that I was allowed to have this evening with my friends that I did not want the evening to end. I invited the guests to see the house.

I brought my guests to the house at about 12:30 A.M. Charlie was nearly always out, never returning until one or two in the morning. We were in the drawing room and started to play the Victrola and the organ, no doubt acting silly as young people do. However, Charlie evidently had come home early, for he summoned me from the top of the stairs. He demanded that I "get that wild bunch of people out of here—get them out, and get them out quick. What do you think this is, a whorehouse?"

I was then forced to end the party abruptly and had to hear him lecture me about my behavior. I was really brokenhearted by his lack of patience and understanding. Inevitably, he called me a "gold digger" and a "Mexican whore" and a whole assortment of other names. I brought up the subject of divorce. "We will divorce when I'm good and ready to divorce and strictly on my terms" was his response. I naturally assumed by this that he wanted *The Circus* released before we divorced, not wanting to risk any bad publicity that might affect its worldwide box office. I was to realize only later that he was then in the process of hiding away much of his financial assets. I also learned later that the studio electricians had placed a bugging device in my bedroom. Charlie was attempting to find out anything he could to prepare himself for our inevitable divorce.

In the summer of 1926, I took some short trips to Catalina and Coronado. Charlie was near completion on *The Circus*, which he had hoped to have finished by the end of the year. He wanted the children and me out of the house. He told me, "Go away some place for a while. I can't work or create while you are here."

I responded, "Charlie, I don't understand. I never see you or annoy you."

"That isn't true. It is just the fact that you are here, and I am supposed to give the usual attention to a home and family. It annoys me and irritates me, and I cannot work."

Charlie never telephoned or asked about us while the children and I were gone. I had asked him once by telephone to join us for a day or so on one of these excursions—Charlie Jr. had just learned to walk—but he curtly declined, saying it was too expensive.

During an extended period in which the children and I were at the Cove Way house, Charlie invited Albert Einstein[4] and his wife over for dinner. At age seventeen, in 1926, I really did not appreciate the greatness of Professor Einstein. His appearance certainly did not impress me. His grey hair hung down over his shoulders, his eyelids drooped, and his English was, at best, fractured. Mrs. Einstein had to frequently help out as interpreter. The two men had very little to say to each other until they got on the subject of music. They then chatted amiably about Brahms, Bach, and Beethoven. Charlie played the organ and violin, to which Einstein applauded vigorously. Of course, I had nothing to contribute. As I look back on those days with Charlie, I realize how much of a dullard I must have been.

It was autumn before Merna finally telephoned me again. She was highly apologetic and went to great lengths to explain why she had failed to call me. "I've been so busy working on this

---

4. Albert Einstein (1879–1955) was the German-born physicist who formulated the "general theory of relativity" in 1916. He was awarded the Nobel Prize in physics in 1921. He and his second wife, Elsa Einstein Lowenthal (1874–1936), who was also his cousin, had married in 1919.

picture with Charlie," she said. "Even on the days Charlie doesn't shoot he wants the cast and crew at the studio in case he changes his mind. You know what he's like."

I did not think I was going to be so forgiving after so many months of not hearing from her, but I relented. She came to the house once or twice, saw the children, but never stayed very long. She appeared to be more than just preoccupied with her work in *The Circus.* One day she telephoned to say she would like for the two of us to get together for an evening.

"I thought this coming Sunday, if you're going to be home, I'd come and spend the night," Merna said. "I can't make it for the weekend. I've got a date Saturday night. I've been dating an interesting man. He's charming and rich. I've been getting attention like you wouldn't believe since I've been working for the great Charlie Chaplin."

"I'll be glad to see you," I said. "It will be like the old days, having you sleep over."

On Sunday, Merna and I had dinner in front of the fireplace. I was glad to have her company. Her brick-red hair and blue-green eyes appeared more than just pretty. I thought she was starting to have the glow of a movie star. I also noticed a glittering diamond bracelet on her wrist. "A gift from your rich boyfriend?" I inquired.

Merna's fair complexion suddenly reddened. "Yes," she said quickly, "ah, no," she added. "Charlie gave me this bracelet for being so cooperative. I didn't want to tell you because I thought maybe you'd think there was something going on between us and, of course, there isn't. Charlie paid me a wonderful compliment," she continued. "He said I was so pretty and so charming that he'd like to use me as Josephine in a Napoleon picture he's planning to make after *The Circus.*"

My heartbeat accelerated. My old friend! Not just some floozie or film actress with whom he had a superficial relationship! This was Merna Kennedy, my oldest friend and the girl I had recommended for the part in the picture. So Mama was *not* right. There was no hope for this marriage.

We were upstairs, nearly ready for bed, when it dawned on me that I should not have to put up with this anymore. I got out of my bed. Merna clutched my arm and said, "Lillita, believe me— please."

Charlie had come in. I heard him in his room. I crossed the room after I had freed myself from Merna's grasp. I went through the bathroom that connected Charlie's room and mine. As I entered his room, Charlie was taking off his coat. He could see that I was agitated. "What's the matter?" he said.

"Charlie, I've had it with you, and I think I'm going to leave you. I've known for a long time that you've been having affairs with different women, but having an affair with Merna is the last straw."

Charlie appeared momentarily at a loss for words, so I continued.

"I know how tight you are with money. That diamond bracelet is all the proof I need, and that business about how she would make a wonderful Josephine just makes me sick. When I think of all the words of love you used to get me into bed . . ."

Charlie finally spoke. "Let me educate you a little," he interrupted. "Sex doesn't necessarily mean love."

"But you told me that you loved me before we were married," I said.

"Yes, I said that and I meant it, but when you forced me into a marriage with that money-grubbing family of yours, I lost that feeling. As to sex, I find you appealing. That doesn't mean I love you. Anyway," he continued, "you may find marriage to me isn't as bad as if I were to expose your good Catholic doctor. He accepted $25,000 to falsify Charles Jr.'s birth certificate. That fact could ruin the pious doctor."

I was appalled and at a loss for words.

"Tell you what, I'll give you and your mother some money and you can go anywhere you want—Mexico, Hawaii, Europe, anywhere—and think it over."

Mama and I decided that a trip to Honolulu, Hawaii, would be the best location for a short holiday to think things over. Charlie Jr. traveled with us. Sydney stayed at home with his nurse as he was much too young to join us. We sailed on the SS *City of Los Angeles* on 7 November 1926 for a planned holiday of several weeks. Charlie came down to Los Angeles Harbor to see us off "for appearances' sake." We were mobbed by photographers. The star of the impromptu photo shoot was not Charlie but rather Charlie Jr., as he had never been seen by the press before. It was the first, and last, time the three of us would be photographed together.

Despite all of the activity on board the ship—the parties, the deck games, the prolonged plans for a costume ball coming up—I still had ample time to review and evaluate my many relationships with Charles Chaplin. Standing at the rail watching a shuffleboard contest in progress, I wondered whether I could be entirely objective in my judgment of him. In our first relationship Charlie was like a father to me. I had always needed a father, and I had one briefly in my stepfather Hal Parker, but that had not been enough. Charlie then had that role—but again, only briefly—for my mother and he had had a misunderstanding that led to the cancellation of my contract from the Charlie Chaplin Film Company. Then came my adolescence and a girlish dream of romance. I was rehired and told by the attractive Charles Chaplin that I was loved and that I would make a perfect Josephine in a film he was going to produce on Napoleon. This flattery led me into a secret and illicit intimacy with Charlie. He said he loved me. What did a fifteen-year-old girl know of love? At this point, nature stepped in and took over. In a short time I was pregnant with Charlie's child. An ugly episode followed when Charlie made it clear he did not want to marry me. He had said to me, "I've been involved twice and almost paid the penalty for having sex with underaged girls— one I had to marry; the other became my mistress and leading lady. I'm afraid that if this information leaks out to the press, they will try to destroy me." But my family would have none of that excuse.

Marriage, I thought at the time, would cancel out all the mean words that were said, but it had not. Charlie continued to be mean-spirited. Should I now make allowances for his wretched childhood? Overlook and forgive his intimacy with my best friend—a girl who had been my friend since early childhood? Would I have the stamina in the future to endure the type of hot/cold behavior Charlie had been thrusting on me? But wait, I thought. I have been dwelling on me and my needs, my misfortunes. I now have two children. Am I not obliged to provide them with a home that has love and fidelity? Should I subject them to the knowledge that their father behaves so amorally?

No, I will not—and that was the answer I had been seeking. The realization that I had made this decision was as though I had shed a load that had weighed heavily on my soul for some time. I suddenly felt free. The trip had given me a perspective that enabled me to see clearly—not only myself, but Charlie and his feeble threat—for the very first time.

Charlie's threat that he would expose Dr. Holleran, my family physician, for accepting a bribe to falsify Charlie Jr.'s birth certificate if I did not remain with him as his wife failed to frighten me, for I realized that in doing so he would implicate himself as the instigator of the crime, for the payment could be traced back to him. It was a bluff.

I did not understand at the time, but I later came to the realization that I was never in love with Charlie. I had tremendous hero worship for him, but that is quite different. I do not believe a child of fifteen knows what love is. Charlie was the most extraordinary person I had ever met and a delightful person to be around, which he was, before I was pregnant. He had enormous physical appeal to me, and I should stress that he could be sensitive and warm-hearted—which showed in his work—but his one great fault was his overprotectiveness of his career and the character he created, the Tramp, which was the love of his life. If he thought either of these—his career or the Tramp—were threatened, he was capable of dire behavior, which I experienced from the moment he was informed that I was pregnant. The Charlie of old was wonderful, but that Charlie was no longer in my life.

Mama, however, thought divorce was a mistake. She had an excuse for all of Charlie's bad behavior, including his threatening me with a .38-caliber hand gun. She reminded me that Charlie was an actor and that he was just being "theatrical." He was a difficult man, she conceded, but her past marital mistakes left her convinced I should try harder and be patient for the sake of the children. I disagreed. I thought it best for all concerned, especially the children, to end this unhappy marriage.

My decision made, my mind clear for the first time in quite a while, the time spent in Hawaii was surprisingly pleasant. We stayed at the very nice Moana Hotel in Honolulu, enjoying the sun and surf of Waikiki Beach. The two prominent families of the island entertained us lavishly. The MacInerneys joined the Dillinghams in throwing a welcoming party to end all parties at their elegant home. Their friends from Los Angeles and San Francisco traveled to attend the festivities. The scent of the tuberoses filled the air, a sumptuous buffet was laid out in an elegantly decorated dining room, and soft Hawaiian music was played by a local orchestra. Nothing was too expensive or time-consuming for the wife of the great Charlie Chaplin. It would probably be one of my last events to enjoy in the role of Mrs. Charles Chaplin, and I was going to savor the title's perks.

Mama and I spent three memorable weeks in Hawaii. We visited several famous historical places, napped in the afternoons, and dined at the well-known restaurants in the evening. At the end of our stay, members of the MacInerney and Dillingham families came to the boat to see us off.

We arrived back at Los Angeles Harbor on 26 November 1926. When we returned home, there was disturbing news. Tomi said that Todah had overheard the cook say that Mr. Chaplin was planning to keep baby Sydney if Mrs. Chaplin left the premises.

Charlie was at the studio, so this would be a good time to leave. Tomi helped me get much of the children's clothes together, as well as mine, and Mama called my grandfather to ask him to come and pick us up as soon as possible. The houseboy tried to alert Charlie to what was happening, but he was reached too late—when Charlie came home we were gone.

I am aware of the various accounts regarding the events that led to my leaving Charlie. My divorce complaint, for example, cites that it was a party I gave that carried on late in the evening, causing Charlie to erupt in rage and demand that my guests leave the house. This party actually occurred, as already described, in April 1926—not November 1926—when Charlie allowed a birthday party for me at the Biltmore Hotel that abruptly concluded at the Cove Way house.

Taking into consideration everything that I had been through with Charlie—the suggestion I should jump off the train en route to Los Angeles after the marriage, his wielding a loaded revolver at me, the verbal tirades in which he claimed I was ruining his career, and his affairs with other women—it is absurd that his demanding my guests leave a party at one o'clock in the morning was the last straw for me and the marriage.

As it actually happened, I have related here. Some things I can remember vividly in my life, and the events that led to my leaving Charlie are among them. I do not recall for what reasons the party story was leaked to the press, and later cited in my complaint, as having happened in November 1926 as the defining event that ended the marriage. Perhaps it was legal strategy by my attorneys. However, this present account is how events actually transpired.

A call soon came to me from Charlie. He said softly, "Lita, be sensible. Come back and we can talk."

Charlie had a natural ability to make people feel sorry for him. I was about to decline his invitation when I suddenly felt a tinge of guilt over the abrupt manner in which I left his house. I answered, "I'll come back, Charlie, but never as your wife. I'll come tomorrow morning to talk," and with that I hung up the telephone.

Grandfather drove me to the Cove Way house the next day, and on the way he asked what I was planning to do.

"Oh, I'll see if I can get Charlie to agree to something to avoid a court fight," I answered matter-of-factly.

"Well, now," he said, "don't discuss terms or anything like that. You leave all that to your lawyer. You don't know anything about law, and you may jeopardize your position if you want custody of the children."

Grandfather would have had a fit if he knew what I had planned.

I left Grandfather in the car and entered the house. I met Charlie in the living room. I could not read his mood. He looked a complete blank.

I dispensed with pleasantries and said, "Charlie, I want a divorce. If you give me $10,000, you'll never see me or the boys again, if that's what you want."

Charlie flew into a rage. "Why, you little money-grubbing bitch! If you think for one moment that I would give you one cent of my money, you're crazy. And you can say what you like about me. I can beat you in any suit you level at me. Beware!"

That was the end of the conversation, as far as I was concerned. Although Charlie continued with a stream of profanities toward me, I quietly left. Back in Grandfather's car, he asked what I had accomplished.

"Nothing," I said. "Charlie's reluctant to do anything to avoid a court action. I guess he thinks he has some kind of special power with his money."

"Well," said Grandfather, "I've called your Uncle Edwin in San Francisco. He's a good lawyer, and he's coming down to see you. He'll take care of you."

I listened to Grandfather without emotion. I was too upset, reliving in my mind the latest unpleasant altercation with Charlie Chaplin.

My uncle arrived several days later. Grandfather and I met him at Union Station. He announced that he would be staying at the Biltmore Hotel, as it was conveniently located downtown near the courthouse, but Grandfather insisted that Uncle Edwin stay with us in Beverly Hills.

On the way back to Beverly Hills, Edwin told my grandfather and me that judges generally dislike dealing with out-of-town lawyers and that he would have to team up with a local law firm. It was recommended to him in San Francisco that the firm of Young & Young would be best, so Grandfather and I gave Edwin the authority to ask them to join our legal team.

Lyndol, Milton, and William Young got to work immediately drawing up a divorce complaint. The complete complaint ran forty-two pages, whereas a normal complaint would run only two or three pages. I did not understand much of the complaint, as it was written in legal jargon, but I was aware that a large section was devoted to sexual relations before and during my marriage to Charlie. As was the routine for the entire complaint, the lawyers had asked me about what Charlie had done or asked me to do in the bedroom. Naturally, they sensationalized everything.

"Do we need all this? It's so embarrassing," I said during one of my rare meetings with the entire legal team working on my behalf.

"Yes," said Lyndol Young. "It's important to show how Chaplin disregards the law."

"Are there laws that govern married people's behavior in the bedroom?" I asked.

"Yes," said Lyndol Young, "but remember, much of this took place when you were underage, unmarried, and pregnant. There's a name for this—it's called 'statutory rape'—and it's a criminal offense punishable in the state of California by a considerable prison sentence."

"But I'd think marriage would exonerate the man if he marries the girl," one of the lawyers interjected.

"That would be hard to prove, of course, but it's worth a try to show intent," Uncle Edwin said. "It's very complicated in this case. Anyway, we have to show that while the whole world loves Charlie Chaplin the comedian, the man is a liar and a debaucher. You must trust our judgment, Lillita," my uncle concluded. "We know what we're doing and for what reason."

The divorce complaint was filed on 10 January 1927. Charlie

heard of its contents while traveling to New York to escape being subpoenaed by my attorneys as well as by the Internal Revenue Service. Charlie had other troubles coming down on him at this time besides our divorce. The Internal Revenue Service had descended on him and his interests, charging that he and his studio owed over a million dollars in unpaid back taxes. Charlie's property was placed into receivership. It was reported that Charlie's problems put him to bed with a nervous breakdown at the Fifth Avenue apartment of Nathan Burkan, his attorney. Burkan expressed to my attorneys a desire to settle, but a settlement was not forthcoming. It was my understanding that Charlie was unable to deal with the situation.

Charlie's attorneys failed to answer my complaint for divorce for nearly six months as they were trying to settle for sums of money Uncle Edwin found unsuitable. Charlie's attorneys wanted to give me $25 a week in temporary support—an absurd sum—and Uncle Edwin wanted $1,000 a week. Charlie's attorneys suggested a divorce settlement of $200,000. Uncle Edwin was holding out for a million dollars. In the meantime, my lawyers went about investigating Charlie's finances while Charlie's attorneys attempted in vain to build a case that I was an unfit mother. It was during this period of endless depositions that we learned that Charlie had bugged my bedroom in an effort to get any information on me that might help him in the future for our divorce. Also, a former cook admitted that Charlie had paid him five dollars to leave his room in the basement of Cove Way so that he and Marion Davies could use the bed. The Japanese chef also remembered the date: 30 March 1926, while I was upstairs giving birth to Sydney. The shock of these revelations was stupefying to me—especially about Marion Davies, whom I had considered, until that time, a friend.

I obtained an alimony order from the courts for a total of $14,400 to cover counsel fees and $4,000 a month for support of the children. However, the money was not immediately forthcoming, as Charlie had not posted the million-dollar bond required to lift the receivership placed over his fortune by the Internal Revenue Service. The press and my lawyers had a field day with this, as my grandfather, with his modest income, was paying for our support. The children and I were depicted by the press as starving. Charlie was portrayed as heartless for not supporting his wife and children. This appearance of neglect did much to harm Charlie's reputation with the public and to label him as frugal and mean. In response, some women's clubs wanted Charlie's films banned and took up collections for the Chaplin children milk fund. Abroad, Charlie received support from French intellectuals who signed a lengthy petition stating, among other things, that Charles Chaplin was beyond reproach.[5]

Charlie and his lawyers were unable to build a case against me. Their strategy to win public sympathy was to defame me and my family by filtering to the press material that referred to me as an illiterate peon from the gutters of Mexico. I thought my grandfather would have a stroke when he read one such piece. "What an insult to your ancestors!" he raved. "How dare anyone print such a deliberate falsehood."

These dreadful falsehoods have persisted over the years. They could not be further from the truth. I am, on my mother's side of the family, the ninth generation to be born in California. In fact, I come from the most fabulous of California Spanish families. I am a descendant, on my mother's side, of the Antonio María Lugo family. The Lugos, who were from Andelucia, Spain, brought the first horses to this country and were one of the first families to be given a land grant from the king of Spain. My great-grandmother was María Merced,[6] who, with her sister, Francisca, owned Rancho Cucamonga and Rancho Santa Ana del Chino in California when these were vast properties with great vineyards. Alvarado, Pico, Rimpau, and Sepúlveda are other family names. In more recent times, I am also the grand-niece of a former governor of California, Henry T. Gage.[7]

My mother was also treated badly by Charlie and his publicity department during this period. She was portrayed as a domineer-

---

5. Chaplin found strong support abroad from a group of French intellectuals in the form of a manifesto entitled "Hands Off Love" that appeared in *Transition*, an English-language literary quarterly published in Paris in the summer of 1927.

6. María Merced Williams Rains Carrillo Fernandez (1839–1907). For a detailed history of María Merced and Lita's ancestry, see Esther Boulton Black, *Rancho Cucamonga and Doña Merced* (Redlands, CA: San Bernardino County Museum Association, 1975).

7. Henry Tifft Gage (1852–1924) was the twentieth governor of California, from 1899 to 1903. Gage was later appointed to the diplomatic post of U. S. Ambassador to Portugal. Lita's great-aunt, Francisca ("Fannie") Victoria Rains, married Gage in 1880.

ing stage mother who orchestrated the relationship between Charlie and me and forced herself in his home as soon as we were married. This is simply not true.

Mama never moved into Charlie's house on her own accord after we were married. It was solely at Charlie's invitation. He wanted to be free to do as he pleased and evidently felt guilty about leaving me alone in the house with the servants. Charlie first brought up the idea of Mama living with us when I was pregnant with Charlie Jr. Soon after Mama and I were brought back to the Cove Way house for Charlie Jr.'s birth, Charlie said, "Why don't you have your mother come and live with us? She wouldn't interfere with us. She can take care of Charlie Jr., and you wouldn't be alone."

Unfortunately, the press and public seemed all too willing to accept the cliché Charlie's publicity department put forth of the overbearing mother-in-law who, with her "gold-digging" relatives, had orchestrated the marriage, and poor Charlie was the mistreated little genius—a victim of circumstances. As to the charge that she was a stage mother who pushed temptation in Charlie Chaplin's path, I can only restate that from the very beginning, when she first met with Charlie and Chuck Riesner outside our home, she was more interested in my education and my being properly chaperoned than building a career for me as an actress. As for the period of my married life, she was always one of Charlie's defenders. No matter how horrendous his actions were toward me, Mama was constantly telling me to "have patience, Lillita, he will change."

Mama and I were both disturbed about how we were portrayed in the press, but we could do little to change public opinion. Charlie Chaplin was the most famous and beloved man in the world. No one wanted to believe he could be capable of such bad behavior. I understood this even then, as I remember when I was at the studio working on *The Kid* how awful we all thought Mildred Harris was for putting Charlie through that divorce she brought against him. I knew public opinion would always be for Charlie.

The children, Mama, and I lived for about a month in a rented house at 713 Linden Drive before the court allowed us, in February, to have temporary use of Charlie's Cove Way house. The court also reduced my monthly support to $3,000 a month, most of which was spent on maintaining the large estate. It was strange living in Charlie's house without Charlie or Kono present. It was during this period that I received many letters from the public, some supportive and some hostile, regarding the divorce proceedings.

Unable to come to an out-of-court settlement with my attorneys, Charlie and his lawyers finally answered my divorce complaint on 2 June 1926. He did not ask for a divorce but requested custody of the children. In his answer, Charlie denied every charge. Moreover, he counterattacked by suggesting that I drank and was having a relationship with another man, which was absolutely false. This changed my stupefaction to indignation. When Uncle Edwin suggested that we force action by threatening to name the "five prominent moving picture women" and Marion Davies as the "certain prominent moving picture actress" referred to in my divorce complaint, I agreed. I went to see Marion at her home. I did not bother to discuss her affair with Charlie. We had no friendship, I now realized, and I found myself unsympathetic toward her. I told her that my attorneys were going to make public Charlie's extramarital affairs, the Charlie Chaplin–Marion Davies affair first among them, unless Charlie came to a settlement agreement.

"W. R. would go crazy!" Marion wailed, visibly shaken. I left her with a glass of champagne in one hand and the telephone receiver in the other. No doubt she called both Charlie and Hearst. It did the trick, for in a few days Charlie was ready to settle.

The lawyers agreed on a settlement, which was approved by Judge Walter Guerin. On 22 August 1927, I was awarded an interlocutory judgment of divorce on grounds of extreme cruelty, custody of my two children, and a sizeable amount of money —$825,000, which included $100,000 in trust for each of the two boys to be established by Charlie, the income from which was to be given over to me monthly for support of the children and the capital of which was to be paid over to the boys when they were thirty-five years of age. Until the trust fund was established, Charlie paid $1,000 a month for the support of the boys. Charlie received reasonable visitation rights.

I was handed a check that very day for $375,000, the balance due over a period of three years. I immediately gave $80,000 to my mother and told her to use it as she pleased. She had been through so much with me, and I felt I had disappointed her after the nice upbringing she had given me. Approximately $200,000 of my settlement went to my attorneys: the Youngs, Uncle Edwin, and George Beebe, who was my attorney for a short period after my separation.

The newspapers had a field day. Gavin McNab, one of Charlie's attorneys, had called the proceedings "The Second Gold Rush." My divorce settlement was the highest such sum ever given in California history until that time. I could not help thinking that day, and many days since then, that because Charlie was so stubborn, and because of his complete disregard for the value of the mother of his two children, he had to pay nearly a million dollars, instead of the $10,000 I had asked for one day in November 1926.

In August 1927, my marriage was dissolved, although the interlocutory decree was not final until 1928. I was not yet out of my teens and was still somewhat naive in some ways. I would have to depend on my grandfather for crucial advice. Uncle Edwin had gone back to San Francisco, but we were still crowded at Grandfather's house. The children, Mama, and I needed a home.

Grandfather suggested that I buy the corner lot at 523 Beverly Drive, next to his house at 521 Beverly Drive, which was then up for sale. I could build a house on the lot of my own liking, be near my grandparents and enjoy the nice area. The house would be at the corner of Beverly Drive and Carmelita Avenue, not far from the Beverly Hills Hotel.

I thought it was a great idea and bought the property, but I had no idea whom I should commission to design the house. The real estate agent who sold me the lot recommended a builder by the name of Roy Seldon Price. Price had designed many wonderful houses and was very famous.

I met with Price and liked his ideas. He was excited to undertake the project, as he had never had to contend with a corner lot. I was also pleased with Grandfather's negotiating skills, for he was able to procure the lot and Price's services for substantially less than their original asking prices. Harold Grieve, whom Price had recommended, was engaged as interior decorator.

Following my sordid divorce, I was determined to rebuild my life and self-esteem. The house was a reflection of this idea. I believe my motive in wanting a home—a house elegant enough to perhaps offset the horrendous publicity the divorce proceedings had put me through—was in my subconscious mind.

And so I desired to have this house, the envy of many, which I hoped would change the public's opinion for whom they might support. It appeared as if half of the public had sided with Charlie and half had sided with me. The house helped raise my self-esteem, which had been severely damaged during the separation and divorce from Charlie.

The house was an eighteen-room Monterey-type structure. It had six master bedrooms, and each of the master bedrooms had its own bathroom. The house had a beautiful dining room with a floor of hand-laid blocks of highly polished oak and a plaster-relief ceiling. The entry hall had imported English wallpaper depicting hounds chasing a fox. The kitchen was enormous, and the refrigeration section ran the entire length of the room. The pantry had service for twenty-four in the best china, silverware, and glassware. On one side of the entry hall was a small room with office needs; on the other was a bathroom with a mirrored wall.

There was an upstairs kitchen and living room. The children's two rooms had a connecting bathroom that was installed with fixtures in miniature—the bathtub, toilet, and basin fixtures were all child sized. The children's breakfast room was illustrated with hand-painted figures of animals.

Mama took the master bedroom that led to the inner courtyard garden. I had a suite composed of one of the five master bedrooms with the upstairs den. All of the bedrooms opened out onto a veranda encircling the second floor of the house. Mama's room was decorated in pink and blue, her favorite colors. Mine was a pale green with satin ceiling and walls.

Tomi and Todah, the couple who had helped us since the days of hiding at the Whitley Heights house when I was pregnant with Charlie Jr., moved in with us. Their quarters were above the four-car garage. Todah was extremely pleased with the well-equipped kitchen he had in which to work.

We even had an organ console installed in the house. Mr. Grieve had sold me on the organ. Music was always so important to me and my family. The idea of having such an instrument was reminiscent of the player piano Grandfather had when I was a little girl. Indeed, this particular pipe organ could be played either manually or with a series of buttons that, when activated, would play whatever music it was programmed to play, much like a player piano.

The house had an outdoor swimming pool. An elaborate garden was designed, with Cécile Bruner rose vines strung along the trellis that connected the house with the pool's dressing rooms. Beautiful pansies adorned the inner garden.

It was during the construction of the house that Mama and I went east to New York City, with a visit to Washington, D.C., in September 1927. Neither Mama nor I had ever been to the East Coast before. We left the boys in California in the care of my grandparents. It was quite a trip, for I was young, rich, and famous and wanted to live it up after all I had been through. There were plenty of social events. In October, I went to Washington, where I was presented to President Coolidge by William Spry, the former governor of Utah, then in the position of U.S. land commissioner. Mama and I also went on a spending spree that severely depleted the settlement money.

When we returned to California, I was thrilled with the completed house, and the thought of the cost did not bother me. The grand total for the lot, house, and garden came to $90,000. We had a housewarming party with champagne and a buffet dinner.

A few years later I was delighted to read in the book *Los Angeles in 7 Days* the following description of the house I built: "At 523 Beverly Drive was one of the loveliest of the homes, a perfect example of the Monterey type, where Lita Grey Chaplin lives with her two little boys."[8]

We had had a glorious year in the house on Beverly Drive, when a man who had made an appointment to see me knocked on my door. His name was Harry Weber of the Weber-Simon Agency, an outstanding theatrical agency in New York's Palace Theatre Building, whom I had met at a party in New York.

Over lunch, Harry explained that the purpose of his visit was to ask whether I might be interested in signing with the Radio-Keith-Orpheum vaudeville circuit as an act to be billed as "Lita Grey Chaplin: Songs to Remember."

I told Harry that, although I came from a musical family, I did not have the proper background to become a professional theater engagement. I had no professional stage experience. Harry

---

8. Lanier Bartlett and Virginia Stivers Bartlett, *Los Angeles in 7 Days* (New York: Robert M. McBride & Company, 1932), p. 114. One cannot underestimate the importance of this brief quote on Lita's self-esteem. It is suggestive that, along with her Webster's dictionary and one-volume encyclopedia, her copy of *Los Angeles in 7 Days* remained on her bedside table at all times, until her death in 1995.

seemed undeterred. He extended me an offer of $2,500 a week. His circuit bosses believed that with a colorful set behind me, a good wardrobe, and excellent song material, I could be sold as "a name from Hollywood."

I was interested in his offer, and he further elaborated his ideas. I would sing popular songs in an elaborate set dressed with gold drapes and red stairs. Two pianos would grace the stage. I would have a stunning wardrobe. The circuit would handle all the publicity. An advance would be made to me if I were unable or unwilling to handle the necessary expenses up front.

"I'll have to think it over" was my response.

I discussed the possibilities first with Mama, for she would be the one left behind to supervise the running of the household and the care of the children.

"I think you should discuss it with your grandfather," Mama said. "He knows more about contracts, finances, and so forth, than I do."

Knowing how Grandfather had consistently felt about any of his family appearing on the stage, I approached him gingerly. After I had explained Harry Weber's offer in detail, I was surprised by Grandfather's response.

"I'm glad you've come to me about this," he said. "I've been doing some serious thinking about the advice I gave you to buy the lot and build a house on it. That, I now realize, was bad advice on my part. I've seen from your bills that the overhead for operating a house of this type is outrageous for your means. I don't think you should turn down this offer—you can't afford to turn it down."

Grandfather recommended that I should rent out my beloved Beverly Drive home and find a small, modest bungalow for the children, Mama, and myself. Tomi and Todah could come during the day, and with the children's income paying their half-share I would be furthering my financial interests substantially month by month.

That settled the matter. I agreed to my grandfather's plan. We had quite an emotional moment as I told him he should not feel guilty in the least for his advice to buy the lot and build a house. I told him how much I loved him and appreciated his support through the years. It was only since my marriage that I had begun to appreciate the stability he gave to my life. I was glad we had that talk, for Grandfather was to die while I was on the road, less than a year later, on 2 April 1929.

We had a lot to do now. I informed Harry of my intentions to accept his offer and join the circuit. A lumberman from Seattle signed a year's lease for the Beverly Hills house—he would be moving in the following month. A bungalow on Rossmore Avenue was rented. It had three bedrooms so Tomi and Todah could be live-in help. Tomi and Todah helped us move.

Harry came back to California with the circuit's signed contract for my signature. Since I had notified him of my willingness to accept his offer, he had been interviewing pianists and talking to potential set designers.

Plans for the act moved along. The special song material was catchy, and the set was beautiful—with gold drapes that opened over red stairs and two pianos, as Harry had described to me on our first meeting.

The tryout house, used mainly for looking at new acts for the circuit, was an old small theater in Long Beach, California. The circuit would send their representative there to pass judgment on me. If they liked my act, I was in business.

I was terribly nervous in Long Beach, anticipating the opening night of my act. Everything had gone all right so far, but actually facing an audience gave me pause. Fortunately, my two pianists, Pat Casey and Roland Becker, and their wives were able to ease my mind at the theater as well as at the hotel in which we were staying.

We had strung together some popular songs with special material for the opening. I knew the material well but was still nervous.

My opening night was 5 October 1928. It was eight o'clock, and I stood in the wings of the theater shaking. My entrance music was played by the pit band, and to my surprise I remembered all the lyrics, sang all the songs as I had done in rehearsals, walked off the stage after my closing number, and the audience applauded. I took a bow, walked off, and came back for another bow. I stood as the curtain closed before me.

I was a hit. The audience was still applauding for me to take another bow. Instead, I went to the dressing room. I had had enough applause. Pat and Roland hugged me, and after changing clothes we left for a late snack at the hotel.

The circuit accepted my act. I was relieved, but I knew I was an amateur. Over time I would learn the tricks of walking on stage, taking bows, and developing a rapport with an audience. In the interim, I had a beautiful set, a nice smile, and an excellent stage wardrobe.

It was the end of 1928, less than a year before the stock market crash, and I was about to embark on a career as a performer.

Epilogue

In October 1928, Lita Grey Chaplin began what was to be nearly a decade of work on the Radio-Keith-Orpheum vaudeville circuit. In the late 1920s, her act was composed of a special introductory song, followed by such popular ballads as "Baby, Oh Where Can You Be?" and "Bring Back My Mother to Me," with "Till We Meet Again" as a closing song. Her act was accompanied by two pianists—Roland Becker and Pat Casey—on a set that consisted of a red staircase and gold curtain. Her wardrobe was equally ornate: long sequined and beaded gowns and elaborate jewelry. She was an immediate critical and popular success.

The lavishness of her vaudeville act was a reflection of her off-stage life. Lita's excessive spending, along with poor money management and the stock market crash of October 1929, eliminated much of her divorce settlement fortune. She was soon dependent on the salary she made as a vaudeville talent, which was reduced from $2,500 to $1,500 a week as a result of the Depression. Her income was supplemented by renting her Beverly Drive home; among her famous tenants over the years were Clark Gable,[1] Jack Benny,[2] Eddie Cantor,[3] Walter Winchell,[4] and William Powell[5]

---

1. Clark Gable (William Clark Gable) (1901–1960) was the motion picture actor known as "The King of Hollywood" and is best remembered as Rhett Butler in the film version of *Gone with the Wind* (1939).

2. Jack Benny (Benjamin Kubelsky) (1894–1974) was a beloved vaudeville, radio, and television comedian. *The Jack Benny Program* (1950–1965) was a television favorite.

3. Eddie Cantor (Edward Israel Iskowitz) (1892–1964) was a popular vaudeville, stage, film, radio, and television entertainer.

4. Walter Winchell (1897–1972) was a syndicated gossip columnist and radio commentator.

5. William Powell (1892–1984) was a suave stage and screen actor best known for playing Nick Charles in the film *The Thin Man* (1934) and the five film sequels.

before she eventually sold the property. Her children lived with their grandmother, supported by the income their father provided until the establishment of their trust funds. At first Lillian Grey had traveled with Lita on the vaudeville circuit, leaving the children in the care of nurses and Lita's grandmother. Lillian, however, quickly tired of the traveling and returned to California to care for the children. Lita eventually hired Gladys Thompson as her dresser and help for on the road. Gladys, who called Lita "Skipper," remained a life long friend.

After her divorce, Lita had romances with film actor Roy D'Arcy,[6] announcing a "trial engagement" in October 1928. The romance lasted less than a year, and D'Arcy remarried his former wife. A relationship with Phil Baker,[7] a well-known Los Angeles musical comedy actor, was also reported in the press. They announced their engagement in the autumn of 1929, but that too was short-lived.

In March 1930, Lita made her first trip abroad as a holiday from Radio-Keith-Orpheum. While she was in Paris, she was introduced to Georges Carpentier,[8] the former boxing champion. There was an immediate attraction, but Lita disliked the idea of being "the other woman," as Carpentier was married and had a daughter. The more she turned him down, the more Carpentier pursued her. The former champion eventually defeated Lita's lingering doubts. Carpentier's wife, Georgette, raised no objections to her husband's extramarital affair. Indeed, she too had a lover but was reluctant to divorce Carpentier for religious reasons. Lita and Carpentier had a happy relationship that lasted five years.

Lita's affair with Carpentier was not widely reported in the press because of his marriage. However, the two did make head-

---

6. Roy D'Arcy (Roy Guisti) (1894–1969) was a vaudeville, stage, and film actor best known for his villainous roles in silent films. His most notable screen credit is Erich von Stroheim's *The Merry Widow* (1925), in which he plays Crown Prince Mirko.

7. Phil Baker (1896–1963) was a successful stage, film, and radio comedian.

8. Georges Carpentier (1894–1975) was a French boxer who held the world's light heavyweight championship from 1920 to 1922. The 1921 boxing match between Carpentier and Jack Dempsey, in which Carpentier was knocked out in the fourth round, was called "The Fight of the Century." Carpentier retired from boxing in 1924 and was an attraction in vaudeville and films before becoming a Parisian restaurateur. Carpentier moved freely among cosmopolitan society and had been a friend of Charles Chaplin's since 1921.

lines in January 1931 when they were robbed by four young men, armed with revolvers, as they stepped into their car after Lita's appearance at a Bronx, New York, vaudeville theater. The men had seen her act and were attracted to the expensive rings, bracelets, and necklace that she wore onstage. Abducted in Lita's own limousine, the couple was driven for more than a mile before being released unharmed.

It was the influence of Carpentier that gave Lita the idea that her children should live in France for an extended period to learn the language and broaden their education. While Lita was back touring in the States, Charles Jr. and Sydney went to Nice in December 1931 for nearly a year with their grandmother where they learned to speak fluent French.

Despite Lita's successful career and relationship with Carpentier, Charles Chaplin retained a very central role in Lita's life. She chose to keep the name he had given her—Lita Grey Chaplin—and there were his sons. Chaplin had not exercised his visiting rights since the time of their separation in November 1926. Nearly three years later, in September 1929, Chaplin did see his children again. The visit was at the instigation of Louisa Curry, Lita's maternal grandmother, who made the arrangements in the absence of Lita and her mother, who were then out of town. Chaplin, however, was not to see them again until 1932. Chaplin did take an interest in their lives, through his attorneys. Of particular interest to him was the way the child support money was being spent.

In 1932, Lita's salary as a vaudeville entertainer had dropped to $550 a week. She had become a pleasing contralto singer, but she was no longer a novelty; her reception was no longer pronounced over other acts. She had incorporated impressions, such as of Sophie Tucker, into her act, and would sing songs that referred to her being the former wife of Charlie Chaplin. "Without a Man" was a song she liked in particular.

Her diminishing income made an offer from Fox Film Corporation alluring. On 22 June 1932, Fox Film Corporation and Lita Grey Chaplin signed a contract to make a film, which carried an option for other films, that would involve Lita and her two sons. Lita would receive $35,000: $15,000 for her acting services and $10,000 each for the services of her children. The initial project was tentatively a film adaptation of the New York stage play *The*

Little Teacher, to be directed by David Butler.[9] Lita came west from New York, rented a house at 224 North Rossmore Avenue in Hollywood, and cabled to her mother to bring the children home to Hollywood from Nice. In July 1932, Butler made extensive tests with the children. Fox mounted a publicity campaign announcing the forthcoming screen debuts of little Charlie and "Tommy" Chaplin.

Lita and the children, however, would never act in the film. On 25 August 1932, Chaplin, through his attorney Loyd Wright, filed a petition objecting to his sons appearing in films. The divorced parents appeared in court on 27 August. At a further hearing on 2 September, Judge H. Parker Wood ruled in Chaplin's favor. Public opinion sided with Chaplin, believing that the boys should lead a normal childhood. Lita persisted in the matter, requesting a new hearing the next day. The father's opinion was upheld. Lita made a third attempt in October, with her petition in court in which she appealed to Chaplin to reconsider, attaching a copy of a ten-page letter that she had mailed Chaplin in which she attempted to explain why it was so important to have the children and her in films. She wrote:

> In the divorce action I was put in a most unfavorable and unfair light. . . . Even today, there is still a great part of the public still willing to believe anything detrimental to me on my account. I know and you know . . . the charges that I was a "little Mexican gold-digger, without education and refinement" and many other far worse accusations are still ringing and still believed. . . . The principal reason for my study and my going into vaudeville was because it gave me the opportunity to appear before the public in the hope that I might, by such contact with the public, be able to remove at least the impression that I was coarse, vulgar and uneducated.

Chaplin was unmoved, contending Lita's epistle to be overlong, overwrought, but most of all inaccurate. He was annoyed that Lita's attorney-uncle had subpoenaed him (he was served the subpoena while calling on his sons on 15 October) to appear again in

---

9. David Butler (1894–1979) began as an actor, most notably in the film *7th Heaven* (1927), before becoming a motion picture and television director. Butler developed a reputation for his ability to direct child performers, directing four of Shirley Temple's best films for Fox.

court on a matter he considered resolved. On 26 October, both parents appeared in court, where the case was decided again in Chaplin's favor. In later years, Lita saw the wisdom in Chaplin's conviction against a film career for their young children. However, she maintained the belief that her former husband was motivated less by paternal concern than with the idea of actors with the name Chaplin appearing in films that he did not control.

Although Chaplin had prevented his sons from appearing in the films at Fox, Lita on her own made two films during this period. *Mr. Broadway* and a Vitaphone two-reeler called *Seasoned Greetings* were both made in New York between vaudeville engagements and released in 1933.

The children continued to aggravate the lingering hostility between the former husband and wife. After Chaplin had established the trust funds for the boys in April 1933, Chaplin, through his attorneys, was constantly questioning Lita's administration of the boys' trust funds. A year after the Fox Film Corporation court battle, Lita was summoned to court in September 1933 by Chaplin to explain the children's expenses. Lita always saw this as harassment. Chaplin had the boys' expenditures cut and a weekly savings account set up for them. Although there was never any finding of impropriety, she hired an accountant, Julia Bergh, to administer and account for all the children's expenses. The itemized and detailed accountings prepared by Bergh, down to the children's $2.50 haircuts, effectively stopped Chaplin's questioning.

Lita's attorneys suggested that the boys should be sent to military school. Chaplin also favored the idea, as Lita, her mother, or Chaplin could arrange to have Charles Jr. and Sydney home on weekends with little contact between the two hostile camps. The boys were enrolled in Black-Foxe Military Institute in Hollywood.

Although an apartment in the Southgate Building in New York was Lita Grey Chaplin's home base for several years, she tried to see her children as often as she could. On one such visit to Hollywood, she arranged to have a party for her sons at the Ambassador Hotel in Los Angeles, where she first met Paulette Goddard.[10] Lita later remembered:

10. Paulette Goddard (Marion Goddard Levy) (1910–1990) was the common-law wife of Charles Chaplin from 1936 to 1942, playing The Gamin in *Modern Times* (1936) and Hannah in *The Great Dictator* (1940). She later married actor Burgess Meredith (marriage dissolved) and novelist Erich Maria Remarque.

I arranged to have a private room at the Ambassador Hotel for a party for the boys. It consisted of about fifteen boys from Black-Foxe, with party favors, cake, and the things small children like at a party. Before I came west by train, I had telegrammed Charlie that I was having a party for the boys and would he like to attend, just to be polite. He surprised me by coming. I opened the door of the party room at the Ambassador and there was Charlie, tanned and looking very well. He acted like an old friend, very pleasant—after all the terrible stuff we had been through—he was just as polite as he could be.

I offered Charlie a glass of champagne. He said, "I think I better leave now. I have Paulette waiting in the car outside, and she is probably getting impatient."

I said to him, "Why don't you invite her up? Maybe she would enjoy a glass of champagne? I'd love to meet her."

"Would that be all right?" he said like a timid little boy, totally unlike the man I had married.

He brought in Paulette Goddard. I had never seen such a beautiful woman, with her dark, soft, shoulder-length hair. She wore a black velvet dress and a string of pearls. While Charlie was visiting with the children, Paulette and I had a pleasant conversation.

"You probably don't remember this," she said to me, "but I used to model clothes in New York, and I used to model clothes for you."

The comment endeared her to me right away. I don't think most people in her position would have admitted that. She was humble and very likable.

Paulette was wonderful to my two boys. I really don't think her relationship with Charlie would have lasted as long as it did if it hadn't been for my children because she had such a good time with the kids. She would take them down to San Diego on Charlie's boat, the *Panacea*, or skiing. She would always send me a little note, keeping me informed of what the boys were doing. Paulette also encouraged Charlie to develop a relationship with the boys, which might not have existed without her.

Lita had been drinking socially since her divorce from Chaplin, in an effort to appear older and sophisticated. After she chose to end her affair with Carpentier, who was himself busy with his own vaudeville engagements, she began to drink heavily and in turn sleep very little.

In 1935, already an alcoholic, she began the national tour of the musical comedy *Life Begins at 8:40*, costarring Milton Berle.[11] The show was not a success, closing after eight weeks. She changed her representation, leaving Harry Weber for Lou Irwin,[12] who handled the very top variety entertainers. Irwin booked Lita to open the Stork Club in New York. The success of her Stork Club engagement allowed Irwin to negotiate for her to play London's Cafe de Paris as part of an arrangement that would require her to play throughout the British Isles through the Gaumont British Theatres.

Lita sailed for England on the SS *Lafayette* in November 1935 for appearances in London, where her new special material, "I'm the Wife of the Life of the Party" and "I Was Only Looking for a Flat," was well received by English audiences and critics. By her own account, her Cafe de Paris engagement was the highlight of her entire professional career. In the spring of 1936, Lita toured Britain with Frank Loesser[13] replacing Irving Actman as her pianist. On Easter Sunday 1936, Lita collapsed on stage in Glasgow, Scotland, with her first nervous breakdown, the result of alcohol abuse and physical exhaustion. She remained in the hospital for several days in Glasgow before she was brought to Los Angeles for further medical treatment.

Lita would explain in later life that she was then harboring a neurosis caused by Chaplin's rejection of her over ten years earlier, which she found to be highly traumatic. When Lita broke her body down by excessive drinking and a demanding vaudeville career, the neurosis, she would explain, had overtaken her.

Lita lived in a house in the San Fernando Valley with her mother and grandmother during her convalescence. The following several months were a period of seclusion for Lita, particularly after she blurted out to Charles Jr. the actual facts of her marriage to his father and that the date of his birth had been falsified. Lita had kept the true history of the unhappy union from the children up

---

11. Milton Berle (Milton Berlinger) (b. 1908) is the comedian best-known for his groundbreaking television work in the 1940s and 1950s that earned him the moniker "Mr. Television."

12. Lou Irwin (1895–1978) was an agent who represented many prominent vaudeville, stage, radio, television, and motion picture talents.

13. Frank Loesser (Henry Loesser) (1910–1969) was a songwriter turned musical comedy writer who wrote the music and lyrics to the musicals *Guys and Dolls* (1950) and *How to Succeed in Business without Really Trying* (1961).

until that time. Her son Sydney remembers that during the nervous breakdown Lita would calmly tell him that his father and Mr. Hearst were spying on her and trying to poison her.

With Lita still not well but improving, her great-aunt, Fannie Gage, came to visit with Henry Aguirre Jr.,[14] a tap dancer. Aguirre felt sorry for Lita and called on her regularly after their first meeting. On one such occasion, Lita asked Henry to marry her, for she felt if someone could get her away from her scornful mother and grandmother—who kept telling her that if she had not been in show business she would not be in her present condition—she could get well. Lita and Aguirre went to Santa Ana, California, where they were secretly married on 21 September 1936. Aguirre's doctor, Dr. Edward Franklin, had Lita well in three months with a therapy that consisted of, among other things, calcium gluconate injections. As soon as Lita recovered her health, she wanted to end her marriage to Aguirre. Aguirre, however, wanted to continue as husband and wife. In May 1937, Lita's contested suit of divorce was unsuccessful. The ensuing complications made headlines. Lita had charged extreme cruelty, claiming Aguirre had said, in November of the previous year, in the presence of friends, that she was "the meanest woman in the world." Aguirre's answer denied her charges and did not ask for a divorce. Judge Charles S. Burnell denied Lita's decree on the grounds of insufficient evidence and reprimanded her for the "peculiar Hollywood custom of short marriages" with particular reference to her. Lita found more evidence against Aguirre in the testimony of her mother as a witness, and on 1 July 1937 she was granted an interlocutory decree of divorce from Aguirre.

Feeling she had recovered completely and living at the Ravenswood apartment building in Hollywood, Lita met Arthur Day[15] at a party. She was attracted to the wit and charm of Day, who was a man of much intelligence but little ambition. Day became her manager and, after a year's courtship, her husband. They were married in Manhattan Beach, California, on 5 July 1938. While on their honeymoon at St. Catherine's Hotel on Catalina Island,

14. Henry Aguirre Jr. (b. 1910) was the second husband of Lita Grey Chaplin.

15. Arthur Franceway Day Jr. (1909–1985) was the third husband of Lita Grey Chaplin.

they were informed by the press that their marriage was invalid, for Lita's interlocutory decree of divorce from Henry Aguirre had not yet become final. Under California law at that time, a year and a day had to elapse before a final decree could be granted. One headline read, "All She Could Say Was 'Oops.'" They were quietly remarried three days later, on 8 July 1938.

Lita and Arthur Day adopted a baby boy in 1940 whom they named Robert Arthur Day. Lita gave up her nightclub career and settled down in a house in the San Fernando Valley on five-and-a-half acres of land with a swimming pool, citrus trees, and the two St. Bernard dogs, Samson and Delilah, that Paulette Goddard had given Charles Jr. and Sydney for Christmas but that Chaplin refused to keep at his home.

Lita's marriage to Day would have lasted longer had it not been for Day's drinking. His frequent parties and bad example caused Lita to start drinking beer and wine. She was soon drinking heavily again, which culminated with an illness while on a visit to New York in 1943. Day sent Lita, severely ill from alcoholism and depression, back to California, where her mother and Gladys Thompson met her at the train station. At five feet eight inches, Lita weighed just ninety pounds.

With another failed marriage and with Charles Jr. and Sydney serving in the army—Charles Jr. in the 89th Infantry Division and Sydney in the 65th Infantry Division—Lita was physically and emotionally at a low point. It was during the Second World War that Lita had her last encounter with Chaplin, who had recently married Oona O'Neill.[16] Lita later remembered:

> I called Charlie and I said, "You know we have two wonderful children. We went through a lot of pain—the both of us—I think we ought to be friends. I think we ought to be civil to each other." He said, "I agree." He came down to the house that I had built and picked me up and took me for a long ride to the beach. I was ill, and

---

16. Oona O'Neill Chaplin (1925–1991), the daughter of playwright Eugene O'Neill, married Charles Chaplin on 16 June 1943. Their marriage withstood all the troubles that beset them, and they had eight children: Geraldine Leigh (b. 1944), Michael John (b. 1946), Josephine Hannah (b. 1949), Victoria (b. 1951), Eugene Anthony (b. 1953), Jane Cecil (b. 1957), Annette Emily (b. 1959), and Christopher James (b. 1962). Lady Chaplin (Chaplin was knighted in 1975) chose not to remarry after Chaplin's death on Christmas Day 1977.

told him so, and shared with him my fear that I might not get better,
although I would try and get help. He gave me encouragement and
said to me, "Lita, if it's any consolation to you, I'd like to tell you
now that there are only two women that I've really loved in my life,
you and the girl I'm married to now."

It is suggestive that Lita held on to Chaplin's statement to the
end of her life. She later reflected:

I looked upon his remark as vindication. He acted the way he did
toward me not because he didn't love me, but he did it to protect
what he created. That's the only explanation I can come to. All the
bitterness of the divorce and all the rejection of the marriage and all
this stuff, I finally got old enough to understand what motivated him
to be so malicious. His real love was the Tramp, the character he
created. That was the love of his life, the Tramp and his career.
Anything that threatened the career would bring out the worst in
him. I had to grow up quite a bit in order to understand this.

Lita entered a sanitarium for alcoholism and severe depression.
Dr. Albert Best, Dr. Edward Franklin's successor, conducted an
aggressive course of treatment including shock therapy. Arthur
Day's mother raised Bobby Day, the child Lita and Arthur had
adopted. Lita had little contact with her adopted son after the couple parted in July 1946. Lita and Arthur Day divorced in September 1948.

After prolonged care, Lita regained her health and became determined to rebuild her singing career. She met Danny Arnold,[17]
whom she hired to handle her nightclub bookings and accompany
her on the road. Lita and Arnold were also romantically involved
during this period. When the travel expenses no longer made her
nightclub career profitable, she made her last appearance as a performer in the film *The Devil's Sleep* (1949), with Arnold cowrit-
ing the script as well as being the film's assistant director.
Although Lita and Danny Arnold would end their romantic relationship, their strong friendship continued to the end of his life in

---

17. Danny Arnold (1925–1995) was a television writer and producer who was
the creative force behind the successful television series *Barney Miller* (1975–
1982). In the 1960s, Lita wanted to write a fictionalized version of her humorous
nightclub experiences with Arnold in a novel she had tentatively entitled *Canned
Heat*.

1995, and he helped Lita financially whenever she needed assistance.

In 1950, Lita opened the Lita Grey Chaplin Talent Agency and worked for a short time as an agent. The overhead forced her to close the agency after only two years with a large debt, which took her several years to pay off completely. However, she took pride in the fact that she was able to help such struggling young actors as David Janssen,[18] getting him his first contract with Universal.

After the failure of the Lita Grey Chaplin Talent Agency, Lita moved in with Charles Jr. and her mother. She could not live with Charles Jr. for long, as his own severe alcoholism would have caused her to relapse. When Charles Chaplin's reentry permit was rescinded in September 1952, while sailing to London on the SS *Queen Elizabeth* to attend the premiere of his film *Limelight*, Lita was subpoenaed by the Federal Bureau of Investigation. She was questioned on 20 October 1952, but refused to help the bureau in its attempt to build a case against her former husband. It was during this period, when Chaplin's name was making headlines, that Lita started to write her account of her marriage to Charles Chaplin. She also began volunteer work—at the invitation of Ida Mayer Cummings, the sister of Louis B. Mayer—at the Jewish Home for the Aging. Lita also took up card playing, which she would enjoy throughout the rest of her life.

It was on one such evening playing cards that an actor friend introduced her to Pat Longo,[19] who was then a part-time big band musician working as a loan officer for the Union Bank and Trust Company. Lita and Longo began dating and on 22 September 1956 were married at the Little Brown Church in the Valley. They lived in a small house at 8276 Gould Avenue, in the Laurel Canyon section of Hollywood. Lita became a housewife once again, a role she enjoyed.

It was during her marriage to Longo that she seriously began the writing of her autobiography, which she called *Trilby Doesn't Have Anything on Me*. Her manuscript, which took nearly ten years for her to complete, ran six hundred pages. Her marriage to

---

18. David Janssen (David Harold Meyer) (1930–1980) was a television and film actor best known for his starring role in the television series *The Fugitive* (1963–1967).

19. Pat Joseph Longo (Patsy Pizzolongo) (b. 1929) was the fourth husband of Lita Grey Chaplin.

Longo ended just as her book went to press, for Longo had fallen in love with another woman. They separated amicably (Lita even helped him pack his things) in February 1966 and divorced in July 1966. Lita authorized the publication of *My Life with Chaplin*, as the book was retitled, in September 1966. The book was mainly the creation of her coauthor, Morton Cooper, who rewrote her manuscript. Although she was unhappy with the inaccuracies and distortions of the text, she did not protest, for it was a low point in her life financially and she did not want to do anything to jeopardize the book's being published. The book sold well, but not as well as the publisher had hoped. Many critics at the time thought the book was distasteful in its intimate revelations.

As a result of his alcoholism, Charles Chaplin Jr. died suddenly on 20 March 1968 in the Hollywood home he shared with his grandmother. He had just been released from the hospital, where he was treated for a broken ankle. His body was severely damaged by alcohol, and his heart just stopped that morning. He collapsed on the bathroom floor where paramedics were unable to revive him. His death was a great personal loss, both for Lita and her mother, who had lived with Charles Jr. for most of his life. Following her son's death, a sober Arthur Day returned to Lita's life. In an effort to rebuild her life and to maintain a steady income, in November 1970 Lita began work at Robinson's department store in Beverly Hills, working as a sales clerk in better ladies' sportswear.

In February 1975, Lita moved into a two-bedroom, third-floor apartment at 8440 Fountain Avenue, West Hollywood, with Arthur Day, platonically. This apartment would be her home until her death twenty years later. Until she was no longer able to give her the care she needed at the very end of her life, Lillian Grey lived with Lita and Arthur. Lillian was later moved to a nursing home where she died in 1985, aged ninety-seven. Arthur Day also died that year. Lita's work at Robinson's proved to be a solace during her bereavement. A fall at work, however, forced her retirement in February 1986.

In her last decade, Lita was sought out by those interested in her marriage to Charles Chaplin and the early days of Hollywood. She attended several Cinecon conventions, an annual meeting of cinema enthusiasts held in Los Angeles. She also began writing notes and assembling material as the initial step to writing a second, and more accurate, account of her marriage to Chaplin.

An appearance at the University of Southern California in 1993, where she discussed Charlie Chaplin after a screening of *The Gold Rush,* introduced Lita to many students who became her friends and were regularly invited over to her apartment to play poker. She acted in one friend's short student film, called *Bookends,* and was the subject of another friend's student film project. From these young friends Lita discovered that she was now regarded as a vital witness to early film history.

Lita became a showpiece at Chaplin-related events. She was invited to attend the Los Angeles press show and premiere of Richard Attenborough's *Chaplin* in 1992 and the American premiere of the restored silent version of *The Gold Rush* in 1994, where, to her astonishment, she was treated as a celebrity. Although she gave surprisingly few interviews in her long life, her last years saw Lita helping many people interested in Chaplin and her brief marriage to him. Her first major interview was with Kevin Brownlow and David Gill for their documentary *Unknown Chaplin* (1983), recorded in March 1981. She allowed several others over the next fourteen years, one of the last for the CBS/Fox laser disc version of *The Gold Rush*, which was taped in November 1993.

Lita Grey Chaplin spent her last year in her modest apartment working on her new book, answering the fan mail she still received, planning the next poker game, and doing the *Los Angeles Times* crossword puzzle over the telephone with her friend Adolph Levy, a retired lawyer. Sydney Chaplin was a dutiful son, paying the majority of her expenses and driving up from Palm Springs to visit her at least once a month.

The death of her friend Danny Arnold in August 1995 precipitated her last illness. It began with nausea that kept her home, although she would still see friends who came to call on her and work on the manuscript of her book, albeit at a reduced level. Most of her energy was spent in an attempt to get well. She attributed the nausea to being upset at Arnold's death. Her nurse, Carmen DeJesus, would prepare the "healthful" drinks and foods she believed would alleviate her discomfort and perhaps make her feel better. Video cassettes of Charlie Chaplin films, many of which she had not seen before, also put Lita in good spirits.

After a few months, it was clear that she should seek medical attention, although she did not feel strong enough to leave her apartment. In late October, she had a series of tests performed that revealed she had a small malignancy on the right side of her chest. Lita opted for a six-week course of radiation treatments, and she was optimistic at first. In early December, she became so ill during the night that her nurse rushed her to the hospital. She never came home. Terminally ill and requiring care she could not receive at her apartment, Lita was taken to the Motion Picture and Television Fund Country House and Hospital in Woodland Hills, California, where she deteriorated quickly. In the early morning of 29 December 1995, Lillita MacMurray, who had spent the majority of her life as Lita Grey Chaplin, died. As were her wishes, she was cremated, and no services were performed.

Introduction to the Chaplin Divorce Documents

Just a few months before she died, Lita Grey Chaplin reflected on the divorce complaint she had filed against her then husband, Charles Chaplin, nearly seventy years before. "I was eighteen years old when the complaint was drawn, and the lawyers had completely taken charge of the case, putting everything in their language and exaggerating it. It was such an ugly document that they sold it on street corners. I'm not saying that it is untruthful; I'm merely saying that I am not proud of it because I could have exercised better judgment.

"The complaint is not inaccurate," she continued, "but it is worded in such a way that it is exaggerated. It expresses things that occurred that should not be mentioned in polite society, particularly the parts referring to activities in the bedroom." She concluded, "It is hard for me to discuss it because I can't deny the things happened, but I can say that I am ashamed of making it public."

It remains an extraordinary document. An unusual forty-two pages in length, the complaint for divorce filed by Lillita Louise Chaplin, plaintiff, against Charles Spencer Chaplin, et al., defendants, contains allegations so shocking that within three days of its filing, opportunists were selling it throughout downtown Los Angeles (and eventually throughout the world) as a steamy pamphlet under such titles as *The Complaint of Lita*, *Charles Chaplin's Divorce Case*, and *Complaint of the Young Movie Star against Her Elderly Husband (And Famous Film Magnate)*.

Then, as now, divorce complaints generally ran only a few

pages, briefly delineating the facts of the union (number of children, length of time together, date of the dissolution, etc.), a statement of the grounds for divorce (adultery, abandonment, or, in today's no-fault regimes, "irreconcilable differences"), and a request for the relief sought (divorce and custody). The complaint filed by Lita Grey Chaplin was different—designed not only to sway a judge but to so sully Charles Chaplin's greatest asset, his reputation with his audience, as to force him into a large settlement with his young wife.

The complaint accomplished both purposes. Within hours of its filing on 10 January 1927, Lita's lawyers had convinced Superior Court Judge Walton J. Wood to issue a temporary restraining order tying up almost the entirety of Charles Chaplin's fortune, estimated at that time to be anywhere from six to sixteen million dollars. Lita's lawyers had designed the suit to accomplish this purpose, naming not only the Chaplin Studios, Inc., the Charles Chaplin Film Corporation, United Artists Corporation, and various banks as defendants but also a host of Chaplin's financial associates from Toraichi Kono (Chaplin's valet) to Defendant "Doe Two" (film producer Samuel Goldwyn). Lita's lawyers had cast a wide net under the assumption that Chaplin had already made considerable efforts to hide a great deal of his assets. In 1927, Charles Chaplin was one of the richest men in Hollywood and, indeed, one of the wealthiest men in the world.

Not only was the public privy to the contents of the complaint on the street, but the popular press made the salacious divorce filing their headline—displacing such stories as the landing of U. S. Marines in Nicaragua, the threat of war with Mexico, and the Teapot Dome scandal. The morning these headlines broke, a mob descended on the county clerk's office, demanding (as the law provided) to exercise their right to view the public complaint. As a precautionary measure, R. F. Gragg, chief deputy county clerk, finally ordered his subordinates to lock up the document for fear that it would be torn to pieces prior to trial.

The complaint accused Chaplin of crimes and indiscretions of the worst kind: seduction of a minor, statutory rape, sexual perversion, soliciting abortions, and threats of murder. So base and perverted were his alleged actions that Lita's lawyers often failed to name them outright, opting instead to use indirect language such as:

throughout the entire married life of said parties and at times too numerous for plaintiff to more particularly specify, defendant has solicited, urged and demanded that plaintiff submit to, perform and commit such acts and things for the gratification of defendant's said abnormal, unnatural, perverted and degenerate sexual desires, as to be too revolting, indecent and immoral to set forth in detail in this complaint . . . the aforesaid solicitations and demands were so revolting, degrading and offensive to plaintiff, and were such infamous personal indignities, and showed such a lack of respect, and such contempt for plaintiff as a wife and a woman, that they were a shock to her refined sensibilities, repulsive to her moral instincts, and abhorrent to her conception of moral and personal decency.

The complaint did, however, name specific acts of perversion that Chaplin had allegedly undertaken. Notable among these was the charge that Chaplin ordered his wife to violate Section 288a of the criminal code, California's Oral Sex Perversion statute prohibiting, "Any person participating in the act of copulating the mouth of one person with the sexual organ of another." The penalty for such an act was upward of fifteen years in the state penitentiary.

Although the complaint left open the question as to whether Lita gave in to her husband's alleged perversions, it did relate the following: "That defendant at no time during their cohabitation, entered or maintained with plaintiff, the normal and ordinary social relations and matrimonial intercourse [later exposition revealing this to mean sexual intercourse], usually existing between man and wife." If this were indeed the case, the careful reader of the complaint might surmise that the couple's two sons were born of immaculate conception.

The final question left open by the document was the identity of the "certain prominent moving picture actress" with whom the complaint alleged Chaplin had an affair and the "five prominent moving picture women" whose "degenerate" actions with him he had allegedly used to taunt his wife. Years later, Lita herself listed the identities of the women. "I had several women who were intimate with Charlie during the marriage whom my attorneys were prepared to call and testify," she said. "This, of course, would never happen, as Marion Davies [consort to the powerful publishing magnate William Randolph Hearst] was at the head of the list. She was the 'certain prominent moving picture actress' of my divorce complaint. The 'five prominent moving picture women' were Edna Purviance, Pola Negri, Claire Windsor,[1] Peggy Hopkins Joyce,[2] and Merna Kennedy."

In the end, the complaint had won Lita a huge settlement and damaged Chaplin's reputation. On 22 August 1927, Lita Grey Chaplin was granted an interlocutory decree of divorce, custody of her two sons, and $825,000 ($625,000 for herself and $100,000 for each son in the form of a trust), the largest divorce settlement in California legal history until that time. The story once again made worldwide headlines, eclipsing even the execution of Sacco and Vanzetti.

Although Charles Chaplin would go on to create such cinematic masterpieces as *City Lights, Modern Times, The Great Dictator, Monsieur Verdoux,* and *Limelight,* the lingering allegations in the divorce complaint would continue to haunt him. Lita explained:

> Many years after the divorce, the United States government with that awful man, J. Edgar Hoover, of the F. B. I. were after Charlie. They were desperately trying to build a case of moral turpitude against him, citing his affairs with underage girls. Charlie left to attend the premiere of *Limelight* in London, and they wouldn't let him back in the country. In the event that Charlie wanted to fight the charges, the government needed some evidence to support their ridiculous claims. The government subpoenaed me in 1952, and they wanted to use my old divorce complaint from 1927 to build their case of moral turpitude because it contained intimate details of my sex life with him. I said, "I'm sorry gentlemen, but I am an adult now and I didn't draw the complaint. It is true that most of the content is correct. However, the way it is presented, the words used, the descriptions of sex, was all drawn up by my attorneys. I can't cooperate with you. Besides, I have two wonderful children by Charlie and I don't want to be responsible for keeping him out of this

1. Claire Windsor (Claire Viola Cronk) (1897–1972) was the beautiful blond actress of silent films with whom Charles Chaplin was sexually involved. Chaplin severed the relationship after he found himself part of Windsor's own staged "disappearance," orchestrated as a publicity stunt.

2. Peggy Hopkins Joyce (Margaret Upton) (1893–1957) had married and divorced five millionaires before arriving in Hollywood in 1922 seeking a career in films. The term "gold digger" was coined for Joyce in the 1920s. It was Chaplin who profited from his short liaison with the notorious Joyce; her stories of her Parisian love life became the basis for his film *A Woman of Paris* (1923).

country." I later got thanks from Oona Chaplin for turning them down.

The extraordinary divorce complaint filed by Lita in the matter of Chaplin vs. Chaplin, Charles Chaplin's answer of 2 June 1927 (summarily denying each of his wife's allegations), Charles Chaplin's cross-complaint, Lita's answer, and various court orders follow in their entirety, reproduced from the original copies. Obvious typographical errors have been amended. Otherwise, the text follows that of the original documents.

IN THE
SUPERIOR COURT OF THE
STATE OF CALIFORNIA
IN AND FOR THE
COUNTY OF LOS ANGELES

No. D-52298

LILLITA LOUISE CHAPLIN,

Plaintiff,

vs.

CHARLES SPENCER CHAPLIN;
THE CHAPLIN STUDIOS, INC., a corporation;
CHARLES CHAPLIN FILM CORPORATION, a corporation;
T. KONO;
ALFRED REEVES;
FIRST NATIONAL BANK OF LOS ANGELES, a corporation;
BANK OF ITALY, a corporation;
SECURITY TRUST & SAVINGS BANK OF LOS ANGELES,
a corporation;
FARMERS & MERCHANTS NATIONAL BANK, a corporation;
UNITED ARTISTS CORPORATION, a corporation;
DOE ONE;[1]
DOE TWO;[2]
DOE THREE;
DOE ONE COMPANY, a corporation;
DOE TWO COMPANY, a corporation;
DOE THREE COMPANY, a corporation.

Defendants.

---

1. Loyd Wright, Charles Chaplin's attorney.
2. Samuel Goldwyn.

COMPLAINT FOR DIVORCE

Plaintiff above named complains of defendants, and for cause of action alleges:

I.

That plaintiff has been for more than one year immediately preceding the commencement of this action, and now is, a bona fide resident of the County of Los Angeles, State of California.

II.

That for the purpose of preventing repetition, the use of the term "defendant" herein will apply and refer to the defendant "Charles Spencer Chaplin" unless otherwise indicated.

III.

For the statistical purposes required by Section 426a of the Code of Civil Procedure of California, plaintiff alleges as follows:

1.—That plaintiff and defendant intermarried at Empalme, in the State of Sonora, Republic of Mexico.

2.—That the date of said marriage was the 25th day of November, 1924.

3.—That the date of the separation of plaintiff and defendant was the 30th day of November, 1926.

4.—That the number of years from the date of the marriage of plaintiff and defendant to the date of their separation is two years and five days.

5.—That there are two children as issue of said marriage, to-wit: Charles Spencer Chaplin, Jr., and Sydney Earl Chaplin.

6.—That the age of said Charles Spencer Chaplin, Jr., is about eighteen months, and the age of said Sydney Earl Chaplin, about nine months.

IV.

Plaintiff alleges that ever since the date of said marriage, defendant has treated plaintiff in a cruel and inhuman manner, and has wrongfully inflicted upon her great and grievous mental suffering and anguish.

V.

That the aforesaid cruel and inhuman treatment of plaintiff by defendant consists of the following specific acts and conduct, to-wit:

(1) That on board the train by which plaintiff and defendant were returning from Mexico, the evening of the day upon which they were married, defendant said to some of his friends who were accompanying them, and within the hearing of plaintiff and others, "Well, boys, this is better than the penitentiary; but it won't last long".

That on the date plaintiff and defendant returned to Los Angeles from Mexico after said marriage, they went to defendant's home for lunch. At said time and place defendant said to plaintiff, "This marriage won't last long. I will make you so damn sick of me that you won't want to live with me".

(2) That during the month of May, 1924, plaintiff and defendant became engaged to be married; that at said time, plaintiff was a virtuous and inexperienced girl, about two months past the age of sixteen years; that thereafter and during said engagement, defendant seduced plaintiff under promise of marriage; that as a result of said seduction, plaintiff became and was pregnant with child at the time of said marriage; that upon the discovery by defendant of said delicate condition of plaintiff, defendant delayed the consummation of said promise of marriage for so long a time in an effort to induce plaintiff to prevent the birth of said child by submitting herself to a criminal operation, and so conducted himself with reference thereto, that plaintiff's said physical condition became and was publicly and generally known at the time of said marriage by reason of the great and wide publicity given to all the facts and circumstances surrounding said marriage; that plaintiff, at all of the times aforesaid, refused to consent and concede to defendant's said wishes and demands with reference to the performance of said operation, solely for the reason that the same was, and would have been, in her judgment and belief, a great social, legal and moral wrong, and on account thereof, contrary,

repugnant and abhorrent to her instincts of motherhood and to her sense and duty of maternal protection and preservation.

That at the time of said marriage plaintiff loved defendant and believed in his love and affection for her, and entered into said marriage willingly on that account, believing that defendant intended to and would carry out his obligations as to said marriage in good faith, and would protect plaintiff and her reputation by thereafter treating her with respect, consideration, love, and conjugal kindness before the world.

That notwithstanding said willingness on plaintiff's part, she had, at the time of said marriage, no practical or reasonable alternative except to enter into the same on account of the facts and circumstances above mentioned. That on the other hand plaintiff is informed and believes, and upon such information and belief alleges the fact to be that defendant entered into said marriage without any intention of carrying out his legal and marital obligations under the said contract, but for the sole and selfish purpose of protecting himself from criminal prosecution for a felony, and with the intent of thereafter carrying out such a deliberate, uniform and unreasonable course of conduct towards plaintiff as to make a continuance of the said marriage relation impossible;

That notwithstanding the aforesaid facts, conditions and circumstances, and the fact that defendant willingly entered into said marriage with full knowledge thereof, defendant has, throughout the entire married life of said parties, and at times and on occasions too numerous to make it possible for plaintiff to give the exact times and circumstances with any greater certainty, wrongfully, falsely, brutally and cruelly accused her and charged her with forcing him to enter into said marriage relation for the purpose of "holding him up," and of "getting money out of him;" that he has likewise in said connection and at such times, accused her on account of said marriage, with being a "gold-digger" and a "blackmailer;" with disgracing him, ruining his career and with standing in the way of his professional success; that on many and diverse of said occasions he has told her that the relation of marriage militated against his success; that she knew he wanted to defer said marriage; that if she had not been selfish and had loved him, she would have "gotten rid" of said baby, as many other women had done for him.

Plaintiff further alleges the following as more specific instances of the aforesaid treatment and conduct:

(a) That while on the train returning from Mexico, the first night of their marriage, plaintiff went into defendant's compartment; as soon as she opened the door, he cried out at her contemptuously and loudly enough that others on said train heard him, "What are you coming in here for? You made me marry you." That plaintiff went out crying.

(b) That on or about the 5th day of January, 1925, defendant came home about 1:30 o'clock A. M., and went into plaintiff's room while she was asleep, and wakened her and commenced to upbraid, reproach and condemn her on account of their said marriage; that at said time plaintiff was in a delicate condition, as aforesaid, and nervous from loss of sleep, and exhausted by excitement and turmoil, and commenced to cry. That she said to defendant: "I am very sorry; but it is not my fault, and I don't see how I can help it. Please let me rest, and don't talk to me any more tonight about it, and I will talk to you in the morning." That defendant replied in an angry and domineering voice: "We'll talk about it right now." That defendant thereupon remained in said room and continued to abuse and condemn plaintiff, as aforesaid, until five o'clock.

(c) That on or about the 15th day of January, 1925, when defendant was preparing to go out, plaintiff began to cry and complained to him about never seeing him, or going out with him, and always being left alone. That defendant thereupon said to her in a sneering, sarcastic tone of voice: "Well, what different kind of treatment can you expect? I didn't marry you because I wanted to; but because you made me."

That the aforesaid treatment of plaintiff by defendant, together with his acts and conduct hereinafter set forth and occurring before the 1st day of February, 1925, kept plaintiff in such a continual state of mental suffering, turmoil and anguish, and on account thereof, in such a continual state of physical unrest, that her said condition was noticed by defendant's physician[3] when said physician had an opportunity of observing defendant's said attitude toward plaintiff and the effect thereof upon her; that said physician, at said time, immediately advised defendant in plaintiff's presence, that it would be dangerous for her to remain in the environment of her home until after her baby was born. That plaintiff

---

3. Dr. Cecil Reynolds.

said she did not want to leave; that all she wanted was peace and quiet; that she would not leave and let defendant charge her with desertion. That said physician thereupon told plaintiff that she could not stand the existing conditions, and would have to get away, and offered to call her own doctor into consultation, and to sign jointly with him, a written statement protecting her against any blame.

That as a result thereof and upon the aforesaid statement having been signed, on or about the 1st day of February, 1925, plaintiff and her mother procured a house by themselves, where they remained for several months.

(3) That defendant at no time during their cohabitation, entered or maintained with plaintiff, the normal and ordinary social relations and matrimonial intercourse, usually existing between man and wife.

In this connection plaintiff alleges with regard to the sexual relations heretofore existing between said parties, that the defendant's attitude, conduct and manifestations of interest therein, have been abnormal, unnatural, perverted, degenerate and indecent, as shown by the following particulars, to-wit:

That throughout the entire married life of said parties and at times too numerous for plaintiff to more particularly specify, defendant has solicited, urged and demanded that plaintiff submit to, perform and commit such acts and things for the gratification of defendant's said abnormal, unnatural, perverted and degenerate sexual desires, as to be too revolting, indecent and immoral to set forth in detail in this complaint. That the aforesaid solicitations and demands were so revolting, degrading and offensive to plaintiff, and were such infamous personal indignities, and showed such a lack of respect, and such a contempt for plaintiff as a wife and a woman, that they were a shock to her refined sensibilities, repulsive to her moral instincts, and abhorrent to her conception of moral and personal decency.

That the aforesaid open solicitations and demands were the culmination of a course of conduct in respect thereto on defendant's part, which commenced shortly after said marriage, and which included his reading to plaintiff from books on such subjects, conversing with her thereon, and recounting to her in detail his personal experiences with five prominent moving picture women involving such practices.[4]

That the aforesaid course of conduct was of such duration and of such a character, that plaintiff is informed and believes, and upon such information and belief alleges the fact be, that it was the result of a deliberate and general intention and plan on the part of defendant, to undermine and distort plaintiff's normal sexual impulses and desires, demoralize her standards of decency, and degrade her conception of morals, for the gratification of defendant's aforesaid unnatural desires, and his said solicitations and demands in reference thereto.

That the aforesaid acts, conduct, solicitations and demands of defendant, in addition to their aforesaid effect upon plaintiff, were the cause of continual friction, unhappiness, quarreling and unpleasantness between said parties, and resulted in a further disagreeable and neglectful attitude on defendant's part toward plaintiff on account of her persistent refusal to yield or accede to defendant's said demands and solicitations.

(a) Plaintiff alleges further in this connection, that approximately six months before the separation of said parties, defendant was home in the afternoon shortly before dinner, and continued his solicitations and demands that plaintiff commit the act of sex perversion defined by Section 288a of the Penal Code of California. That defendant became enraged at plaintiff's refusal and said to her: "All married people do those kind of things. You are my wife and you have to do what I want you to do. I can get a divorce from you for refusing to do this." That upon plaintiff's continued refusal, defendant abruptly left the house and plaintiff did not see him again until the next day.

(b) That approximately four months before said separation, defendant named a girl[5] of their acquaintance, and told plaintiff that he had heard things about said girl which caused him to believe that she might be willing to commit acts of sexual perversion; and

4. Edna Purviance, Pola Negri, Claire Windsor, Peggy Hopkins Joyce, and Merna Kennedy. Lita and her attorneys were also suspicious of Charles Chaplin's relationship with actress Betty Morrisey, whom they subpoenaed for a deposition.

5. Andrea Gatesbry, who was introduced to Lita and Charles Chaplin by Elinor Glyn.

Complaint for Divorce

asked plaintiff to invite her up to the house some time, telling plaintiff that they could have some "fun" with her.

With respect to the character of the social and personal relations and matrimonial intercourse existing between said parties, plaintiff alleges the following particulars, to-wit:

(a) That during the first two months after said marriage, defendant took plaintiff out with him not more than three or four times, according to her best recollection and belief. That on said occasions, he bluntly and contemptuously told plaintiff that he wanted her to go with him for the sake of appearances; that he could not afford to have the public think he was neglecting her. That under the aforesaid humiliating circumstances, plaintiff went with defendant whenever he requested it, with the exception hereinafter mentioned, in an effort to protect him against any adverse public criticism or comment, and to overcome his said antagonism toward her and said marriage.

(b) That during said time defendant had not more than two or three meals at home with plaintiff. That it was his custom to come home late at night and go to his room, and she would see nothing of him.

(c) That when plaintiff left defendant's home on or about the 1st day of February, 1925, as aforesaid, she had not seen defendant for several days prior thereto; and did not see him at the time of her departure.

That during the time that plaintiff lived away from defendant's home, as aforesaid, defendant had dinner at said temporary residence of plaintiff twice; and stopped in to see her about once a week, and never telephoned her. That during a portion of said time he took plaintiff out, as aforesaid, about once a week in public.

(d) That the general conditions described in subdivisions (a), (b), and (c), continued to exist after plaintiff's first baby was born, up to and until the time of the separation herein set forth.

(e) That plaintiff was at Coronado for a month, with her babies, during the summer of 1926; that during said time defendant never telephoned her or came to see her and said babies.

(f) That while plaintiff was at Coronado, as aforesaid, she telephoned defendant one Saturday morning and asked him if she could come home and spend the weekend with him. Defendant told her not to come; that it would be too expensive. That the morning thereafter, plaintiff read in the newspaper an account of a large party given by defendant at the family home on the Saturday night referred to.

(g) That during the summer of 1926, plaintiff and her babies spent a month at Catalina. That during said time defendant never came to see her and the babies; and never called her on the telephone. That during said time plaintiff frequently telephoned defendant and urged him to come down and spend a few days with them.

(h) That on several occasions during the past year, defendant has said to plaintiff: "Go away some place for a while; I can't work or create when you are here. You are ruining my career." That on one such occasion plaintiff replied to defendant: "Why, Charlie, I don't understand how I interfere with your work. I never see you or annoy you." And he replied in a tone of exasperation: "That isn't it. It is just the fact that you are here; and I am supposed to give the usual attention to a home and family. It annoys me, and irritates me; and I cannot work."

(i) That recently plaintiff took a trip to Honolulu, at the request of defendant. That plaintiff was away at said time for several weeks with her eldest baby. That plaintiff cabled defendant when she would return; that defendant did not meet the steamer, and she did not see him until the day after her arrival.

(j) That on Christmas Day, 1925, defendant promised plaintiff that he would have Christmas dinner at home with her. That defendant started to leave the house about five o'clock in the afternoon. That plaintiff thereupon said: "Dinner will be ready at seven; you will be back now, won't you?" That defendant promised to return at seven; that plaintiff did not see or hear from him until about two o'clock the next morning, when he came home intoxicated.

(4) That defendant has never shown a normal, usual or proper fatherly interest in, or affection for the two minor children of plaintiff and defendant. In this connection, and in addition to the allegations heretofore made bearing upon the aforesaid specifications of extreme cruelty, plaintiff alleges as follows:

(a) That it was defendant's general practice and custom during said marriage to come home late at night and leave in the morning without going to see said children.

That during the month of October, 1926, according to plaintiff's best recollection and belief, defendant did not go in to see his said children for a period of two weeks consecutively, although he was at the home as usual during said time.

(b) That shortly after the birth of the second baby, the exact date of which plaintiff is unable to state, she asked defendant to build an addition onto the house for necessary room for said children. That defendant curtly refused without manifesting any interest in the subject; that the only reason given for his said refusal was the following statement: "This is *my* home; and I am not going to spoil it."

(c) That since the separation of plaintiff and defendant on the 30th day of November, 1926, to the date of the filing of this complaint, defendant has neither furnished nor contributed any money to enable plaintiff to provide said babies with the common necessaries of life, excepting by the payment of one milk bill amounting to twenty-seven dollars. That plaintiff, during said time, has been entirely without money with which to provide said babies with the proper care, attention and nourishment, which fact was well known to defendant; that during said time defendant has been requested on several occasions, to furnish plaintiff with the necessary money for said purpose. That during said entire time defendant has left plaintiff to the extremity of borrowing money from her friends, and relying upon the charity of her family in order to properly care for said babies.

That during said time defendant has visited said babies only once. That at Christmastime defendant failed to visit said babies, and notwithstanding the fact that every facility and courtesy has been extended and shown to defendant in respect to visiting said children.

(5) That during the cohabitation of plaintiff and defendant, defendant has told plaintiff on occasions too numerous to specify with more particularity and certainty, that he did not believe in the custom of marriage or in the marriage relation; that he could not tolerate the conventional restraint which they imposed; and that he believed it was proper and right for a woman to bear children to a man out of wedlock.

That he has likewise ridiculed and scoffed at plaintiff's adherence to and belief in conventional moral and social standards, with reference to marriage, the relation of the sexes and the bringing of children into the world; and has made light of the moral and statutory laws in reference thereto.

In this connection, defendant at one time told plaintiff that a certain couple who had five children, were not married; and in connection therewith, he said: "That is the ideal way for a man and a woman to live together."

(6) That during the entire aforesaid married life of said parties, defendant has openly, both publicly and privately, associated with other women, to plaintiff's great humiliation and distress, and to her exclusion and neglect; that defendant has maintained and continued such associations under a claim of right to do so; and that reports and information of such associations continuously reached plaintiff.

(a) That during the first month of their marriage and while plaintiff was pregnant as aforesaid, plaintiff was informed and believed that defendant was spending a very great portion of his time in the company of a certain prominent moving picture actress.[6] That plaintiff asked defendant if this were true, and he bluntly and boastingly said, "Yes, it is true; and I am in love with her, and don't care who knows it. I am going to see her when I want to, and whether you like it or not. I don't love you; and I am only living with you because I had to marry you."

That shortly thereafter, defendant wanted plaintiff to go with him to said woman's house and meet her; telling plaintiff at said time that she was a wonderful woman and plaintiff would like her. That under the circumstances, plaintiff refused to go. That thereafter on many occasions, defendant insisted that plaintiff go with him to said woman's house.

That these commands were made with such stress and under such peculiar circumstances that plaintiff, whether with any justification or not, feared that defendant intended to do her some great bodily harm in connection therewith, and persisted in her refusal to go. That in every such instance defendant left the house and stated that he was going without her.

That on one such occasion defendant wanted plaintiff to go to said house with him for dinner. That plaintiff said, "Why do you keep insisting that I go there? You know that I don't want to go and don't want to meet her." Defendant replied: "You will have to meet her. You are my wife, and you can't refuse to meet my friends, or I won't live with you. If you don't go with me, I'll fix you." That defendant's attitude and demeanor were so threatening on this occasion, that plaintiff feared such bodily harm, that when

---

6. Marion Davies.

defendant then left said house, leaving plaintiff alone, she went to her grandfather's; but returned home later in the evening.

That the next day thereafter, defendant said to plaintiff sneeringly and exultantly: "I know what you did last night when I left; and I have just been waiting to get you to leave this house. Now I have got it on you."

That at the aforesaid times, plaintiff was with child as aforesaid, and not yet seventeen years of age.

In this connection plaintiff further alleges that the only place defendant ever showed any personal interest in having plaintiff go with him, during their entire married life, was the home of the woman aforesaid; and the only friend he was ever particularly concerned about having plaintiff meet, during said time, was said woman; that said woman was the only friend of defendant that plaintiff ever refused to meet; that said woman's home was the only place plaintiff ever refused to go with defendant.

(b) That plaintiff is informed and believes and upon such information and belief alleges the fact to be, that in or about the month of May, 1925, and while plaintiff was temporarily away from defendant's house as aforesaid, the automobile of a certain woman was at defendant's house and stood in front thereof alone for several hours on four consecutive days. That on one of said occasions, said automobile was there as aforesaid, as late as ten o'clock at night.

(c) That at one time, during said marriage, the date of which plaintiff is unable to fix, she had been out of town for several days, and when she returned her key would not open the door and she was unable to get into the house. Thereafter plaintiff found that this was on account of the fact that the lock had been changed on the door; that thereafter she spoke to defendant about changing of said lock, and he jokingly said: "I guess the servants were trying to protect me."

(7) That defendant left plaintiff alone the greater portion of the time, and entirely dependent upon herself, her family and her own friends, for her entertainment and diversion. That defendant rarely came home until very late at night; and only on very few occasions spent the evening at home with plaintiff. That during the last six months that plaintiff and defendant lived together, defendant never spent an evening at home with her and the babies. That on occasions when defendant came home early, and plaintiff had guests, he refused to come in and meet or speak to said guests.

That plaintiff has had house guests at her home for as long as a week at a time, without said guests meeting or seeing her husband.

That in the following specific instances, without knowing anything, or very little about plaintiff's guests, defendant has made slurring and insulting remarks to her about them, to wit:

(a) That at one time, the approximate date of which plaintiff is unable to fix, she had three guests at her home spending the evening—a mother, her son, and the son's fiancée. The mother was an old friend of plaintiff and her family. Defendant was out, and did not return home until late.

The next day defendant said to plaintiff in an insinuating manner: "I know who was here last night. I saw you through a window and had a witness with me." That plaintiff, ignoring defendant's manner, laughed, and said: "Why, Charlie—only Mr. _____ was here; and his mother and fiancée were with him."

Defendant appeared in a very surly mood, and replied: "Yes? I know about the fiancee part of it. She is his sister and is trying to cover up the nature of his visits. You are no better than a prostitute, and much less sincere—having men around like that."

(b) That shortly after the occurrence set forth hereinabove in subdivision (a), of specification 7, plaintiff went to the home of the woman therein referred to, with defendant, and became acquainted with her.

That thereafter plaintiff went to said woman's home several times alone. That when defendant heard of this, he became very angry with plaintiff, and told her that he did not want her to associate with the woman referred to—that she was no good. He said: "Whenever you get like her and her kind, I'll be through with you."

(c) That on the 29th day of November, 1926, plaintiff brought some guests home with her, about 12:30 A. M., with whom she had been dining, to show them defendant's house. That plaintiff did not expect defendant to be home that early, and she did not know that he was home. That a few minutes after plaintiff and said guests arrived, defendant came to the head of the stairs and called plaintiff, in a very rude and peremptory manner, and within the hearing of said guests.

That plaintiff immediately left the room and ran up the stairs to where defendant was standing; that defendant said to her: "Get that wild bunch of people out of here—get them out, and get them out quick. What do you think this is, a whorehouse?"

That plaintiff thereupon dismissed said guests immediately.

(8) That defendant, on innumerable occasions, has abused, condemned, reproached and upbraided plaintiff, both for the conception and birth of their two children; and has likewise charged her, on account of her refusal to prevent the latter, with ruining his career, and with the lack of proper consideration and affection for him.

In this connection, plaintiff more specifically alleges:

That as soon as defendant found that the second baby had been conceived, he insisted that plaintiff take illegal and immoral steps to prevent its birth, saying, that he did not want any more children.

That plaintiff refused to do as defendant demanded, and he accused her of being selfish; telling her at said time that other women had done that much for him without any hesitation; and of one moving picture actress, whom, he stated, had such an operation performed twice for him.[7]

That at another time defendant said to plaintiff in this connection, and in an insulting manner: "What do you want to do; populate Los Angeles?"

(9) That during the entire married life of plaintiff and defendant, he has insisted and maintained the attitude and determination, that when it was convenient for him, that plaintiff must get a divorce, but in strict accordance with his dictation and instruction; and that, upon that condition alone, would he make any provision for her support. That up to the time plaintiff separated from defendant on the 30th day of November, 1926, she was so completely intimidated by threats, that she was afraid to do anything with reference to leaving him or getting a divorce, without his sanction and approval. That the threats resorted to and used by defendant for the purpose aforesaid, were threats of great bodily harm; threats that he would ruin her reputation with the power of his money; and threats that she would never get a cent for her support, excepting what he was willing to give her, if he had to buy perjured testimony to defeat her action, or had to take all his property and get out of the United States, to prevent it.

In this connection defendant at one time told plaintiff that if she

---

7. Edna Purviance.

ever commenced a divorce action against him, except in accordance with his wishes, that when he got through with her, with his money, plaintiff's own family would have nothing further to do with her.

(9½) That on one occasion, defendant suggested that plaintiff take her own life; and on another occasion he picked up a loaded revolver and menacingly threatened to kill her.

(a) In the first instance above referred to, about two weeks after said marriage, defendant and plaintiff were in defendant's bedroom at his house, and defendant had been reciting to her the terrible position he was in on account of said marriage; that at said time and on account thereof, plaintiff was in a state of great mental excitement, and was hysterical and despondent. That she said to him: "I don't see what we can do but try and make the best of it." That defendant was sitting on the bed, and reaching over to a small table, picked up a loaded revolver, and holding it out in his hand, said: "There is one way to end it all." That plaintiff became frightened and said to him: "Put down that revolver, it might go off; and don't talk that way, it is silly." That defendant replied: "It isn't silly—you can't tell. I might get suddenly crazy anytime, and kill you."

(b) The other instance above referred to, occurred November 29th, 1926, at the family home. That at said time defendant had objected to the presence in the house of some guests of plaintiff, as above mentioned, and after said guests had left, plaintiff and her mother had gone to plaintiff's room. That shortly thereafter, defendant came to the door of said room and called to plaintiff, and told her to come to his room, that he wanted to see her.

That plaintiff thereupon went into defendant's room, and when she entered, defendant said to her, in an angry and threatening tone of voice: "What do you mean by wakening me with all those people here?" Plaintiff replied that she did not think he would be home yet, or she would not have brought anyone home with her. That plaintiff further said: "I am sorry—I did not expect to do any harm. But I am not going to stand this kind of treatment; it is too humiliating to endure."

That defendant thereupon rushed over to a small table next to his bed, waving his arms in the air, and picked up a loaded revolver lying on said table, and rushed toward plaintiff in a threatening and excited manner, crying: "I will kill you if you dare to leave this house; or tell the newspapers anything about this." That plaintiff turned and ran from said room.

That plaintiff was, and became so alarmed, and so in fear of great bodily harm on account thereof, that the next day she left the home and residence of plaintiff and defendant and has not returned thereto.

(10) That plaintiff is informed and believes, and upon such information and belief alleges the fact to be, that defendant has maintained an unjustifiable system of espionage upon her, during the greater portion of their married life, in an effort to secure evidence for a divorce against her.

(11) That plaintiff is informed and believes, and upon such information and belief alleges the fact to be, that defendant has knowingly made false statements to immediate friends and acquaintances of his, to justify his obvious neglect of plaintiff, reflecting upon her character, breeding, gentility and education; and has attributed to her base, ulterior and mercenary motives in marrying him.

(a) That a certain prominent moving picture actress, who is an intimate friend of defendant, told plaintiff, about a year after her marriage to defendant, that she was surprised to find plaintiff the kind of a person that she was; that defendant had told her, and also a certain friend of hers, that plaintiff was a person of no education or breeding; that she was a "gold digger;" that she was crude; and that she had only married defendant to get money out of him.

(b) That one evening about three months after said marriage, defendant came into plaintiff's room, and, leaving the door open, commenced to accuse plaintiff of forcing him to marry her to get money out of him, with blackmailing him; and with not caring for him.

That after said abuse had continued for some time, the gong in the hall downstairs rang, and a certain doctor friend of defendant's came upstairs. That defendant appeared to be surprised to see said friend. That thereafter defendant continued to rave about blackmail in the presence of said doctor, and to further abuse plaintiff to such an extent that she became hysterical.

That plaintiff thereupon turned to said doctor, and in defendant's presence said: "Can you imagine a man talking like that, when he knows that he offered me a half million dollars to get rid of this baby by an abortion, and I refused to do it."

That thereafter said doctor told plaintiff that he had come into said house at the above mentioned time with said defendant; that he was downstairs during the entire aforesaid conversation; and that he had been invited to said house for the purpose of being convinced that plaintiff was not sincere in her affection for defendant, but was only trying to get money out of him.

(12) That during the month of June, 1926, defendant told plaintiff that after the picture he was then working on was completed, would be a good time for her to get a divorce as hereinabove set forth; that at said time he told plaintiff that she would never get any more for her support and maintenance than he was willing to give her voluntarily; that he had all of his property and income so tied up that she could never get a cent through the courts; that he could go to Europe and make pictures there just as well, and that he would do it if she did not do just as he said.

That at said time he said to her: "Why—even the house we are living in is not in my name; and I had it put out of my name to protect me against women."

(a) That about a month later plaintiff complained to defendant and told him that she could not stand the conditions under which she was living. That he replied: "If you get spunky, and do anything that will reflect on me, or cause a scandal—I have enough money to do anything; and I can pay somebody to lie about you if it is necessary, to prevent you from ever getting a cent." That he also said at this time: "If you ever commence a suit for divorce against me, don't expect the servants to testify for you, even if you are right. I pay them, and they will say what I tell them to say."

VI.

That plaintiff is informed and believes, and upon such information and belief alleges the fact to be, that in public opinion, the reflection upon her reputation, character, innocence and worth as a woman, wife and mother, arising out of facts and circumstances in connection with the aforesaid seduction and publicity given thereto, will be augmented and intensified, and has been augmented and intensified, by defendant's aforesaid failure to carry out the obligations of said marriage in good faith; and his failure to treat plaintiff with conjugal kindness, consideration and love, after the assumption of said obligations. That plaintiff believes, and at all times since said marriage has believed, that on account thereof a wrongful and unjustified impression would and will exist in the public mind that plaintiff was morally at fault in connection with said seduction, or was otherwise unfit as a wife, because of defendant's failure to accept and honor her as such.

And that, on that account, plaintiff has undergone peculiar, unusual and aggravated mental suffering, and has had inflicted upon her a peculiar and unusual personal injury and wrong, by reason of defendant's aforesaid extreme cruelty.

VII.

That plaintiff is informed and believes, and upon such information and belief alleges the fact to be, that defendant's said failure to carry out the marriage contract entered into as aforesaid in good faith; and his said failure to treat plaintiff with conjugal kindness, respect and consideration as his wife, and as the mother of his said children, thereby causing a separation and divorce, without fault on her part, has deprived and will deprive plaintiff of the only natural, adequate and possible, shelter, protection and justification, for her relations with defendant before their marriage; and has and will deprive her of the only natural, adequate and effective compensation for the wrong suffered by her on account of the aforesaid seduction, and the injury done to her reputation on account of the publicity given thereto as aforesaid.

That on account of plaintiff's aforesaid belief, she has submitted to the cruel treatment of defendant herein set forth for a long period of time; and has suffered and will suffer on account thereof, peculiar, unusual and aggravated mental anguish and distress; and has suffered a peculiar, aggravated and unusual personal wrong and injury, on account of being deprived of the protection and security afforded by her marriage relation with defendant.

VIII.

Plaintiff is informed and believes, and upon such information and belief alleges the fact to be, that immediately after said marriage, said defendant commenced to pursue, and continued to pursue, during the entire cohabitation of said parties, a deliberate, willful, uniform course of cruel treatment of the plaintiff, with the wrongful intent and purpose of compelling her to seek a divorce; in connection with a deliberate and uniform course of conduct with the wrongful intent and purpose of so intimidating said plaintiff that she would not seek such divorce except upon terms and conditions, and at such time and in such a manner as should be consistent with said defendant's wishes and dictation; and to thereby defeat the ends and purposes of said marriage contrary to law and public policy. And that the cruel and inhuman treatment of plaintiff by defendant, and the mental pain, suffering and anguish wrongfully inflicted upon plaintiff thereby, as hereinabove alleged and set forth, was the result of the aforesaid deliberate intent and purpose of said defendant.

IX.

That plaintiff is informed and believes, and upon such information and belief alleges the fact to be, that said defendant entered into said marriage with plaintiff without any intention of carrying out the moral, personal and marital obligations imposed upon him by said marriage; but that he entered into said marriage, and thereby further imposed upon the youth and innocence of plaintiff and her love and affection for him, and upon her belief and confidence in his promises and representations of love and affection for her, and upon her good faith in entering into said marriage, for the sole purpose of protecting himself from the consequences of his illegal, wrongful and immoral infliction of wrong and injury upon plaintiff before said marriage as herein set forth.

X.

That plaintiff is a woman of refinement, and education, and with high moral standards, and of a loving nature and affectionate and sensitive disposition; that at the time of said marriage she was an innocent unsophisticated girl except in her relations with defendant, as herein set forth, and that at said time she had never been out in the company of any man alone, with the exception of defendant.

XI.

Plaintiff alleges that at all times during the period of her cohabitation with defendant in said marriage relation, she has conducted herself toward defendant as a kind, considerate, loyal and loving wife; and has fully observed and performed the duties and obligations of a wife to defendant; and that during said time, notwithstanding the aforesaid cruel and inhuman treatment of her by said defendant, she has endeavored to the best of her ability to overcome defendant's aforesaid attitude toward her, their children and said marriage.

XII.

That the aforesaid minor children of plaintiff and defendant are now in the custody of plaintiff, and plaintiff is a fit and proper person to have and be awarded the custody, care and control of said children; and said plaintiff is willing and desirous of assuming the responsibility of the custody, care and education of said children.

That defendant is an unfit person to have the care, custody and control of the children of said marriage; or to control or direct their education.

XIII.

That at all times herein mentioned defendant, The Chaplin Studios, Inc., was, and now is a corporation duly organized and existing under and by virtue of the laws of the State of California, with its principal place of business in the City of Los Angeles, State of California.

That at all times herein mentioned the defendant, Charles Chaplin Film Corporation, was, and now is a corporation, duly organized and existing under and by virtue of the laws of the State of Delaware, with its principal place of business in the City of Los Angeles, State of California.

That at all times herein mentioned the defendant, First National Bank of Los Angeles, was, and now is a national banking association, duly organized and existing under and by virtue of the laws of the United States of America, with its principal place of business in the City of Los Angeles, State of California.

That at all times herein mentioned the defendant, Security Trust & Savings Bank of Los Angeles, was and now is a corporation duly organized and existing under and by virtue of the laws of the State of California, with its principal place of business in the City of Los Angeles, State of California.

That at all times herein mentioned the defendant, Farmers & Merchants National Bank, was, and now is, a national banking association, duly organized and existing under and by virtue of the laws of the United States of America, and has its principal place of business in the City of Los Angeles, State of California.

That at all times herein mentioned the defendant, Bank of Italy, was, and now is, a corporation duly organized and existing under and by virtue of the laws of the State of California, with its principal place of business in the City of Los Angeles, State of California.

That at all times herein mentioned, defendant, United Artists Corporation, was, and now is, a corporation duly organized and existing under and by virtue of the laws of the State of _____; that said corporation maintains a place of business in the City of Los Angeles, State of California.

That at all times herein mentioned, defendants Doe One Company, Doe Two Company, and Doe Three Company, were, and now are, corporations duly organized and existing under and by virtue of the laws of the State of California.

XIV.

That the defendants, Doe One, Doe Two, Doe Three, Doe One Company, Doe Two Company and Doe Three Company, are sued herein under fictitious names, their true names to the plaintiff being unknown, and plaintiff will ask leave to insert their true names herein when ascertained.

XV.

That plaintiff is informed and believes and therefore alleges that the defendants, Doe One, Doe Two, Doe Three, Doe One Company, a corporation, Doe Two Company, a corporation, and Doe

Three Company, a corporation, have in their possession and/or under their control community property which belongs to the plaintiff and defendant and/or separate property of the defendant.

That plaintiff is informed and believes and therefore alleges that the defendant, United Artists Corporation, a corporation, has entered into a contract with the defendant and/or the defendant, The Chaplin Studios, Inc., and/or the defendant Charles Chaplin Film Corporation, a corporation, for the purchase and release of those certain motion pictures entitled *The Gold Rush* and *The Circus*, which said motion pictures are the community property of plaintiff and defendant; that said defendant United Artists Corporation, a corporation, has received and pending the trial of this action will continue to receive large sums of money from the releasing of said motion pictures known as *The Gold Rush* and *The Circus* which sums of money are the community property of plaintiff and defendant.

XVI.

That the defendants, T. Kono, and Alfred Reeves, at all times mentioned herein were, and now are, employed by the defendants, Charles Spencer Chaplin and/or The Chaplin Studios, Inc., and/or Charles Chaplin Film Corporation, and that said first named defendants were, and are, under the control and direction of the defendant. That plaintiff is informed and believes and upon such information and belief alleges that for several years preceding the filing of this action, said defendants, T. Kono and Alfred Reeves, have had, and now have, in their possession and/or under their control a large amount of property belonging to defendant, Charles Spencer Chaplin, The Chaplin Studios, Inc., a corporation, and the Charles Chaplin Film Corporation, a corporation. Plaintiff does not know and is unable to ascertain the description, character or value of said property.

Plaintiff is informed and believes and therefore alleges that said property in the possession or under the control of said defendants, T. Kono and Alfred Reeves, includes community property of plaintiff and defendant, as well as separate property of said defendant, Charles Spencer Chaplin, and consists of bonds, stocks, securities, real estate and money.

That plaintiff is informed and believes and therefore alleges that defendant at all times mentioned herein has maintained and now maintains a safety deposit box at the banking offices of the following named defendant banks: First National Bank of Los Angeles, Security Trust & Savings Bank of Los Angeles, Farmers & Merchants National Bank, and Bank of Italy.

Plaintiff is informed and believes and therefore alleges that the defendants, T. Kono, Alfred Reeves, The Chaplin Studios, Inc. and Charles Chaplin Film Corporation have maintained and now maintain safety deposit boxes at the offices of the following named defendant banks: First National Bank of Los Angeles, Security Trust & Savings Bank of Los Angeles, Farmers & Merchants National Bank, and Bank of Italy. That said defendant, and defendants, T. Kono, and Alfred Reeves, The Chaplin Studios, Inc. and Charles Chaplin Film Corporation, have concealed and now conceal in said safety deposit boxes, stocks, bonds, other securities and money, and other personal property; that said property consists of community property of plaintiff and defendant and separate property of defendant.

XVII.

That plaintiff is informed and believes and therefore alleges that defendants, The Chaplin Studios, Inc. and Charles Chaplin Film Corporation, a corporation, were organized several years prior to the filing of this complaint by the defendant for the purpose of affording defendant a convenient instrument or vehicle through which he could transact his personal and individual business; that said corporations have been maintained and used by defendant, and are being maintained and used by defendant for the purpose of holding and concealing the community and separate property of the defendant, in order to defeat and prevent the enforcement of plaintiff's claims, rights and interest therein and thereto; that said corporations have in their possession and/or under their control, and standing in their names community property of plaintiff and defendant, and separate property of defendant.

That defendant owns and/or controls substantially all of the issued and outstanding capital stock of said defendant corporations, The Chaplin Studios, Inc. and Charles Chaplin Film Corporation, and that the directors and officers of said defendant corporations are under the direction and control of defendant in all matters pertaining to said corporations, and said property.

XVIII.

That there is community property belonging to plaintiff and defendant situated in the County of Los Angeles, State of California and elsewhere, consisting of real estate, stocks, bonds, securities, money and other personal property, including two motion pictures entitled *The Gold Rush* and *The Circus*, and the proceeds derived and to be derived therefrom; that plaintiff is informed and believes and therefore alleges that the total value of the community property of plaintiff and defendant is upwards of the sum of Ten Million Dollars.

XIX.

That defendant has separate property situated in the County of Los Angeles, State of California, and elsewhere, consisting of real estate, stocks, bonds, securities, money and other personal property; that the legal description of said real estate which is situated in the County of Los Angeles, State of California, is as follows:

1. Lots twenty-four (24) and twenty-five (25) Tract three-three-five-seven (3357), as per Map recorded in Book 37, Pages sixteen (16) and seventeen (17) of Maps, Records of Los Angeles County, standing of record in the name of the defendant Chaplin Studios, Inc.

2. Lot One (1) and the West one hundred forty-two and eighty one hundredths (142.80) feet of Lot Two (2) of Tonner & Garbut Subdivision, of the S. W. Little Tract, as per Map recorded in Book 19, page 30 of Miscellaneous Records, Records of Los Angeles County, except the south Twenty-five (25) feet thereof included within the boundary of De Longpre Avenue, (formerly Wilson Avenue), standing of record in the name of the defendant The Chaplin Studios, Inc.

That plaintiff is informed and believes and therefore alleges that the value of defendant's separate property is upwards of the sum of Six Million Dollars.

XX.

That plaintiff is informed and believes and therefore alleges that ever since the marriage of plaintiff and defendant, defendant has received and now receives a salary of $250,000 per year, in connection with his services and activities as an artist and director in the motion picture business, which said salary is the community property of plaintiff and defendant, and that in addition to said salary, defendant receives an income from other sources than said salary of upwards of $300,000 per year.

XXI.

That defendant has threatened to remove said property and the whole thereof from the jurisdiction of this court and to otherwise dispose of, conceal, transfer, and encumber said property for the purpose of defeating plaintiff's rights and claims thereto as his wife, and for the purpose of embarrassing, hindering and delaying the satisfaction and payment of any orders made herein for the support and maintenance of plaintiff and her said children and for suit money to enable plaintiff to prosecute this action, and to prevent the enforcement of any decree or judgment made herein affecting plaintiff's rights or claims in and to said property, and providing for the permanent support and maintenance of plaintiff and said children. That plaintiff is informed and believes and therefore alleges that said defendant intends to, and will, unless restrained by order of Court from so doing, carry out his said threats as hereinabove alleged, by, through and with the co-operation, instrumentality and assistance of said defendants, T. Kono, Alfred Reeves, The Chaplin Studios, Inc. and Charles Chaplin Film Corporation, a corporation.

That the aforesaid community property and funds and the separate property of defendant have been so commingled, and have been so concealed in the names and in the possession of said defendants, T. Kono, Alfred Reeves, The Chaplin Studios, Inc. and Charles Chaplin Film Corporation, a corporation, that on account thereof, it is and will be necessary for said defendant and said defendant corporations to render an account of all property and assets standing in their names and/or in their possession and/or under their control, in order that the Court may properly determine

the character, extent and value of the community property of
plaintiff and defendant, and may determine the character, source
and value, and the real, equitable and beneficial ownership of the
property and assets held by said corporations, and said other defendants, or in their possession or under their control.

XXII.

That plaintiff is informed and believes and therefore alleges that
said defendants, T. Kono, Alfred Reeves, The Chaplin Studios,
Inc., a corporation, Charles Chaplin Film Corporation, a corporation, unless restrained by order of Court from so doing, will hin-
der, delay, harass and embarrass plaintiff by selling, transferring,
conveying, concealing and otherwise disposing of, or mortgaging,
hypothecating or otherwise encumbering said community property of plaintiff and defendant and said separate property of defendant, or some part thereof.

That plaintiff is informed and believes and therefore alleges that
unless said defendants, The First National Bank of Los Angeles,
a corporation, the Bank of Italy, a corporation, Security Trust &
Savings Bank of Los Angeles, a corporation, Farmers & Merchants National Bank, a corporation, and each of them, are restrained by order of Court from so doing, will permit the
defendants, Charles Spencer Chaplin, and/or The Chaplin Studios,
Inc., a corporation, and/or Charles Chaplin Film Corporation, a
corporation, and/or T. Kono, and/or Alfred Reeves, to withdraw
money on deposit in said defendant banks, or some of them, which
said deposits, plaintiff is informed and believes and therefore alleges, stand in the name of defendants Charles Spencer Chaplin,
and/or The Chaplin Studios, Inc., a corporation, and/or Charles
Chaplin Film Corporation, a corporation, and/or T. Kono, and/or
Alfred Reeves, and which said money on deposit in said banks as
aforesaid, is either the community property of plaintiff and defendant, or the separate property of defendant.

That plaintiff is informed and believes and therefore alleges that
unless restrained by order of Court from so doing, that said defendants, The First National Bank of Los Angeles, a corporation, and/
or the Bank of Italy, a corporation, and/or Security Trust & Savings Bank of Los Angeles, a corporation, and/or Farmers & Merchants National Bank, a corporation, will permit said defendants

Charles Spencer Chaplin, The Chaplin Studios, Inc., a corporation, Charles Chaplin Film Corporation, a corporation, T. Kono and Alfred Reeves, to have access to the safety deposit boxes which, it is hereinabove alleged, said last mentioned defendants maintain at said defendant banks, or some of them, and which said safety deposit boxes at said defendant banks, plaintiff is informed and believes and therefore alleges, contain money and personal property which is the community property of plaintiff and defendant or the separate property of defendant.

That plaintiff is informed and believes and therefore alleges that unless defendant United Artists Corporation, a corporation, is restrained by order of Court from so doing, it will pay over and remit to defendant, or defendants The Chaplin Studios, Inc., a corporation, Charles Chaplin Film Corporation, a corporation, or some other person or company for the benefit of defendant, moneys already received and which will be received pending the trial of this action, from the releasing of *The Gold Rush* and *The Circus* as hereinabove alleged, which said money is community property of plaintiff and defendant.

That plaintiff is informed and believes and therefore alleges that unless said defendants, and each of them, hereinabove named, referred to and described, be restrained by this Court as aforesaid, defendant will carry out his said threats as hereinabove alleged, and will remove said property and money from the jurisdiction of this Court.

XXIII.

Plaintiff further alleges that by reason of the fact that defendant will continue to conceal, sequester and cover up the community property of plaintiff and defendant and the separate property of defendant, a Receiver should be appointed herein to take possession of and safe-guard all of the community property of plaintiff and defendant and all of the separate property of defendant within the jurisdiction of this Court.

XXIV.

That plaintiff is informed and believes and therefore alleges that defendant, unless restrained by order of Court from so doing, will endeavor to harass and embarrass plaintiff by attempting to take the minor children of plaintiff and defendant from the present custody of plaintiff.

That plaintiff is informed and believes and therefore alleges that defendant, unless restrained by order of Court from so doing, will harass and embarrass said plaintiff by attempting to visit, annoy, speak to and communicate with plaintiff, and by having plaintiff followed by agents and detectives in the employ of defendant.

XXV.

That it is necessary for plaintiff to engage the services of attorneys to institute and prosecute this action against defendants; that plaintiff is without funds or property to maintain and support said minor children and herself, either permanently or during the pendency of this action, or to pay the costs, expenses and attorneys fees to enable her to prosecute this action.

WHEREFORE, plaintiff prays:

1. That the bonds of matrimony now existing between plaintiff and the defendant Charles Spencer Chaplin be dissolved.

2. That the permanent custody and control of said minor children, Charles Spencer Chaplin, Jr., and Sydney Earl Chaplin, be granted unto plaintiff.

3. That a restraining order, pendente lite, be granted unto plaintiff, enjoining and restraining said defendant, his representatives, agents, bankers, attorneys and servants, from

(a) Taking, or attempting to take, the minor children of plaintiff and said defendant from the custody of plaintiff, or in any manner whatsoever interfering with plaintiff's custody of said minor children.

(b) Visiting, annoying, speaking to, or in any manner whatsoever communicating with, or attempting to visit, annoy, speak to or in any manner whatsoever communicate with plaintiff.

4. That an order, pendente lite, be granted unto plaintiff:

(a) Enjoining and restraining all of the defendants above named, and each of them, and the representatives, agents, bankers, attorneys and servants of said defendant Charles Spencer Chaplin, from selling, transferring, conveying, assigning, or otherwise disposing of, and from mortgaging, hypothecating or otherwise encumbering, all or any part of the community properties, securities, or moneys of the plaintiff and said defendant, and any and all of the separate properties, securities, or moneys of said defendant in their possession or under their control, pending the further order of this Honorable Court, and specifically the following described property, to-wit:

Lots twenty-four (24) and twenty-five (25), Tract Thirty-three hundred fifty-seven (3357), as per Map recorded in Book 37, Pages sixteen (16) and seventeen (17) of Maps, Records of Los Angeles County, standing of record in the name of the defendant The Chaplin Studios, Inc.

Lot One (1) and the West One Hundred Forty-two and eighty one hundredths (142.80) feet of Lot Two (2) of the Tonner & Garbut Subdivision, of the S. W. Little Tract, as per map recorded in Book 19, Page 30 of Miscellaneous Records, Records of Los Angeles County, except the South twenty-five (25) feet thereof included within the boundaries of De Longpre Avenue (formerly Wilson Avenue), standing of record in the name of the defendant The Chaplin Studios, Inc.

All negatives, positive prints, bill-board lithographs, pressbooks, still photographs, cuts, and all and any other publicity matter of or in any way relating to that certain photoplay known as, and entitled *The Circus*; and all contracts appertaining to the sale, release and distribution of said photoplay in any and all countries throughout the entire world, and any and every other thing in any way relating to or appertaining to or connected with the sale, release and distribution of said photoplay.

(b) Enjoining and restraining said defendants First National Bank of Los Angeles, a corporation, Bank of Italy, a corporation, Security Trust & Savings Bank of Los Angeles, a corporation, Farmers & Merchants National Bank, a corporation, United Artists Corporation, a corporation, and each of them, from

(1) Opening, or permitting access to, or permitting the examination or removal by any person whomsoever of any of the contents of, any safety deposit box or boxes, in their respective possession or under their respective control, either directly or indirectly through any subsidiary corporation, which the defendants Charles Spencer Chaplin, The Chaplin Studios, Inc., a corporation, Charles Chaplin Film Corporation, a corporation, T. Kono, Alfred Reeves, or any of them, either alone or jointly with any

other person, co-partnership or corporation, have access to, pending the further order of this Honorable Court;

(2) Honoring any withdrawal or withdrawals, in any manner whatsoever, from or upon any and all banking accounts with them respectively, whether such accounts be term, checking, special savings, or any other character whatsoever, standing in the name of defendants Charles Spencer Chaplin, The Chaplin Studios, Inc., a corporation, Charles Chaplin Film Corporation, a corporation, T. Kono, Alfred Reeves, or any of them, either alone or jointly with any other person, co-partnership or corporation, and belonging to the defendant Charles Spencer Chaplin, as either community property of plaintiff and defendant or as his separate property, pending the further order of this Honorable Court.

(3) Paying out, in any manner whatsoever, to any person whomsoever, any moneys or credits now in their possession or under their control respectively, or which may hereafter come into their possession or under their control respectively, and due, owing or belonging to the defendants Charles Spencer Chaplin, The Chaplin Studios, Inc., a corporation, Charles Chaplin Film Corporation, a corporation, T. Kono and Alfred Reeves, pending the further order of this Honorable Court.

(c) Enjoining and restraining the defendants Charles Spencer Chaplin, The Chaplin Studios, Inc., a corporation, Charles Chaplin Film Corporation, a corporation, T. Kono and Alfred Reeves, and their respective agents, attorneys, bankers and servants respectively, from

(1) Opening, or otherwise gaining access to, or attempting to open or otherwise gain access to, or examining or removing any of the contents of, or attempting to examine or remove any of the contents of, any safe deposit box or boxes wheresoever located to which said defendants, or any of them, either alone or jointly with any other person, co-partnership or corporation, have access.

(2) Withdrawing, or attempting to withdraw, in any manner, shape or form whatsoever, any properties, securities, monies or credits whatsoever standing in the name of said defendants, or any of them, either alone or jointly with any other person, co-partnership or corporation, upon the books of, or which now or hereafter may become due and owing from the defendants United Artists Corporation, a corporation, First National Bank of Los Angeles, a corporation, Bank of Italy, a corporation, Security

Trust & Savings Bank of Los Angeles, a corporation, and Farmers & Merchants National Bank, a corporation, or any other person, co-partnership, firm, corporation or bank, and belonging to the defendant Charles Spencer Chaplin either as community property or as his separate property.

(3) Removing from the State of California, any and all stock books, stock transfer books, account books, check books, checks and bank statements in any way whatsoever appertaining or relating to those two certain photoplays respectively known as, and entitled, *The Gold Rush* and *The Circus*, and to any and all other transactions of said defendants, or any of them, and any and all contracts, correspondence, memoranda and other papers or documents in any way whatsoever appertaining or relating to those two certain photoplays respectively known as and entitled *The Gold Rush* and *The Circus*, and to any and all other transactions of said defendants, or any of them.

5. That all of the defendants above named, and each of them, be compelled to account to this Honorable Court as to the community properties, securities, and moneys of plaintiff and the defendant Charles Spencer Chaplin in their possession or under their control respectively, and as to the separate properties, securities, and moneys of said defendant Charles Spencer Chaplin in their possession or under their control respectively, and for the rents, issues and profits accrued, or to accrue, of and from said community and separate properties, securities and moneys.

6. That this Honorable Court make an order herein directing said defendant to pay plaintiff,

(a) A reasonable sum of money per month, to be fixed by the Court, for the support and maintenance of plaintiff and the minor children of plaintiff and defendant during the pendency of the suit above entitled, consistent with the financial circumstances of the plaintiff and said defendant, their mode of living together during their married life, and their station in life.

(b) A reasonable sum of money, to be fixed by the Court, to enable plaintiff to employ counsel to prosecute this action and compensate said counsel for the services rendered and to be rendered by them to plaintiff.

(c) A reasonable sum of money to be fixed by the Court for costs and expenses to prosecute this action.

7. That this Honorable Court make such assignment of the

community property to the respective parties, in such proportions as the Court, from all of the facts of the case, and the condition of the parties, may deem just, in addition thereto, make such allowance for the support and maintenance of the plaintiff, and the support, maintenance and education of the minor children of plaintiff and said defendant as the Court may deem fair, just and equitable in the premises.

8. That this Honorable Court make an order requiring said defendant to give reasonable security for providing maintenance, or making any payments required under the provisions of Chapter II of The Civil Code of the State of California, and that this Honorable Court enforce the same by the appointment of a Receiver, or by any other remedy applicable to this case, all as provided by Section 140 of Article IV of Chapter II of The Civil Code of California.

9. For such other and further relief as to this Honorable Court may seem meet, just and equitable in the premises.

EDWIN T. MCMURRAY,
YOUNG & YOUNG,
MILTON K. YOUNG,
LYNDOL L. YOUNG,
WILLIAM K. YOUNG,
L. R. BRIGHAM,
Attorneys for plaintiff.

IN THE
SUPERIOR COURT OF THE
STATE OF CALIFORNIA
IN AND FOR THE
COUNTY OF LOS ANGELES

No. D-52298

LILLITA LOUISE CHAPLIN,

Plaintiff,

vs.

CHARLES SPENCER CHAPLIN, et al.,

Defendants.

ANSWER OF DEFENDANT, CHARLES SPENCER CHAPLIN

The defendant, Charles Spencer Chaplin, answering plaintiff's amended complaint on file herein, for himself alone, and for neither of his co-defendants, admits, denies and alleges:

I.

Answering paragraph IV of said complaint, denies that ever since the date of said marriage, or at any other time or at all, the defendant has treated the plaintiff in a cruel or inhuman manner, or has wrongfully or at all inflicted upon her great or any grievous or other mental suffering or anguish, or any suffering or anguish whatsoever.

II.

Answering paragraph V of said complaint, denies that the defendant has in any way, or at all, treated the plaintiff in a cruel or inhuman manner, and denies that any alleged cruel and inhuman, or cruel or inhuman treatment of plaintiff consists of any or either of the specific acts or conduct alleged in said paragraph V, and in particular the defendant denies:

1. Denies that on board the train by which plaintiff and defendant were returning from Mexico, or at any other time or place whatsoever, the evening of the day upon which the plaintiff and defendant were married, or at any other time or at all, the defendant said to some of his friends who were accompanying them, or to any one or at all, either within or without the hearing of plaintiff and others, or any thereof, the following statement: "Well, boys, this is better than the penitentiary; but it won't last long," or any substantially similar statement.

Admits that on the date plaintiff and defendant returned to Los Angeles from Mexico after said marriage, they went to defendant's home for lunch, but denies that at said time and place, or at said time or place, or at any other time or at all, the defendant said to plaintiff, "This marriage won't last long. I will make you so damn sick of me that you won't want to live with me;" or any statement similar thereto.

2. Denies that during the month of May, 1924, plaintiff and defendant became engaged to be married; denies that thereafter and during, or thereafter or during said alleged engagement, defendant seduced plaintiff under promise of marriage; denies that as a result of said alleged seduction plaintiff became or was pregnant with child at the time of said marriage; denies that upon discovery by defendant of said alleged delicate condition of plaintiff, or at any other time, defendant delayed the consummation of said alleged promise of marriage for so long a time, or for any time, in an effort to induce plaintiff to prevent the birth of said child by submitting herself to a criminal operation, or by any other means, and so conducted himself with reference thereto, or so conducted himself with reference thereto, that plaintiff's said alleged physical condition either became or was publicly and generally known, or publicly or generally known at the time of said marriage, either by reason of the great and wide, or great or wide publicity or by reason of anything else whatsoever, given to all or any of any alleged fact or facts or circumstance or circumstances surrounding, or otherwise connected with said marriage; denies that plaintiff at all of the said alleged times, or at any other time or at all,

refused to consent or accede to defendant's alleged wish or wishes, or demand or demands with reference to the performance of said alleged operation; denies that the defendant expressed any wish or demand with reference to the performance of any alleged operation; denies that any such alleged refusal on the part of the plaintiff was solely for the reason that the same was or would have been, in her judgment and belief, or in any judgment or belief, a great or other social, legal or moral wrong and on account thereof, or on account thereof, contrary, repugnant or abhorrent to her instincts of motherhood, or to her sense or duty of maternal protection or preservation, or any thereof; and in connection with the aforesaid denials, and in connection with the allegation contained in subdivision 2 of said paragraph V of said complaint, the defendant alleges that he at no time expressed any wish or demand with reference to the performance of any operation, as alleged in said portion of plaintiff's complaint, or otherwise or at all.

Denies that the defendant entered into said marriage with plaintiff without any intention of carrying out his legal or marital obligations, or that he entered into said marriage for the sole or selfish purpose of protecting himself from criminal prosecution for a felony, or with the intent of thereafter carrying out, or otherwise performing or being engaged in such or any deliberate or uniform or unreasonable course of conduct toward plaintiff as to make a continuance of the said marriage relation impossible, and in that connection the defendant alleges that at the time he entered into the said marriage with the plaintiff, he intended, in all respects, to carry out the obligations devolving upon him as the husband of plaintiff, in good faith, and that he intended in all respects to protect the plaintiff as his wife, and the defendant further alleges that at all times since the said marriage to the plaintiff, he has, with the utmost good faith, carried out his obligations as the husband of the plaintiff, and has in every way treated the plaintiff with kindness, respect and love that a husband owes to his wife.

Denies that the defendant has, throughout the entire married life of said parties, or otherwise or at all, or at any time or upon any occasion, wrongfully or falsely or brutally or cruelly accused or charged the plaintiff with forcing him or otherwise forcing him to enter into said marriage relation for the purpose of "holding him up," or of "getting money out of him," or for any other purpose; denies that he has in said alleged or in any other connection, or at

such alleged time, or at any other time or times or at all, accused
her or charged her on account of said marriage, or on any other
account, with being a "gold digger," or a "blackmailer," or with
disgracing him or ruining his career, or standing in the way of his
professional success; denies that on many or any of said alleged
occasions, or upon any other occasion, the defendant has told
plaintiff that the relation of marriage militated against his success
or that she knew he wanted to defer said marriage, or that if she
had not been selfish and had loved him, or had loved him, she
would have "gotten rid of the said baby as many other women had
done for him," and in that connection the defendant alleges that
he has never at any time or at all, made any such statement or
accusation or charge to the plaintiff; but in that connection the
defendant alleges that on many occasions the plaintiff has told the
defendant that she was not in love with him.

(a) Denies that as soon as she opened a door, or at any other
time or at all, the defendant cried out to her contemptuously and
loudly enough that others on said train heard him, or contemptuously or loudly, or otherwise or at all, the following statement:
"What are you coming in here for? You made me marry you," or
any statement substantially similar thereto; denies that plaintiff
went out of said compartment crying.

(b) Denies that on or about the 5th day of January, 1925, defendant came home about 1:30 o'clock A.M., and went into, or went
into plaintiff's room where she was asleep, or that he went into
her room at all, or wakened her or commenced to or did upbraid,
reproach, condemn, or otherwise accuse or charge her on account
of their said marriage, or on account of anything else whatsoever;
denies that on said alleged occasion, or at any other time or at all,
the plaintiff said to the defendant: "I am very sorry; but it is not
my fault, and I don't see how I can help it. Please let me rest, and
don't talk to me any more tonight about it, and I will talk to you
in the morning," or any statement substantially similar thereto;
denies that defendant replied or otherwise stated in an angry or
domineering tone of voice, or at all, "We'll talk about it right
now," or any statement substantially similar thereto, and denies
that defendant thereupon, or at all, remained in said room, or continued to or did in any manner whatsoever, abuse or condemn
plaintiff until 5:00 o'clock, or that he abused or condemned plaintiff for any period of time whatsoever, or at all.

The Curry home as it looked in 1908. The house stood in the intersection of present-day Cahuenga Boulevard and Highland Avenue in Hollywood. (*Author's collection*)

Lillita MacMurray
aged five in 1913.
(Author's collection)

Lillita MacMurray
photographed at the
Chaplin Studio as
"The Age of
Innocence," 1920.
(Author's collection)

First National exhibitors pose for a group photo at the Chaplin Studio during the production of *The Kid*, 1920. Lillita, as the flirting angel, is in front of Chaplin, who is also in costume. Jackie Coogan is above Chaplin's left shoulder. *(Roy Export Company Establishment)*

The angel dream sequence of *The Kid,* 1921. *(Roy Export Company Establishment)*

Chaplin rehearsing the actors for the angel dream sequence of *The Kid.* Lillita is on the far right. *(Roy Export Company Establishment)*

Chaplin directing Lillita, as the flirting angel with harp in hand, to cry. *(Roy Export Company Establishment)*

The Chaplin Studio photographed after a rare Hollywood snowfall, 1921.
(Roy Export Company Establishment)

Lillita and her mother appear as French maids with Chaplin and Edna
Purviance in *The Idle Class,* 1921. *(Roy Export Company Establishment)*

Lita Grey with Chaplin at the signing of her contract as leading lady for *The Gold Rush,* March 1924. *(Roy Export Company Establishment)*

Lita Grey signing her contract for *The Gold Rush.* From left to right are Eddie Manson, Chuck Riesner, Lillian Spicer, Chaplin, Lita Grey, Jim Tully, Henry Bergman, Eddie Sutherland, and Alf Reeves. *(Roy Export Company Establishment)*

Lita Grey and Chaplin after the signing of her contract. *(Roy Export Company Establishment)*

On location for *The Gold Rush* in Truckee, California. Chaplin and Lita Grey, along with six hundred extras, prepare for the great trek. *(Roy Export Company Establishment)*

Chaplin, appearing unwell from influenza, with Lita Grey in Truckee. *(Roy Export Company Establishment)*

Lita Grey with Chaplin and Sid Grauman in Truckee. *(Roy Export Company Establishment)*

Lita Grey with
Chaplin and Sid
Grauman in Truckee.
*(Roy Export Company
Establishment)*

Lita Grey in Truckee.
*(Roy Export Company
Establishment)*

The newlyweds in
Shorb, California,
November 1924.
(Author's collection)

Charles Chaplin's Cove Way, Beverly Hills, mansion, 1924.
(Author's collection)

Charles Chaplin as Napoleon with Lita Grey Chaplin as Josephine at a fancy-dress party at the Ambassador Hotel, 1925. Also in the group are Marion Davies and John Gilbert (standing on opposite sides of Chaplin), Eleanor Boardman (below Lita), and Irving Thalberg (below Marion Davies). (*Culver Pictures, Inc.*)

Lita Grey and Charles Chaplin at the Hollywood premiere of *Little Annie Rooney*, 1925. *(Author's collection)*

Chaplin and Merna Kennedy in *The Circus*, 1928. *(Roy Export Company Establishment)*

Lita Grey and Charles Chaplin pose with Charles Jr. for appearances' sake prior to departure for Honolulu, Hawaii, November 1926. *(Author's collection)*

Lita Grey Chaplin with her mother, grandfather, and sons Charles Jr. and Sydney after leaving Chaplin, December 1926. *(Author's collection)*

Lita Grey Chaplin with her counsel, January 1927. From left to right are William K. Young, Milton K. Young, Lita Grey Chaplin, Edwin T. McMurray, Lillian Spicer, and Lyndol L. Young. *(Author's collection)*

Lita Grey Chaplin at the time of the divorce proceedings, when she was given temporary use of the Cove Way house, 1927. *(Author's collection)*

Lita Grey Chaplin taking the oath in the divorce suit, August 1927. *(David Robinson collection)*

Lita Grey Chaplin's Beverly Drive home, 1928. *(Author's collection)*

Lita Grey
Chaplin,
1929.
*(Author's
collection)*

Lita Grey
Chaplin,
1930.
*(Author's
collection)*

Lita Grey Chaplin with her children, Charles Jr. (left) and Sydney (right), 1932. (*Author's collection*)

Lita Grey Chaplin, 1934. *(Author's collection)*

Lita Grey Chaplin with her second husband, Henry Aguirre, 1936.
(Author's collection)

Lita Grey Chaplin with her third husband, Arthur Day, 1938.
(Author's collection)

Lita Grey Chaplin, 1946. *(Author's collection)*

Lita Grey Chaplin, 1967. *(Author's collection)*

Charles Chaplin Jr.,
1960. *(Author's
collection)*

Sydney Chaplin,
1990. *(Author's
collection)*

Lita Grey Chaplin with her dog Peachy, 1992. *(Author's collection)*

Lita Grey Chaplin with Jeffrey Vance, 1995. *(Author's collection)*

In connection with this subdivision (b), the defendant alleges that if, on or about the 5th day of January, 1925, the plaintiff was nervous from loss of sleep, or from any other cause, or was exhausted by excitement and turmoil, or was exhausted from any cause whatsoever, or commenced to or did cry, that said nervous condition and said condition of exhaustion and excitement and said crying, or any or either thereof, were in no way caused by any act or word on the part of the defendant, and he was in no way responsible therefor.

(c) Denies that on or about the 15th day of January, 1925, or at any other time, when the defendant was preparing to go out, or at any other time, plaintiff began to cry, or complained to the defendant about never seeing him, and/or going out with him, or always being left alone, or about anything else; denies that thereupon, or at all, the defendant said to her in a sneering, or sarcastic tone of voice, or that he stated to her at all, "Well, what different kind of treatment can you expect? I didn't marry you because I wanted to; but because you made me," or any statement substantially similar thereto; denies that the aforesaid or any treatment of plaintiff by defendant, either together with, or of themselves, his said alleged acts or act, or conduct as alleged to have occurred before the first day of February, 1925, or any act or conduct of the defendant whatsoever, placed or kept the plaintiff in such or any continual or any state or condition of mental or other suffering or turmoil or anguish, that on account thereof or on account of anything whatsoever, in such or any continual or other state of physical or other unrest, that her said alleged or any condition was noticed by defendant's physician when said physician had an opportunity of observing defendant's said alleged attitude toward plaintiff, or the effect thereof upon her, or at any other time or at all; denies that said physician, at said time, or at any other time, immediately or ever advised defendant, in plaintiff's presence, that it would be dangerous for plaintiff to remain in the environment of her home until after her baby was born; in connection with this subparagraph of subdivision (c), as hereinabove last set forth, the defendant alleges that prior to said first day of February, 1925, this defendant, as the husband of the plaintiff, felt impelled to, and did call to the attention of the plaintiff certain conduct in which she had been engaged, and which conduct this defendant resented and criticized; that by reason of the said criticism, the plaintiff sought, by pretext, to find some reason for leaving the home which the defendant provided for himself and the plaintiff, and in which home there was provided all the comforts necessary to the complete comfort and happiness of the plaintiff and the defendant, and the plaintiff asserted to the defendant that the said home was big and gloomy, and that she did not care to live in it; that after the plaintiff had made said statements to the defendant, the defendant, out of consideration for the physical condition in which the said plaintiff then was, invited the mother of the plaintiff to come and live with the plaintiff and the defendant at the home then maintained by this defendant for himself and plaintiff, and the mother of the plaintiff did come and live with plaintiff and defendant.

That notwithstanding the previous criticism directed by this defendant toward the said plaintiff, on account of her conduct as aforesaid, the said plaintiff persisted in continuing to do certain things which had previously given rise to just criticism on the part of this defendant, and the said plaintiff, after realizing the position which this defendant maintained toward the said conduct of the plaintiff, finally informed the defendant that she wanted to live separate and apart from the defendant, and that the atmosphere of the household was getting her nervous, and that it would be better for both the plaintiff and the defendant if they did live separate and apart.

Denies that plaintiff said she did not want to leave. Admits that plaintiff would not leave and let defendant charge her with desertion, and alleges that it had never been suggested that such a charge should be made. In this connection, the defendant alleges that he had made no objection to the proposed plan of the plaintiff to leave the house and live separate and apart from the defendant, but notwithstanding that fact, the plaintiff insisted on having her physician come to the home of plaintiff and defendant, which visit of the physician the plaintiff stated to the defendant, was for technical reasons, and because the said plaintiff did not want the said defendant to charge her, or have opportunity to charge her with desertion or abandonment.

Denies that said physician thereupon, or at all, told plaintiff that she could not stand the existing or any conditions, or that she would have to go away. Denies that as a result thereof, or upon the aforesaid statement having been signed on or about the first day of February, 1925, the plaintiff and her mother procured a house by themselves, where they remained for several months or for any period; and in this connection, the defendant admits that on or about the first day of February, 1925, the plaintiff and her mother, with the knowledge and consent of the defendant, procured a home for occupancy by themselves, and that the said plaintiff and her mother, with the knowledge and consent of the defendant, lived and remained in said home for a period of several weeks.

In connection with those matters hereinabove last set forth, this defendant alleges that the aforesaid statement which was signed by the said physicians, was signed entirely at the request of the plaintiff, and only because she stated that it was her desire to leave the house and the home which the defendant had provided for her, and to live separate and apart from the defendant, but at the same time, she did not want to have the defendant charge her with desertion.

Further and in this connection, the defendant alleges:

That during the time that the plaintiff and her mother were occupying the home to which they removed, the defendant visited the said plaintiff at frequent intervals, and that said visits were made on the most friendly and lovable basis. That the relationship between the said plaintiff and this defendant during said period of time was most intimate. That on several occasions this defendant took friends with him to call upon the said plaintiff, and that after a few weeks, the said plaintiff, of her own free will, returned to the defendant's home, which had previously been occupied by the said plaintiff and defendant, and at said time informed the defendant that she no longer desired to live separate and apart from the defendant, and that she desired his companionship and the comfort of his home, and after said return, the plaintiff continued to reside in said home and to live with the defendant continuously until the separation of these parties on November 30, 1926.

3. Denies that defendant at no time during the cohabitation of plaintiff and defendant, entered or maintained with plaintiff the normal or ordinary social relations and matrimonial intercourse or matrimonial intercourse, usually existing between man and wife; denies that prior to the filing of the complaint herein, the defendant's attitude or conduct or manifestation of interest with regard to the sexual relations existing between the parties have been or were abnormal, unnatural, perverted, degenerate or indecent, as

shown by those particulars alleged in plaintiff's said complaint, or otherwise or at all, and in particular denies that throughout the entire married life of said parties, or at any time since the marriage of said parties, or otherwise, or at all, or at any time whatsoever, the defendant solicited, urged, demanded, suggested or requested that plaintiff submit to, perform or commit or otherwise engage in such act or acts or thing or things for the gratification of defendant's said alleged abnormal, unnatural, perverted, degenerate or indecent or other sexual desire or desires, as to be too or otherwise revolting, indecent or immoral to set forth in detail in said complaint, and further denies that the defendant ever, or at all, solicited, urged, demanded, suggested or requested that plaintiff submit to, perform, commit or otherwise engage in any act or thing in any way abnormal or unnatural or perverted or degenerate or indecent.

Denies that said alleged or any solicitation or solicitations or demand or demands or suggestion or request on the part of this defendant were in any way or manner so, or otherwise revolting, degrading or offensive to plaintiff, or were of such infamous personal indignities, or of any type or character of indignity, or showed such or any lack of respect, or such or any contempt for plaintiff as a wife or as a woman, that they were, or any of them was, or that they were or that any of them was calculated to be a shock to her refined or other sensibilities, or repulsive to her moral or other instincts, or abhorrent to her conception of moral or personal decency, and the defendant particularly denies that he ever made of or to the plaintiff, either expressly or impliedly any solicitation or demand or request or suggestion that was in any way revolting or degrading or offensive or indecent.

Denies that any of said alleged solicitations and demands, or any solicitation or demand, were the culmination of, or any part of a course of conduct or any conduct on the part of the defendant, or that any said alleged solicitations and demands commenced shortly after said marriage, or ever commenced at all, or were ever made in any manner whatsoever, and denies that the defendant ever read to the plaintiff from books or any book on such or kindred subjects, or that he ever conversed with her thereon, or upon any subject in any way abnormal, unnatural, perverted, or degenerate or indecent, or ever recounted to her in detail, or otherwise, his alleged personal, or any experience or experiences with five or any prominent moving picture women involving such practices, or with any person whomsoever.

Denies that said alleged course of conduct, or any course of conduct, or any conduct at all on the part of the defendant, was of such or any duration, or of such or any character that the same was the result of a deliberate or general intention or plan or of any intention or plan on the part of the defendant to undermine or distort or otherwise effect plaintiff's normal, or other sexual impulses or desires, or impulse or desire, or demoralize or otherwise injuriously affect her standards of decency, or degrade or otherwise injuriously affect her conception or ideas of morals, for the gratification of defendant's said alleged desires, or for any other purpose whatsoever, or at all, or his said alleged solicitations and demands, or solicitation or demand in reference thereto, or in reference to any other thing whatsoever, and in that connection this defendant alleges that no such conduct as alleged in the plaintiff's complaint, or otherwise or at all, was ever engaged in any manner whatsoever by this defendant, for any purpose whatsoever, or at all. In that connection, this defendant alleges that the plaintiff is the mother of two children begotten of this defendant, and that she has at all times lived with this defendant, at the home of this defendant, since the marriage of said parties until the date of the separation as alleged in said complaint, except for the few weeks during which the plaintiff and her mother lived separate and apart from this defendant, as hereinabove set forth; that during all of said time, said plaintiff and this defendant were guests together in the homes of defendant's friends; that on many occasions they attended dinner parties together at the homes of friends of the defendant, and likewise during said time said plaintiff and this defendant entertained guests in the home of the parties hereto, gave week-end parties and otherwise were hosts together at many parties which their friends attended. That on many occasions this defendant took said plaintiff to theaters, opening performances of motion pictures, and to other public performances and functions, and otherwise during said time she professed for this defendant, and claimed to have as to him, feelings of respect and admiration as a man and as her husband; that likewise, during all of said time, in the privacy of their own home and in their own relations as husband and wife, said plaintiff professed to entertain for this defendant an attitude and feeling of respect usually existing in a wife toward and for her husband.

Denies that said alleged acts, conduct, solicitations or demands of defendant, as set forth in plaintiff's said complaint, or any act, conduct, solicitation, demand, suggestion or request of this defendant were the cause of or resulted in continual or any friction or unhappiness or quarreling or unpleasantness between said parties, or resulted in a further or any disagreeable or neglected attitude on the part of this defendant toward said plaintiff, either on account of any alleged persistent refusal to yield or accede to defendant's said alleged demands or solicitations, or on account of any other thing whatsoever, and in that connection this defendant alleges that the said plaintiff never at any time persisted, or otherwise refused to yield or accede to any demands or solicitations on the part of this defendant, for the reason that no such demands or solicitations or demand or solicitation or request or suggestion was ever made by this defendant of or upon the plaintiff.

(a) Denies that approximately six months before the separation of the said parties, or at any other time or otherwise or at all, the defendant continued or ever made any solicitations and demands, or solicitation or demand or request or suggestion that plaintiff commit the act defined by Section 288a of the Penal Code of the State of California. Denies that defendant ever became enraged at plaintiff's alleged refusal to accede to any such demand or solicitation, (and denies that any such refusal was ever made for the reason that no such demand or solicitation was ever made or suggested), and denies that defendant said to her: "All married people do those kind of things. You are my wife and you have to do what I want you to do. I can get a divorce from you for refusing to do this," or any statement substantially similar thereto, or any statement at all. Denies that plaintiff continued to refuse, or ever refused, and denies that upon plaintiff's alleged continued or any refusal, defendant abruptly left the house, or that plaintiff did not see him again until the next day, and in that connection, the defendant alleges that if he ever abruptly left the house, and if the plaintiff ever failed to see him until a day following, it was not because of any reason or thing as alleged and set forth in plaintiff's complaint.

(b) Denies that approximately four months before said separation, or at any other time, or otherwise or at all, the defendant named a girl of their acquaintance, or any other person, and told plaintiff, or told plaintiff, that he had heard things, or anything, about said girl, or any person, which caused him to believe, or that he did believe, that she, or any other person, might be willing or was willing to commit an act or acts of sexual perversion, or that he asked plaintiff to invite her, or any other person, up to the house or any other place some time, or any other time, or that he told plaintiff that they or either of them could have some "fun" with her, or any one else.

With respect to the character of the social and personal relations and matrimonial intercourse existing between said plaintiff and defendant, and in particular with reference to those particulars set forth in the plaintiff's complaint, this defendant admits, denies and alleges:

(a) Denies that during the first two months after said marriage, the defendant took plaintiff out with him not more than three or four times, but on the contrary, this defendant took said plaintiff with him both to the private homes of his friends, and to many public functions, and in addition thereto, many friends of the parties hereto were invited to and were received as guests at the home of the defendant and said plaintiff, which said occasions included week-end parties, opening performances of motion pictures, and many other such occasions. Denies that on any occasion or at all, the defendant bluntly and contemptuously, or bluntly or contemptuously, or otherwise or at all, told plaintiff that he wanted her to go with him for the sake of appearances, or for any other similar reasons, or that he told plaintiff that he could not afford to have the public think that he was neglecting her, but on the contrary, the defendant alleges that during said time he was making diligent effort, in good faith, to have his friends become acquainted with and become interested in the said plaintiff, so that the married life of the parties hereto would be happy, and that the plaintiff would be contented as his wife; denies that the plaintiff ever went with the defendant under any humiliating circumstances or circumstance whatsoever, or that she ever made any effort to protect him against any adverse public criticism or any other criticism, or comment, or to overcome his said alleged or any antagonism toward her or said marriage, and in that connection this defendant alleges that the plaintiff never went with the defendant upon any occasion where there existed any humiliating circumstances or conditions, and further alleges that the plaintiff at no time ever advised or informed this defendant that any humiliating circumstances existed, or that she considered or regarded any conduct or act on the part of this defendant, or on the part of his friends as humiliating, or that she accompanied the defendant upon any occasion for the purpose of protecting this defendant from adverse public criticism or comment, or for the purpose of overcoming any alleged antagonism toward said plaintiff or toward the marriage of these parties.

(b) Denies that during said time defendant had not more than two or three meals at home with plaintiff, or that it was his custom to come home late at night, and/or to go to his room without seeing the plaintiff, but on the contrary, and in that connection, this defendant alleges that during said time referred to in said subparagraph of plaintiff's complaint, this defendant was actively engaged in his profession and in the direction and production of a motion picture, all of which facts were and are well known to the plaintiff, and that it was necessary, in carrying out his said professional duties and activities, that he depart from his home very early in the morning, and at an hour in the morning when the plaintiff was still asleep, and likewise this defendant, because of said duties was required to remain at his work at the studio until about 7:00 o'clock in the evening, which fact was also well known to the plaintiff. That during said time, and at the conclusion of his day's work, this defendant telephoned daily to the plaintiff for the purpose of ascertaining what plans, if any, the plaintiff had made for the evening and whether or not this defendant should go to his home for the evening meal, but that on several of such occasions, plaintiff was not at home when this defendant called on the telephone, and frequently, on such occasions, the plaintiff offered some excuse or pretext for not having this defendant come to his home for the evening meal, and informed this defendant that she was going out, or was going to the home of her grandmother, or was having a party of friends whom she thought would not interest this defendant, or that she had made plans to have her evening meal away from home. That during said period of time, said plaintiff never at any time complained to this defendant concerning the fact that the professional duties and activities of this defendant required him to be absent from the home, as hereinabove alleged, but on the contrary, seemed thoroughly satisfied with the conduct of this defendant in that regard, and seemed entirely satisfied that this defendant was thus devoting himself to his professional duties and activities.

(c) Denies that during the time that plaintiff lived away from the defendant's home, the defendant had dinner at the said temporary residence of plaintiff only twice, or that he stopped in to see her not more than once a week, or that he never telephoned to her, or that during only a portion of said time he took the plaintiff out about once a week in public, but on the contrary and in that connection, this defendant alleges that the departure of the said plaintiff from the home of plaintiff and defendant was the result of the plaintiff's own desire, and her own expressed wish, and that in discussing her departure, the said plaintiff informed and advised this defendant that she would find a suitable place to live, and that when she had prepared it for habitation, she would communicate that fact to this defendant and would let him know where the said place was located; that at said time, said plaintiff informed this defendant that she felt that she and this defendant would be happier if they lived apart; that she was nervous and that her nervous condition might be made better by a temporary separation. That the plaintiff at said time led this defendant to believe, and this defendant did believe, that said plaintiff did not care to see this defendant at frequent intervals, or at all, following her departure from the home; that in all matters connected with the said departure of the plaintiff from the home of these parties, this defendant, out of respect for the plaintiff, and because of her condition, acceded to her wishes as expressed to this defendant; that notwithstanding the fact that the plaintiff had led this defendant to believe, and that he did believe that the plaintiff did not care to see him, this defendant frequently telephoned to the plaintiff and inquired of her concerning her personal welfare; that not long after the said departure of the plaintiff from the home of these parties, said plaintiff communicated to this defendant her desire to have the defendant come to see her, and that in response to said communication, this defendant called upon the said plaintiff and thereafter he continued to see her, and in all respects, to the best of his ability, provided the plaintiff with the comforts of life and with every attention.

(d) Denies that the general or any conditions or condition described or alleged in subdivisions (a), (b) and (c) of subdivision 3 of paragraph V, or any or either of said subdivisions, continued to or ever did exist, either before or after plaintiff's first baby was born, or up to or until the time of the separation of the parties on November 30, 1926, or otherwise, or at all.

(e) Admits that while the plaintiff was at Coronado, for a month, during the summer of 1926, the defendant did not go to Coronado, but denies that during said time the defendant never telephoned to plaintiff. In that connection the defendant alleges that at the time the plaintiff and the two babies left for Coronado, this defendant was very busily and actively engaged in his professional duties as a producer of motion pictures, and the plaintiff well knew, at the time of her departure, that it would not be possible for this defendant to visit her at Coronado. That at the time of the departure, she informed this defendant that she did not know just where she would stop, and that he should not telephone to her until she had found a house and communicated with him, and had advised him where he could reach her by telephone. That the plaintiff well knew that because of the fact that at that time the defendant had from two hundred to three hundred people actually working, it would be impossible for this defendant to leave his work and go to Coronado, and that at the time of her departure she professed to be entirely satisfied and happy at the prospect of her trip, and offered no complaint whatsoever to this defendant because of the fact that he could not go to Coronado; that upon one occasion while at Coronado, the plaintiff did telephone to this defendant, and requested him to come to Coronado for the week-end, and upon being advised by this defendant that it would be impossible for him to go because he was so busy with his work, the plaintiff replied that she was having a lovely time and was quite happy.

(f) Denies that while plaintiff was at Coronado, she telephoned to the defendant one Saturday morning, or at any other time, or asked him if she could come home and spend the week-end with him, and denies that the defendant on said, or upon any occasion, told her not to come. In that connection, this defendant alleges that on one occasion the plaintiff telephoned to this defendant and asked him to come to Coronado for the week-end, to which this defendant replied that he was so busy with his work that it would be impossible for him to go, to which she replied that she was having a lovely time, and was very happy; that on said occasion this defendant asked the plaintiff to come to Los Angeles, as some people were going to be at the house, and that upon being so advised, the plaintiff stated that she would come, but in fact, the plaintiff did not attend and did not further communicate with this defendant.

(g) Admits that during the summer of 1926, the plaintiff and the children of these parties spent a month at Catalina, and admits that during said time the defendant did not go to Catalina, and did not call the plaintiff on the telephone, but in that connection, this defendant alleges that by an agreement and understanding between these parties, it was decided that it would be both pleasant and beneficial to the plaintiff and to the children, for them to spend a month at Catalina; that at said time, the defendant was busily engaged and engrossed in the duties of his profession and in the work of a motion picture production, and at the time of the departure of the plaintiff and the children for Catalina, it was agreed between these parties that because of the existing duties of the defendant's work, he would make no attempt to go to Catalina. That it was also understood, and it was decided between these parties that as frequently as possible, the plaintiff would telephone to the defendant and as a matter of fact, the plaintiff did telephone to the defendant, in accordance with the understanding between the parties, every other day during the time she was in Catalina. That at no time during her stay in Catalina did the plaintiff offer any complaint whatsoever, or express any dissatisfaction over the fact that it was impossible for the defendant to visit her at Catalina, but on the contrary seemed thoroughly satisfied and happy with the arrangement which had been agreed upon between these parties with regard to her stay at Catalina.

(h) Denies that on several occasions, or on any occasion, during the year just prior to the filing of the complaint herein, or during any other time, the defendant said to the plaintiff, "Go away some place for a while; I can't work or create when you are here. You are ruining my career," or any statement substantially similar thereto. Denies that on one such or on any occasion the plaintiff replied or said to the defendant, "Why, Charlie, I don't understand how I interfere with your work. I never see you or annoy you," or any statement substantially similar thereto. Denies that on said or on any occasion, or in reply to any statement of the plaintiff, this defendant replied in a tone of exasperation, or otherwise or at all, "That isn't it, it is just the fact that you are here; and I am supposed to give the usual attention to a home and family, it annoys me and irritates me; and I can't work," or any statement substantially similar thereto. In this connection this defendant alleges that during said time, the plaintiff well knew that the defendant was busily engaged in the work of his profession and she at all times well knew of the demands and requirements made upon this defendant, and of the necessity of his devoting his undivided attention to the work of his profession; that the plaintiff was well aware that in order for this defendant successfully to produce a good picture, and successfully to enact his part in said picture, that it was necessary and important that he concentrate upon his work, and devote his every attention to it. That during said time this defendant explained to the plaintiff that it was vitally important that he give his undivided attention to his motion picture production, and to this explanation or statement she replied, "I want to go away and do something;" that thereupon this defendant told the plaintiff that it was his desire that she have her friends come to the house, and give all the parties that she liked, because he wanted her to be entirely happy. During said time the said plaintiff both invited and received many of her friends at the house, and almost nightly entertained parties of her friends, at which from twelve to twenty persons would be present. That after this had continued for some time, the plaintiff advised the defendant that she was tired of entertaining and that she desired to go away for two or three weeks, and it was upon one of such occasions that the plaintiff advised the defendant that she desired to go to Catalina.

(i) Admits that a short time prior to the separation of these parties the plaintiff took a trip to Honolulu, but denies that she went on said trip at the request of the defendant, and in this connection, this defendant alleges that for a long time prior to the time that plaintiff took said trip to Honolulu, the plaintiff and this defendant had been living together very happily, and, although this defendant was busily engaged in his profession, the said parties had spent a great deal of time together and had attended together many parties and other functions at the home of friends and also at public places. During this time, the plaintiff seemed to be very happy, spent a considerable portion of the day at the Ambassador Hotel and other places where she would attend teas and parties and then in the evening she would call this defendant on the telephone at the Studio and they would and did go together to dinner with friends of this defendant or with friends of the plaintiff. As hereinabove alleged this happy relationship had continued for several weeks, when suddenly the plaintiff began to and did indulge in the use of alcoholic beverages, as defendant was informed and

verily believes, and on many occasions, when this defendant telephoned to the home of these parties to arrange for dinner together
with plaintiff, he would be informed that she was out and had been
out for some time. On these occasions when she was absent from
the home, she did not take the children of these parties but at all
of said times absented herself from the home and likewise from
the care of the said children. Upon many occasions, prior to her
departure for Honolulu, the plaintiff returned to the home of plaintiff and defendant in the early hours of the morning and on these
occasions, this defendant would try to reason with plaintiff and
point out to her that she was not conducting herself in a proper
manner and that it would cause unfavorable criticism and comment and that if plaintiff had a proper regard for this defendant as
her husband, she would not engage in such conduct. This defendant likewise advised the plaintiff that it was very unwise, from
all standpoints, for her to indulge in excessive use of intoxicating
beverages and advised and requested her to refrain from such use.
After this course of conduct had been carried on by the plaintiff
for some time, and as a result of the very late hours kept by plaintiff, she caught a cold in her ear and as a result thereof had to be
taken to a hospital for an immediate operation on her ear, all of
which caused this defendant great worry and anxiety. However,
almost immediately upon leaving the hospital she again absented
herself from the home of these parties and came home very late
at night in an intoxicated condition. This defendant again tried to
reason with the plaintiff and point out to her the fact that by such
conduct she was ruining her health and that it was very ill-advised
to do such things and very dangerous to her health to so conduct
herself so soon after leaving the hospital and so soon after having
the operation on her ear.

That during said time and after this course of conduct had been
engaged in by plaintiff for some time, this defendant was advised
that the plaintiff, on most of these occasions, was associating with
a particular group of persons, some of whom were very indiscreet
and some of whom likewise indulged in intoxicating beverages to
excess.

That during said time this defendant was informed that the
plaintiff had been frequently associating with a certain automobile
salesman in Hollywood, California, without the consent or knowledge of this defendant. That upon being informed of this fact, this

defendant informed the said plaintiff that he had received these reports concerning her association with the said automobile salesman. That the attitude and manner of the plaintiff, when confronted with this information, was very cold and indifferent and it became very apparent to this defendant that the plaintiff no longer cared to continue the happy relationship which had been in existence between these parties for some time prior to the time when the aforesaid course of conduct became a habit with the plaintiff.

That at the time when this defendant confronted the plaintiff with the information that he had learned of her association with the aforesaid automobile salesman, a further discussion was had. That this defendant believed that if something should occur to sever the relationship of the plaintiff and some of those persons, including the said salesman, with whom she had been associating, that she would change her course of conduct and the happy relationship between these parties could again be established. That in order to accomplish the aforesaid purpose, and in order to separate the plaintiff from some of these companions, this defendant suggested to the plaintiff that she take a trip and that if she took such a trip she would perhaps get over the infatuation which apparently existed between herself and the said automobile salesman, but the plaintiff declined to take such a trip and stated that she wanted to remain in Los Angeles. That thereafter and for some time the plaintiff did remain in Los Angeles and notwithstanding the protests of this defendant, she continued her association with the aforesaid automobile salesman and with other persons with whom this defendant had requested the plaintiff not to associate. After this had continued for some time, the plaintiff very suddenly, and without any previous discussion of the matter, told this defendant that she desired to take a trip to Honolulu, and the defendant believing that such a trip would result in a severance of the relations as heretofore set forth, acquiesced in the plan and told the plaintiff that he thought such a trip would be a very fine thing for her.

(j) Denies that on Christmas Day, 1925, the defendant promised plaintiff that he would return home in the evening for dinner with plaintiff and denies that when the defendant came home he was in an intoxicated condition, and in this connection this defendant alleges that he is not in any way addicted to the use of intoxicating liquor.

4. Denies that defendant has never shown a normal, usual or

proper fatherly interest in or affection for the children of plaintiff and defendant, but on the contrary alleges that he has at all times exhibited for the said children, and each of them, a normal, usual, proper and affectionate fatherly interest.

(a) Denies that it was the defendant's general practice and custom, or general practice or custom, or practice or custom at all, to come home late at night and leave in the morning, or leave in the morning without going in to see said children, but on the contrary and in that regard this defendant alleges that this defendant saw his said children practically every day, although he admits that upon a few occasions, and entirely because of the fact that his professional duties and activities required him to be at the Studio until late in the evening and also required him to leave his home early in the morning, he did not see said children, because at the time he came to his home said children were asleep and they were still asleep at the time he left in the morning and he did not consider that a proper regard for the interest of the said children would permit him to awaken them.

Denies that during the month of October, 1926, or at any other time, the defendant failed to go in to see his children for a period of two weeks consecutively, or for any other consecutive period of days, and in this connection this defendant alleges that during the time that the children were kept at the home of these parties by the plaintiff, that this defendant went in to see the children daily, with the exception of not more than one or two occasions, and that the only time or times when the defendant failed to see the said children were upon those occasions when the plaintiff took the said children to the home of the plaintiff's grandmother and placed them in the care and custody of her said grandmother.

(b) Admits that after the birth of the second baby, plaintiff and this defendant had a conversation upon the subject of building an addition to their house for the purpose of providing a special nursery for the children, but denies that defendant curtly or otherwise refused to build said addition or that he gave as an alleged reason for such alleged refusal the following statement: "This is *my* home and I am not going to spoil it." In that connection, this defendant alleges that after the second baby was born, the plaintiff and defendant had a conversation regarding the building of a special nursery and an addition to their house, in which conversation the plaintiff suggested that this be done right away. This defendant advised the plaintiff that in his opinion it would be better to wait until after the picture, upon which the defendant was then working, was completed, when the plaintiff and defendant would take a trip abroad together and that during the time that the family and the children were absent from the house the alterations and addition to the house could be made without subjecting the parties and the children to the necessary annoyance and inconvenience attendant upon the making of such alterations and addition; that this defendant thought that it was for the best interest of the children that the alterations be made while they were absent from the house and that no inconvenience or discomfort whatsoever would be or could be occasioned to the said children because of any delay in building such addition to the house. That the aforesaid suggestion made by this defendant to the plaintiff regarding the time of making such alterations and addition to the said house was entirely acquiesced in by the plaintiff and the plaintiff stated to this defendant that she thought it was a good idea and was desirable to make the alterations while these parties were away from the house.

(c) Answering subdivision (c) of subparagraph 4 of paragraph V of plaintiff's said complaint, this defendant alleges that the separation of plaintiff and this defendant on the 30th day of November, 1926, was occasioned entirely by the act of the plaintiff and without any just cause or reason, and without the knowledge and consent of this defendant. That the first knowledge that this defendant had of said separation was when he was informed on the telephone by one of his servants that this plaintiff was packing up her clothing and that she had sent the children of these parties away from the family home. That immediately upon being thus informed, this defendant communicated with the plaintiff and protested against her departure from the family home and both requested and demanded that she return to the family home and bring the children with her and remain with the said children in the family home. That the only reply by the plaintiff to this request and demand of this defendant was that this defendant should see her lawyer.

That within two or three days after the departure of the plaintiff from the family home, as aforesaid, an attorney at law representing this defendant advised the attorney who was then representing the plaintiff that whatever was necessary for the support, care and maintenance of the children of these parties would be gladly and cheerfully furnished and that all that the plaintiff or her said attorney needed to do in that regard was to advise this defendant's attorney what sum would be necessary; and in that regard the defendant further alleges that neither the plaintiff nor her said attorney or attorneys, although requested so to do, have ever advised or suggested to this defendant or to the attorney or attorneys representing this defendant what sum would be necessary for the proper support of the children, except that on one occasion, as this defendant is informed and believes and therefore alleges, an attorney representing the plaintiff stated to an attorney representing this defendant that he wanted all that the defendant had.

The defendant further alleges that he has always been ready willing and able to provide for the care, maintenance and support of the said children, which fact has at all times been well known to plaintiff and to plaintiff's attorneys, and that since the voluntary departure of the plaintiff from the family home, and without any order whatsoever from the above entitled court, this defendant has contributed to and for the proper support and maintenance of his said children.

Further answering said allegation, and with reference to the visits to his children since the departure of the plaintiff from the family home, this defendant alleges that immediately upon the said departure of plaintiff, this defendant requested and demanded that the plaintiff return to the family home and bring the children with her; that the children were his just as much as they were the plaintiff's and he demanded that the children be returned to his home where they could be properly taken care of; that after the departure of the plaintiff, she took the said children and each of them to the home of her grandparents and that this defendant demanded of plaintiff the privilege of frequently seeing and visiting the said children, but said privilege was denied this defendant by the plaintiff until the same had been arranged for by attorneys representing these parties. That when this defendant finally obtained such permission and consent, and went to the home of plaintiff's grandparents to see his said children, he was compelled by the plaintiff to visit said children in the immediate presence and under the notice and observation of the mother and grandparents of the plaintiff, each and all of whom exhibited and manifested an openly hostile attitude toward this defendant and robbed this defendant of the pleasure of his visit with the said children and made it impossible for this defendant to bestow upon his said children that fatherly affection and interest which it was and has always been and still is his desire to do. That if this defendant thereafter failed to visit his said children, it was only because and it was because of the fact that the plaintiff insisted that he could not see the said children except in the immediate presence and under the notice and observation of her family as aforesaid and that under such circumstances, and in order to prevent further friction and unpleasantness he considered it advisable that he refrain from any further visits.

5. Denies that during the cohabitation of plaintiff and defendant or at any other time, the defendant told the plaintiff on any occasion or at any time whatsoever that he did not believe or does not believe in the custom of marriage or in the marriage relation or that he could not or did not tolerate the conventional or other restraint which marriage or the marriage relation imposed or that he believed it was proper or right for a woman to bear children out of wedlock.

Denies that he has ever ridiculed or scoffed at or otherwise criticized plaintiff's alleged adherence to or belief in conventional or other moral or social standards with reference to marriage or the relation of the sexes or the bringing of a child or children into the world or has made light of or otherwise criticized the moral or statutory laws or any law in or with reference thereto.

Denies that at any time whatsoever this defendant told the plaintiff that a certain or any couple who had five children or any children, were not married or that in connection therewith or at all this defendant said to plaintiff, "That is the ideal way for a man and woman to live together," or any statement substantially similar thereto.

6. Denies that during the entire married life of said parties or during any portion of said time, the defendant has openly or at all, or publicly or privately associated with other women or with any other woman or that any such alleged association has resulted in any great or any humiliation or distress to plaintiff or to her exclusion or neglect and denies that defendant has either made or begun or maintained or continued such or any alleged associations under any claim of right to do so, or otherwise or at all.

This defendant has no information or belief sufficient to enable him to answer thereto and basing his denial upon that ground, denies all and every part of the following allegation in subparagraph 6 of said paragraph V of said complaint, which said allegation is as follows: "and that reports and information of such associations continuously reached plaintiff," and in that connection this defendant alleges that if any report or reports or information whatsoever of any alleged associations between this defendant and any other woman or women came to the notice or knowledge of the plaintiff, that such alleged reports and information and any and all thereof were without any foundation in fact and were and are untrue.

(a) This defendant has no information or belief sufficient to enable him to answer thereto and basing his denial upon that ground, denies all and every part of the following allegation contained in subdivision (a) of subparagraph 6 of said paragraph V of plaintiff's said complaint, which allegation is as follows: "That during the first month of their marriage and while plaintiff was pregnant as aforesaid, plaintiff was informed and believed that defendant was spending a very great portion of his time in the company of a certain prominent moving picture actress," and in that connection this defendant alleges that if the plaintiff was so informed or believed, such information and belief was wholly without foundation in fact and was untrue and in that connection this defendant further alleges that at no time since the marriage of plaintiff and this defendant did this defendant spend any great or considerable portion of time or any time whatsoever in the company of any prominent or other moving picture actress or any other woman or women whomsoever, except only such association as was made necessary by reason of the fact that this defendant was engaged in the production and in acting in a motion picture.

Further answering said subdivision of said subparagraph, this defendant denies that plaintiff ever asked defendant if any such alleged information were true and denies that he bluntly or boastingly or at all said or replied, "Yes, it is true; and I am in love with her, and don't care who knows it. I am going to see her when I want to, and whether you like it or not. I don't love you; and I am only living with you because I had to marry you," or any statement substantially similar thereto and further answering, this defendant alleges that no such event ever took place nor was any such statement ever made nor was any conversation with reference to any such or similar incident ever had between these parties.

Denies that shortly thereafter or at any other time or at all this defendant wanted or expressed any desire to have plaintiff go with him to said alleged woman's, or any woman's house or there meet said alleged woman or any woman or that this defendant told plaintiff at said time or at any other time or at all that said alleged woman or any other woman was a wonderful woman and that plaintiff would like her or that plaintiff would like her or anyone else. Denies that the plaintiff ever refused to go with this defendant to any such alleged place and denies that thereafter on many occasions, or at any other time or at all this defendant ever either requested, suggested or insisted that plaintiff go with him to said alleged woman's, or any other woman's house, or any other place to meet any such alleged woman; denies that these or any commands or demands or requests or any thereof were made at all, or were made with such or any stress or under such or any peculiar or other circumstances, that plaintiff either with or without any justification feared that defendant intended to or would do her some great or any bodily or other harm and denies that plaintiff ever had or entertained any such fear or that she ever refused or persisted in any refusal to go with this defendant and further denies that at every or any such alleged instance this defendant left the house or stated that he was going without her and denies that any such instance ever occurred or existed.

Denies that on one such or on any occasion whatsoever this defendant wanted or desired or expressed any such desire to plaintiff that she should or would go with him to said alleged house or to any house whatsoever for dinner or for or upon any other occasion and denies that plaintiff said, "Why do you keep insisting that I go there? You know that I don't want to go and don't want to meet her," or any statement substantially similar thereto and denies that on such or any occasion whatsoever this defendant replied or in any way stated, "You will have to meet her. You are my wife, and you can't refuse to meet my friends, or I won't live with you. If you don't go with me, I'll fix you," or any statement substantially similar thereto and further denies that any such alleged incident or occurrence or statement or conversation ever took place. Denies that on said alleged occasion or upon any occasion whatsoever the defendant's attitude or demeanor was so threatening (and in that connection the defendant alleges that he never at any time maintained or exhibited any threatening attitude or demeanor toward plaintiff) that plaintiff feared such or any bodily or other harm that when defendant then left said home or at any other time, she went to her grandfather's or any other place and/or but returned home later in the evening, and in that connection this defendant alleges that no such thing ever happened as alleged in plaintiff's complaint or otherwise or at all.

Denies that the next day after such alleged incident, or at any other time or at all the defendant said to plaintiff, either sneeringly or exultantly or in any other manner or at all, "I know what you did last night when I left; and I have just been waiting to get you to leave this house. Now I have got it on you," or any statement substantially similar thereto, and in that connection this defendant alleges that no such incident or statement ever took place or was made.

Denies that the only place defendant ever showed any personal interest or any interest in having plaintiff go with him was the home of said alleged woman and denies that the only friend he was ever particularly or otherwise concerned about having plaintiff meet was said alleged woman and denies that said alleged woman was the only friend of defendant that plaintiff ever refused to meet, and denies that plaintiff ever refused to go with said defendant to said alleged woman's house or to any other woman's house and in that connection the defendant alleges that during the entire married life of this defendant and the plaintiff, this defendant always and constantly maintained a proper interest in having the plaintiff meet his friends and on many occasions too innumerable to mention this defendant took the plaintiff to the home of his friends where they were guests together and that the plaintiff never refused to meet any friend of the defendant and never refused to go with defendant to the home of any of his friends and further alleges that there was never any occasion whatsoever for any such refusal ever being made or given and that no such refusal by the plaintiff was ever made or given.

(b) This defendant has no information or belief sufficient to enable him to answer thereto and basing his denial on that ground denies each and every allegation and all thereof contained in subdivision (b) of subparagraph 6 of said paragraph V of said complaint and in particular, this defendant denies that in or about the month of May, 1925, or at any other time or at all, while plaintiff was temporarily or otherwise absent from defendant's house, or at any other time whatsoever or at all, the automobile or other vehicle of a certain or any woman was at defendant's house, or stood in front thereof alone for several hours, or for any period of time whatsoever on four consecutive days or upon any occasion whatsoever. Denies that on one of said alleged occasions, or at any other time or at all, said alleged automobile was at said place as late as ten o'clock at night or for any other period of time whatsoever and in that connection alleges that it is a fact that on many occasions friends of this defendant and of plaintiff came to the home of these parties and that while such friends were there their automobiles remained outside on the driveways at this defendant's home, but that never at any time was there any woman whatsoever alone with this defendant at his home.

(c) Denies that at one time, or at any time or at all, when the plaintiff had been out of town, or at any other time, or when she returned, that plaintiff's key would not open the door, or that plaintiff was unable to get into the house, or that she thereafter, or at all, found or otherwise discovered that the, or any lock on said alleged or any door, had been changed, or that she thereafter spoke to defendant about changing the said lock, or that he jokingly or otherwise said: "I guess the servants are trying to protect me," and in that connection, this defendant alleges that no such incident or occurrence or statement ever happened or was ever said, nor was there any similar incident nor any similar statement made.

(7) Denies that defendant left plaintiff alone during the greater portion of the time, or that he left her entirely or at all dependent upon herself or her family or her friends for her entertainment or diversion, or otherwise, except only for such time and upon such occasions as were made necessary by reason of the fact that the defendant was and is engaged in the motion picture business, and that such business has always, and did during the time since the plaintiff and defendant have been married, require of this defendant a great portion of his time and attention, and that in order for this defendant to have a measure of success in his work and in his profession, it was necessary for him to devote a great portion of his time to his said work and his said business, of all of which facts the plaintiff at all times was well aware. Denies that defendant rarely came home until very late at night, and denies that only on very few occasions this defendant spent the evening at home with plaintiff, but on the contrary alleges that during the

greater portion of the time since the marriage of this defendant and plaintiff, he has spent a great deal of his time with plaintiff and has, with her, entertained their friends in the home of this defendant and plaintiff, and has also gone with this plaintiff to the homes of their friends, and to many public places and to many public functions, all of which is more particularly hereinbefore alleged and set forth. Denies that during the last six months that plaintiff and defendant lived together, or during any other period of the time since the marriage of these parties, the defendant never spent an evening at home with plaintiff and the babies, or the babies. Admits that on a few occasions this defendant declined to go in and meet or speak to certain guests, but in that connection this defendant alleges that when this did occur, it was because of the fact that on such occasions this defendant had been working arduously in the acting and production of a motion picture and would go home completely fatigued and tired out, and that on such occasions, in order for him to preserve his health and be able to continue with his said work, it was necessary for him to retire and rest. That not only did this defendant on a few occasions decline to meet and entertain friends of plaintiff, but likewise on a few occasions he declined to meet with or entertain his own personal friends, all of which facts and the reasons therefor were well understood by the plaintiff and also by said persons.

This defendant has no information or belief sufficient to enable him to answer thereto, and basing his denial on that ground denies the following allegation found in subparagraph (7) of said paragraph V of said complaint, which allegation is as follows: "That plaintiff has had house guests at her home for as long as a week at a time, without said guests meeting or seeing her husband."

Denies that in those specific instances alleged and set forth in said paragraph (7), or otherwise or at all, either with or without knowing anything or very little about plaintiff's guests, or any of them, that the defendant has made or did make slurring or insulting remarks to the plaintiff about said guests, or any of them, and in particular this defendant denies:

(a) This defendant has no information or belief sufficient to enable him to answer thereto, and basing his denial upon that ground, denies all and every part of the following allegation, to-wit: "That at one time, the approximate date of which plaintiff is unable to fix, she had three guests at her home spending the evening,— a mother, her son and the son's fiancée. The mother was an old friend of plaintiff and her family. Defendant was out, and did not return home until late."

Denies that the next day, or at any other time or at all, this defendant said to plaintiff in an insinuating manner, or that he at all said to plaintiff the following statement: "I know who was here last night. I saw you through a window and had a witness with me," or any statement substantially similar thereto. Denies that plaintiff, either with or without ignoring defendant's alleged manner, laughed or said, "Why, Charlie—only Mr. _____ was here; and his mother and fiancée were with him," or any statement substantially similar thereto. Denies that this defendant appeared in a very surly mood, or in any mood whatsoever, or replied or stated: "Yes? I know about the fiancée part of it. She is his sister and is trying to cover up the nature of his visits. You are no better than a prostitute, and much less sincere—having men around like that," or any statement substantially similar thereto, and in connection with the said allegations set forth in subdivision (a) of subparagraph 7 of said paragraph V of said complaint, this defendant alleges that no such incident or occurrence ever took place.

Further answering in that connection, the defendant alleges that defendant had demanded and insisted that plaintiff should not invite or permit the presence of a certain young man to or in the home of these parties, but wholly disregarding the wishes, requests and demands of defendant, plaintiff invited and received said young man and his mother and another woman, to the home of these parties.

(b) Denies that shortly after the alleged occurrence set forth in subdivision (a) of specification 6 of paragraph V of plaintiff's complaint, or at any other time or at all, the plaintiff went to the home of the alleged woman therein referred to, or any other woman, with defendant or became acquainted with her, and denies that thereafter, or at all, plaintiff went to said alleged woman's home several, or any times whatsoever, alone. Denies that when defendant heard of this, (and in this connection the defendant denies that he ever heard of any such occurrence) or at any other time or at all, this defendant became very angry or otherwise angry with or at plaintiff, or told her that he did not want her to associate with said alleged woman referred to—that she was no good, or that this defendant made any statement whatsoever to the plaintiff regarding or concerning said alleged woman, or any one else. Denies that this defendant said, "Whenever you get like her and her kind, I will be through with you," or any statement substantially similar thereto, and in that connection this defendant alleges that no such alleged incident or occurrence ever took place.

(c) Answering subdivision (c) of subparagraph 7 of paragraph V of said complaint, this defendant denies that a few minutes after plaintiff and said guests arrived, defendant came to the head of the stairs and called plaintiff, or called plaintiff in a very or otherwise rude or peremptory manner, and/or within the hearing of said guests. Denies that at said time and place, or at any other time this defendant said to plaintiff, "Get that wild bunch of people out of here—get them out and get them out quick. What do you think this is, a whorehouse?" or any other statement except as hereinafter set forth. In connection with the said allegations, this defendant alleges the following facts:

That upon the return of the plaintiff from her trip to Honolulu, or within two or three days thereafter, the plaintiff stated to this defendant that she desired to entertain a party of guests at her home, being persons whom she had met on the boat coming from Honolulu. This defendant thereupon told the plaintiff that it was entirely agreeable to him, except that he did not desire or agree that plaintiff should entertain her young boy friends. In reply the plaintiff said that this would be a dinner just for a few friends whom she had met on the boat, and this defendant then told plaintiff that she was entirely welcome to do so. During this conversation it was stated, and it was understood by this defendant that plaintiff was going to have the said dinner and entertain the said guests at the home of plaintiff and defendant; however, this defendant discovered that on said evening, the plaintiff did entertain her guests at a dinner at the home of plaintiff and this defendant and on the same evening, and immediately following the dinner at the said home, proceeded to the Biltmore Hotel where she entertained a party of approximately twenty people; that on the day of this evening, this defendant had been arduously at work at the studios and that he went home at about 11:00 o'clock in the evening, and thereupon went to bed. Later, and at about 1:45 or 2:00 o'clock in the morning, (on the same night however) this defendant was awakened by loud noises, loud conversation and loud and raucous laughter, and upon being awakened he heard one of the children crying in the nursery, heard the gramophone, the piano and the pipe organ, all of which instruments were being played at the same time, and after waiting a while to see if the noises would not cease, and when it became apparent that instead of being lessened, the noise was being increased, this defendant decided that something would have to be done, so that the entire household would not be further disturbed, and so that he and the child who was at home that evening, could again go to sleep. At this time, this defendant observed couples going out onto the lawn; and the loud laughter, conversation and general hilarity taking place, indicated to this defendant that at least some of the persons who were there acted as if they were intoxicated. Thereupon, this defendant called his wife upstairs and there asked her what she meant by bringing such a crowd of people to the home that time of night and waking up the entire household, and disturbing the sleep of himself and the child; he further told plaintiff that there was entirely too much noise and hilarity, and that he thought it was entirely out of place, and that he demanded that she request her guests to leave. That thereupon the plaintiff became very angry, but upon further demand of this defendant, she went downstairs and told her guests that it would be necessary for them to leave. That the conversation that this defendant had with plaintiff on said occasion was upstairs, and there was no opportunity whatsoever for any of plaintiff's guests to overhear anything that was said by this defendant, and that if they were informed or advised of anything that defendant said, such information was given entirely by plaintiff.

(8) Answering subparagraph 8 of paragraph V of said complaint, this defendant alleges that all and every part of said allegations are, and each of them is untrue. Denies that this defendant, on any occasion whatsoever, or at all, has abused, condemned, reproached or upbraided or otherwise criticized plaintiff, both or either for the conception or birth of their two children or either of said children, or has likewise or at all charged her or criticized her on account of her refusal to prevent the latter, or on account of anything whatsoever, (and in this connection this defendant alleges that the plaintiff never refused to prevent the latter for the reason that this defendant never at any time made any suggestion that the same be prevented) with ruining his career, or with the lack of proper or any consideration or affection for him, and de-

nies that this defendant on account of any of said things, or on account of anything whatsoever, in any way charged or upbraided or reproached or abused or condemned plaintiff.

Denies that as soon as defendant found that the second baby had been conceived, or at any other time or at all, he insisted or requested or even suggested that plaintiff take illegal or immoral or any other steps or any other action to prevent the birth of said child, or that he said he did not want or desire any more children or another child. Denies that plaintiff refused to do as defendant demanded, and denies that plaintiff refused to do anything whatsoever, or that this defendant made any demand or that he accused or charged plaintiff of being selfish, or that he accused or charged her in any other manner or with any other thing, or that he told her at said time, or at any other time, that other women or any other woman had done that much or anything whatsoever for him, with or without hesitation, or that he told her of one or any moving picture actress, or any other person who, he stated, had such an operation, or any other operation, performed twice, or at all, for him, or for any one else. Denies that at another time or at any time, or at all, this defendant said to plaintiff in this connection, or in any other connection, or at all, or in an insulting manner or in any manner whatsoever: "What do you want to do, populate Los Angeles?" or any statement substantially similar thereto.

(9) Denies that during the entire married life of plaintiff and defendant, or during any period of time whatsoever, this defendant had insisted upon or had maintained an attitude or determination that when it was convenient for him, or at any other time, plaintiff must get a divorce, or that she must get a divorce at all, either in strict accordance with his dictation or instruction, or in any other manner whatsoever; denies that he ever stated or suggested or requested or demanded that only upon that condition, or upon any condition would he make any provision for her support. Denies that up to the time plaintiff separated from defendant on the 30th day of November, 1926, or at any time during said period of time, or otherwise or at all, she was ever completely or otherwise intimidated or in any way influenced by any threat, or that she was afraid to do anything with reference to leaving this defendant or getting a divorce, either with or without his sanction or approval, and in that connection this defendant alleges that he at no time ever made any threat of any nature whatsoever, of or to this plaintiff, or to

any one else, of or concerning her getting a divorce. Denies that any threat or threats were resorted to or used or in any manner made by the defendant for any purpose whatsoever or that any said alleged threat or threats were threats of great bodily harm, or threat or threats that he would ruin her reputation with the power of his money, or otherwise, or threat or threats that she would never get a cent for her support excepting what he was willing to give her, or that he ever threatened or suggested that he would buy perjured or any other testimony to defeat her action, or to be in any way connected with any action, or a threat or threats that he would take all of his property or any part thereof, and get out of the United States, or get out of the United States to prevent it, and in that connection this defendant alleges that no threats of any kind or character were ever made by him to this plaintiff, either to influence her to get a divorce or to influence her in any action whatsoever, or otherwise or at all.

Denies that this defendant ever told plaintiff that if she ever commenced a divorce action against him, except in accordance with his wishes, or with his desire or wish, that when he got through with her, with his money, plaintiff's own family would have nothing further to do with her, and in that connection this defendant alleges that no such statement, or anything similar thereto was ever said by this defendant to the plaintiff.

(9½) Denies that on one occasion, or on any occasion, or at all, the defendant ever suggested that plaintiff take her own life, or any similar suggestion, or that on another occasion or at any time or at all, he picked up a loaded revolver, or picked up any revolver, or menacingly or otherwise threatened to kill plaintiff.

(a) Denies that about two weeks after the said marriage, or at any other time, or otherwise or at all, when the defendant and plaintiff were in defendant's bedroom at his house, or at any other time or place, or when the defendant had been reciting to her the terrible position he was in on account of said marriage, (and in this connection the defendant denies that he ever did recite or otherwise comment upon any position that he was in on account of said marriage); denies that at said time, or at any time, or on account thereof, or on account of anything else whatsoever, the plaintiff was in a state of great or any mental excitement, or was hysterical or despondent. Denies that at said time and place, or at any other time or place, the plaintiff said to this defendant, "I

don't see what we can do but try and make the best of it," or any
statement substantially similar thereto. Denies that at said alleged
time or place, the defendant was sitting on the bed, and denies that
reaching over to a small table, or that he did reach over to a small
table, picked up a loaded revolver, or any revolver, or that he held
it out in his hand, or otherwise exhibited it to plaintiff, and denies
that at said time or place, or at any other time or place, this defendant said, "There is one way to end it all," or any statement substantially similar thereto. Denies that plaintiff became frightened
or that she said to him, "Put down that revolver, it might go off;
and don't talk that way, it is silly," or any statement substantially
similar thereto. Denies that defendant replied, "It isn't silly—you
can't tell. I might get suddenly crazy any time, and kill you," or
any statement substantially similar thereto, and in connection with
the said subdivision of said complaint, and the allegations therein
set forth, this defendant alleges that no such incident ever occurred, nor were any such statements ever made.

(b) Denies that on or about November 29, 1926, when the plaintiff went into defendant's room, defendant said to her, in an angry
or threatening tone of voice, "What do you mean by wakening
me, with all those people here," or that plaintiff replied that she
did not think he would be home yet or she would not have brought
any one home with her, and denies that plaintiff further said, "I
am sorry—I did not expect to do any harm. But I am not going to
stand this kind of treatment; it is too humiliating to endure." Denies that defendant thereupon, or at all rushed over to a small table
next to his bed, or any other place, or that he waved his arms in
the air, or that he picked up a loaded revolver or other revolver
lying on said table, or from any other place, or rushed toward
plaintiff in a threatening or excited manner, or otherwise or at all,
or that he said, "I will kill you if you dare to leave this house; or
tell the newspaper anything about this," and denies that plaintiff
turned or ran from said room, or that plaintiff was or became so,
or at all alarmed or so or at all in fear of great or any bodily
harm, either on account of said alleged statement or on account of
anything whatsoever, that the next day she left the home and residence of plaintiff and defendant.

In connection with those allegations set forth in subdivision (b)
of subparagraph 9½ of paragraph V, this defendant alleges:

That after those things had occurred on the night of November

29, 1926, as are hereinbefore in this answer alleged and set forth, and after the said persons had left the home of the plaintiff and this defendant on said occasion, the plaintiff went to her room and this defendant later knocked at the door and told plaintiff that he wanted to see her. That thereupon plaintiff went into the room of this defendant and there sat on the bed, at which time and place this defendant and plaintiff had a conversation regarding the occurrence of the evening. That this defendant did not act in an angry way or display an angry manner or attitude, but on the contrary, tried in a calm manner to reason with the plaintiff and show her the mistake she was making in conducting herself in the manner that she had, and that it was entirely unfair and unwise to bring such parties of persons to the house at that time in the morning and where they would conduct themselves in such a loud and boisterous manner so as to awaken a sleeping child and the entire household. That this defendant at said time explained to plaintiff that the exactions of his work were of such a character that he could not be thus annoyed and worried, and that in his opinion it was unjust and unfair and cruel for her thus to annoy this defendant and cause him such distress, and he asked the plaintiff why she was seemingly doing everything she could to annoy and worry defendant. In reply, the plaintiff stated that she was tired and would not talk to this defendant, and that she was not going to listen to any preaching on the part of this defendant, and thereupon she left the defendant's room, and this defendant did not again see her.

A few hours later, and before plaintiff and the said child were out of their rooms, this defendant, as usual went to work at the studios, and at about 2:30 o'clock in the afternoon of that day, this defendant was informed, over the telephone, that plaintiff's effects were being packed up and that the babies were going to be taken from the house. That immediately upon receiving such information, this defendant rushed to his home and there and then discovered that plaintiff's clothing and effects, together with the clothing and effects of her mother, had been packed. That plaintiff was not present at the time, but the mother of the plaintiff was present and this defendant asked plaintiff's mother what the packing and the absence of the babies meant, and was informed by plaintiff's mother that she did not know. Thereupon, this defendant inquired of plaintiff's mother as to the whereabouts of the plaintiff, but plaintiff's mother would give no reply. Thereupon, this defendant went to the nursery to inquire regarding the children, and plaintiff's mother informed this defendant that the children had been taken away, and this defendant was further advised that plaintiff's mother and the plaintiff had stated that they were never coming back. Upon receiving this information, this defendant told the mother of the plaintiff that it was his desire that she leave the house, and further told plaintiff's mother that the plaintiff must return to the home immediately and must bring the children with her. Thereupon the plaintiff's mother left the house. Later in the afternoon, the plaintiff telephoned to this defendant and inquired as to whether or not plaintiff's mother was there, and this defendant told plaintiff that her mother was gone, and further told plaintiff that she must come to the house immediately, so that they might talk matters over, and plaintiff promised to come to the house within a half hour. Some time later, and without having returned to the house, the plaintiff again called on the telephone and told this defendant that a man was going to call for her trunks, and this defendant advised plaintiff that nothing would be permitted to leave the house, and that she must come home and must bring the children with her. Thereupon, the plaintiff told this defendant that he had better see her lawyer.

That upon the following day, as this defendant is informed and believes, the said plaintiff, either in person or through her representatives, informed newspaper reporters employed by newspapers published in Los Angeles, that this defendant had created a scene at a party at the house and had humiliated her, and that the parties were separated.

(10) Denies that during the greater portion of the married life of this defendant and plaintiff, or at any other time or at all, defendant has maintained an unjustifiable system of espionage upon her, in an effort to secure evidence for a divorce against plaintiff.

(11) Denies that the defendant has knowingly, or otherwise or at all, made false statements, or any statement, to immediate friends and acquaintances of his, or to any person whomsoever, in any way reflecting upon plaintiff's character, breeding, gentility, or education or otherwise reflecting upon plaintiff, or has attributed to her base, ulterior or mercenary motives, or other motives, in marrying this defendant.

(a) Answering subdivision (a) of subparagraph 11 of paragraph

V of said complaint, this defendant has no information or belief sufficient to enable him to answer thereto, and basing his denial upon that ground denies all and every part of the allegations contained in said subdivision.

And in particular this defendant denies that he ever told a certain prominent moving picture actress, or any other person, about a year after the marriage of these parties, or at any other time or at all, that plaintiff was a person of no education or breeding, or that plaintiff was a gold-digger, or that plaintiff was crude, or that plaintiff had only married defendant to get money out of him, or any statement similar thereto, or any criticism of plaintiff whatsoever.

(b) Denies that one evening about three months after the marriage of these parties, or at any other time or at all, the defendant went into plaintiff's room or any other place, or then or there or at all commenced to or did accuse plaintiff of forcing this defendant to marry her to get money out of this defendant, or with blackmailing him or with not caring for him.

Denies that the said defendant at said time or place, or at any other time or at all abused plaintiff, or that after said alleged abuse had either begun or had continued for some time or for any time whatsoever, or that at said time or place, or at any other time a certain doctor friend of defendant's came upstairs, or that defendant appeared to be surprised to see said friend, or that he did see said friend, or that thereafter the defendant continued to or did at all talk to said friend or in his presence, or in the presence of any one about blackmail, or that he further or at all abused plaintiff to such an extent that she became hysterical, or to any extent whatsoever, or at all.

Denies that at said time and place, or at any other time or at all, plaintiff turned to said doctor and in defendant's presence, or in defendant's presence said, "Can you imagine a man talking like that, when he knows that he offered me a half million dollars to get rid of this baby by an abortion, and I refused to do it," or any statement substantially similar thereto.

Denies that thereafter or at all, the said doctor told plaintiff that he had come into said house at the above mentioned time, or at any other time with said defendant, or that he was downstairs during the entire or any portion of said alleged conversation or any conversation, or that he had been invited to said house or had come to said house for the purpose of being convinced that plaintiff was not sincere in her affection for defendant, but was only trying to get money out of him, and further answering each and every allegation of said subdivision (b) of subparagraph 11, this defendant alleges that no such occurrence ever took place, and that all of the allegations contained in said subdivision are and each of them is untrue, and all and each of them is a fabrication.

(12) Denies that during the month of June, 1926, or at any other time or at all, this defendant told plaintiff that after the picture he was then working on was completed, would be a good time for her to get a divorce, or that any other time would be a good time for her to get a divorce, or that at said alleged time or at any other time he told plaintiff that she would never get any more for her support or maintenance than this defendant was willing to give her voluntarily, or that he had all of his property, or any part thereof, or all or any part of his income so tied up, or at all tied up, that she could never get a cent through the courts, or through any court, or that he could or would go to Europe and make pictures, or make pictures just as well, or that he would do so if she did not do just as he said, and in that connection this defendant alleges that no such conversation ever took place. Denies that at said time, or any other time, this defendant said to plaintiff, "Why, even the house we are living in is not in my name; and I had it put out of my name to protect me against women," or any statement substantially similar thereto.

(a) Denies that about a month later, or at any other time or at all, plaintiff complained to defendant, or told him that she could not stand the condition or any condition under which she was living, and denies that defendant replied, or otherwise stated, "If you get spunky, and do anything that will reflect on me, or cause a scandal—I have enough money to do anything; and I can pay somebody to lie about you if it is necessary, to prevent you from ever getting a cent," or any statement substantially similar thereto; denies that at said alleged time or at any other time or at all, this defendant said to plaintiff, "If you ever commence a suit for divorce against me, don't expect the servants to testify for you, even if you are right. I pay them, and they will say what I tell them to say," or any statement substantially similar thereto.

III.

Answering paragraph VI of said complaint, this defendant denies that in public opinion or in any opinion the reflection upon plaintiff's reputation, character, innocence or worth as a woman, wife or mother, arising out of facts or any fact or circumstances or any circumstance, in connection with said alleged seduction or any publicity given thereto has been or will be either augmented or intensified, or has been augmented or intensified by defendant's alleged failure to carry out the or any obligations, or obligation of said marriage in good faith, or otherwise; denies that there has been any reflection whatsoever in public opinion, upon plaintiff's reputation, character, innocence or worth as a woman, wife or mother, or that any publicity has been given thereto, except such publicity, and any resulting public opinion, for which the plaintiff was and is herself responsible, and in that connection this defendant alleges that if any unfavorable public opinion has been either created or expressed or that if any unfavorable opinion exists in the public mind regarding the plaintiff as a woman, wife or mother, arising out of any facts or circumstances whatsoever connected with the marriage of these parties, that the plaintiff is herself responsible for such things for the reason that she has, without any justification or excuse, untruthfully alleged and has included in the allegations of the complaint and amended complaint on file herein, unnecessary, improper and unwarranted references to facts and circumstances alleged by her to have existed prior to the marriage of these parties.

Denies that the defendant has in any way failed in good faith or otherwise, to carry out the obligations of said marriage; denies that he has failed to treat plaintiff with conjugal kindness, consideration and love, or love at any time whatsoever. Denies that plaintiff believes or has ever believed that on any account whatsoever a wrongful or unjustified impression, or any impression would or has or will exist in the public mind, or in the mind of anyone, that plaintiff was morally or otherwise at fault in connection with the alleged seduction, or was otherwise unfit as a wife because of defendant's alleged failure to accept or honor her as such, and further answering this defendant denies that defendant has ever failed to accept or honor this plaintiff as his wife.

Denies that on that account or on any account whatsoever, or because of anything, plaintiff has undergone peculiar, unusual, or aggravated, or any mental suffering, or any suffering whatsoever, or has had inflicted upon her a peculiar or unusual personal injury or wrong, or any personal injury or wrong, either by reason of defendant's alleged extreme cruelty, or by reason of anything else for which this defendant is or has been responsible, and in that connection this defendant denies that he has in any manner been cruel to or toward plaintiff.

IV.

Answering paragraph VII of said complaint, this defendant denies that he has in any way failed to carry out, in good faith, or otherwise, the marriage contract entered into between plaintiff and this defendant but on the other hand alleges that in all respects and at all times he has in good faith exerted every effort to carry out every obligation imposed upon him as the husband of plaintiff; denies that he has failed to treat plaintiff with conjugal kindness, respect or consideration as his wife or as the mother of his said children or either of them, or that he has thereby or at all caused a separation or a divorce without fault on the part of the plaintiff, or that anything whatsoever for which this defendant is responsible has deprived or will deprive plaintiff of the only or any natural, adequate or possible shelter, protection or justification for her alleged relations with defendant before their marriage, or has or will deprive plaintiff of the only or any natural, adequate or effective compensation for any alleged wrong suffered by her on account of said alleged seduction or for or on account of any alleged injury done to her reputation on account of any publicity given thereto. Denies that on account of plaintiff's said alleged belief, or on account of anything whatsoever, or otherwise or at all, plaintiff has submitted, or has had any occasion to submit to the or any cruel treatment of defendant for a long period of time or for any period of time or at all, or that plaintiff has suffered or will suffer on account of anything whatsoever, peculiar, unusual or aggravated mental anguish or other or any anguish or distress, or has suffered or will suffer peculiar, aggravated or unusual or other or any personal wrong or injury, or any wrong or injury, either on account of being deprived of the alleged protection and security

afforded by her marriage relation with defendant or for or on account of anything else whatsoever.

Further answering said paragraph VII, this defendant alleges
that if any injury whatsoever has been sustained by the plaintiff to
her reputation because of any publicity whatsoever, the plaintiff
and her attorneys are directly and solely responsible therefor by
reason of the unwarranted and unjustifiable inclusion of alleged
facts and circumstances occurring between plaintiff and this defendant prior to their marriage.

V.

Answering paragraph VIII of said complaint, this defendant denies that immediately after said marriage or at any other time, or
at all, said defendant commenced to pursue and continued to pursue or ever has pursued a deliberate or willful or uniform course
of cruel treatment of the plaintiff, or any cruel treatment whatsoever, with the wrongful intent or purpose of compelling her to
seek a divorce, or with any intent or purpose whatsoever or at all,
in connection with a deliberate or uniform course of conduct or
with any course of conduct whatsoever, with the wrongful intent
or purpose or with any intent or purpose of so or otherwise intimidating said plaintiff that she would or would not seek a divorce
except upon the terms and conditions, or terms or conditions or at
such time or in such a manner as should or would be consistent
with said defendant's wishes or dictation or to thereby defeat or
otherwise effect the end or purpose of said marriage, contrary to
law or public policy. Denies that there has been any cruel or inhuman treatment of plaintiff by defendant and denies that the alleged
cruel or inhuman treatment of plaintiff by defendant or any mental
pain or suffering or anguish wrongfully or otherwise alleged to
have been inflicted upon plaintiff thereby or at all, is the result of
any deliberate or other intent or purpose of this defendant, and
in that connection this defendant denies that he has ever either
deliberately or otherwise, or willfully or otherwise with any intent
or purpose whatsoever, inflicted any cruel treatment whatsoever
upon plaintiff, or has in any way intimated plaintiff for any purpose whatsoever.

VI.

Answering paragraph IX of said complaint, this defendant denies that he entered into said marriage with plaintiff without the intention of carrying out his moral or personal or marital obligations imposed upon him by said marriage; denies that he entered into said marriage or in any way imposed upon the youth or innocence of plaintiff, or upon plaintiff at all, or upon her love or affection for him or upon her belief or confidence in any promise or representation of love or affection for plaintiff, or upon her good faith in entering into said marriage, for the sole purpose or for any purpose of protecting himself from any alleged consequences of any alleged illegal, or wrongful or immoral infliction of any wrong or injury upon plaintiff either before or after said marriage, and further answering, this defendant alleges that he entered into said marriage with the intention of doing everything within his power to make the plaintiff happy as his wife and in all respects to make the marriage relation happy and he has at all times since said marriage in good faith done everything within his power to that end.

VI A.

Answering paragraph X of said complaint, this defendant is informed and verily believes that on various and sundry occasions said plaintiff drank liquor to excess, and while under the influence of liquor her conduct became unwomanly, unseemly and undignified in speech and action, in the presence of many persons.

VII.

Answering paragraph XI of said complaint, this defendant denies that at all times during the period of her cohabitation with defendant in said marriage relation, she has conducted herself toward defendant as a kind, considerate, loyal or loving wife or has fully observed or performed the duties or obligations of a wife to defendant, and further answering said paragraph, this defendant denies that he has in any way treated the plaintiff in a cruel or inhuman manner and denies there has been any occasion for or that there has been any endeavor on the part of plaintiff to overcome any alleged attitude of this defendant toward plaintiff, or the children, or either of them, or the said marriage of these parties.

Further answering said paragraph, this defendant admits that during a portion of the time since the marriage of these parties, the plaintiff seemingly conducted herself toward this defendant as a kind, considerate, loyal and loving wife.

VIII.

Answering paragraph XII of said complaint this defendant denies that plaintiff is a fit and proper or fit or proper person to have and be awarded or to have or be awarded the care, custody and control or care, custody or control of the said children or either of them, and further answering paragraph XII of said complaint, this defendant alleges that the plaintiff, voluntarily and without just cause and wicked disregard of and for the future welfare and happiness of the elder of the two children of this defendant and plaintiff, and with full knowledge that by so doing, the said child would inevitably in the future be defamed, disparaged and stigmatized, and would, when grown, suffer reproach, humiliation and dishonor, has included in the complaint filed in the above entitled action an allegation by which she has published to the world that the said child had been conceived out of wedlock. That said allegation in said complaint was made by the said plaintiff with full knowledge and understanding that it was totally and wholly unnecessary for any purpose of stating, in said complaint, an alleged cause of action for a divorce against this defendant, and that said plaintiff made said unnecessary allegation with utter and ruthless disregard for the future comfort and happiness of said child, and solely for the purpose of wounding the feelings and sensibilities of this defendant, and in this regard, this defendant alleges that the above entitled court may and should consider the said conduct on the part of said plaintiff for the purpose of determining whether or not the said plaintiff is in fact a fit or proper person to have and be awarded the custody, care and control of the children of plaintiff and defendant, and each of them, or either of them.

For the further consideration of the court in determining whether or not the plaintiff is a fit and proper person to have the custody of said children, this defendant alleges that during a great portion of the married life of this defendant and plaintiff, the plaintiff has failed to give to the said children or to either of them that care and attention which is usual and normal with a mother, but on the other hand has left the entire care and attention of the said children to a nurse and on many days has even failed to visit said children or inquire concerning their welfare. The defendant is informed and believes and upon such information and belief further alleges that during the time when the plaintiff was in Catalina on the occasion alleged in her complaint, she permitted a space of about five days to intervene during which time she did not see said children nor pay any attention whatsoever to them or their welfare, although there was every opportunity for her to do so. On information and belief this defendant further alleges that on the occasion of the trip taken by the plaintiff to Honolulu, as alleged in her complaint, one of the children of these parties was taken with the plaintiff, and that while on the boat, both going and coming, the plaintiff almost wholly disregarded the said child and would go for many hours without paying any attention whatsoever to it while she attended dances, and otherwise amused herself with certain people on the said boat, and indulged in intoxicating liquors to excess, and that she likewise neglected the said child and disregarded its welfare during the time she was in Honolulu.

Denies this defendant is an unfit person to have the care, custody or control of the children of the said marriage, or either of them, or to control or direct their education, and in this connection this defendant alleges that he is a fit and proper person to have and to be awarded the custody, care and control of the said children, and each of them, or either of them, if the above entitled court should determine that the said children, and each of them, or either of them, should be awarded into the custody of this defendant. That this defendant is ready and willing to receive the custody, care and control of the said children and each of them, or either of them, and is ready, willing and able to give all necessary attention to the said children, but in this connection this defendant further alleges that the interests of the children are paramount and it is the desire of this defendant that the custody and care of said children should be awarded to such party as in the discretion of the above entitled court should be deemed to be proper, in the best interests of the children, and under such circumstances so that neither the plaintiff nor the defendant shall be denied any reasonable opportunity to visit with and enjoy the companionship of the said children, and each of them, or either of them.

VIIIA.

Answering paragraph XIII of said complaint, denies that Charles Chaplin Film Corporation has its principal place of business in the City of Los Angeles, or elsewhere in the State of California.

IX.

Answering paragraph XV of said complaint, denies that the defendants Doe One, Doe Two, Doe Three, Doe One Company, a corporation, Doe Two Company, a corporation, and Doe Three Company, a corporation, or either of the aforesaid defendants, or any defendant whom they may represent, have or have had in their possession, or under their control, any community property whatsoever belonging to this defendant and the plaintiff.

Denies that those certain motion pictures entitled *The Gold Rush* and *The Circus* are, or that either of them is, the community property of this defendant and the plaintiff; denies that defendant United Artists Corporation, a corporation, has received or will continue to receive any sum of money whatsoever either on account of the releasing of said motion pictures known as *The Gold Rush* and *The Circus*, or either of them, or for or on account of anything else whatsoever, which is community property of this defendant and plaintiff.

X.

Answering paragraph XVI of said complaint, this defendant admits that T. Kono is now and has been employed by this defendant and admits that Alfred Reeves is now and has been employed by The Chaplin Studios, Inc. and the Charles Chaplin Film Corporation, a corporation, but denies that Alfred Reeves, at all or any of the times mentioned in the complaint was or is now in the employ of this defendant and denies that either T. Kono or Alfred Reeves was or is under the control or direction of this defendant except that as to the defendant T. Kono, he is the personal servant of this defendant and only as such servant is he or has he been under the control and direction of this defendant; denies that for several years preceding the filing of this action or at any time or at all, save and except as hereinafter alleged, either T. Kono or

Alfred Reeves have had or now have in their possession or under their control a large or any amount of property belonging to this defendant, and in this regard this defendant alleges that long prior to the commencement of the above entitled action, Alfred Reeves had the temporary custody of certain separate property of this defendant of a value not to exceed the sum of $50,000.00; and for lack of information and belief, denies that either T. Kono or Alfred Reeves have had or now have in their possession or under their control a large or any amount of property belonging to The Chaplin Studios, Inc., a corporation, or the Charles Chaplin Film Corporation, a corporation.

Denies that either T. Kono or Alfred Reeves have any property whatsoever either in their possession or under their control belonging to this defendant or that they have, or that either of them has, in their or his possession or under their or his control any community property whatsoever belonging to this defendant and plaintiff or that they have or that either of them has in their or his possession or under their or his control any separate property of this defendant or any bond or bonds, stock or stocks, security or securities, or real estate or money or any other property.

This defendant has no information or belief sufficient to enable him to answer thereto and basing his denial on that ground denies all and every part of the following allegation contained in said paragraph XVI, which said allegation is as follows:

> Plaintiff is informed and believes and therefore alleges that the defendants, T. Kono, Alfred Reeves, The Chaplin Studios, Inc. and Charles Chaplin Film Corporation have maintained and now maintain safety deposit boxes at the offices of the following named defendants banks: First National Bank of Los Angeles, Security Trust & Savings Bank of Los Angeles, Farmers & Merchants National Bank, and Bank of Italy. That said defendant, and defendants T. Kono, and Alfred Reeves, The Chaplin Studios, Inc. and Charles Chaplin Film Corporation, have concealed and now conceal in said safety deposit boxes, stocks, bonds, other securities and money, and other personal property; that said property consists of community property of plaintiff and defendant and separate property of defendant.

In particular, this defendant denies that either he, or T. Kono or Alfred Reeves or The Chaplin Studios, Inc. or Charles Chaplin

Film Corporation, or anyone else have concealed or now conceal in said or any safety deposit boxes, any stocks or bonds or other securities or money or other personal property consisting of community property of this defendant and plaintiff or the separate property of this defendant, and in that connection denies that he or either of the aforesaid persons, firms or corporations have concealed any community property whatsoever or any other property.

XI.

Answering paragraph XVII of said complaint, this defendant admits that The Chaplin Studios, Inc. and Charles Chaplin Film Corporation, a corporation, were organized several years prior to the filing of the complaint in the above entitled action, but denies that either of said corporations was organized by this defendant or by anyone else for the purpose of affording this defendant a convenient instrument or vehicle or other means through which he could transact his personal or individual business; denies that said corporations or either of them have been or are now maintained or used by this defendant or by anyone in his behalf for the purpose of holding or concealing or otherwise controlling or affecting either the community or the separate property of this defendant or for the purpose of defeating or preventing or otherwise affecting the enforcement of plaintiff's claim or claims, right or rights, or interest therein or thereto or for any other purpose which is or could in any way affect any right, claim or interest of the plaintiff in any manner whatsoever; denies that said corporations or either of them have in their possession, or under their control, or standing in their corporate names, any community property of this defendant and plaintiff or any separate property of this defendant.

Denies that this defendant either owns or controls substantially all of the issued or outstanding capital stock of said corporations, to-wit, The Chaplin Studios, Inc. and Charles Chaplin Film Corporation, a corporation, or either of said corporations, except as hereinafter alleged, and denies that the directors or officers of said defendant corporations, or either of them are under the direction or control of this defendant in all or in any matter or matters pertaining to said corporations or either of them, or pertaining to any property whatsoever, save and except such direction and control as defendant was entitled to give and maintain by virtue of his being a stockholder.

Further answering said paragraph XVII, this defendant alleges that both of the aforesaid corporations, to-wit, The Chaplin Studios, Inc. and Charles Chaplin Film Corporation, were organized prior to the marriage of this defendant and plaintiff, the dates of the incorporation of each thereof being as follows, to-wit: The Chaplin Studios, Inc. was incorporated on March 13, 1918 in the State of California and that the Charles Chaplin Film Corporation, a corporation, was incorporated on the 17th day of November, 1924 in the State of Delaware.

That at all times since the commencement of the above entitled action, and for some time prior to the commencement of the said action for divorce, this defendant was not, has not been, nor is he now a stockholder of record on the books of, nor the owner of any stock of The Chaplin Studios, Inc. This defendant is informed and believes and upon that ground alleges that all of the outstanding and issued capital stock of The Chaplin Studios, Inc., a corporation, save and except the qualifying shares of directors, since prior to the commencement of the said action, were held and owned and have at all times since prior to the filing of this action been held and owned and are now held and owned of record on the books of the said The Chaplin Studios, Inc., by and in the name of the Charles Chaplin Film Corporation, a Delaware corporation. That this defendant is the owner and holder of record of not more than one-half of all of the outstanding and issued capital stock of the Charles Chaplin Film Corporation, and that the remaining one-half is owned and has at all times since the incorporation thereof, been owned by others than this defendant. That all of the said stock owned by this defendant in said Charles Chaplin Film Corporation, a corporation, was acquired by him and the same was issued to him in exchange for a partnership interest and his interest in the assets of that certain copartnership hereinafter referred to and that all of the right, title and interest of this defendant in and to said copartnership assets was and is his own separate property.

XII.

Answering paragraph XVIII of said complaint, this defendant admits that there is community property belonging to this defendant and the plaintiff, but denies that the same consists of any real estate or stocks or bonds or securities or personal property, other than money, and denies that two motion pictures entitled *The Gold Rush* and *The Circus*, or either of said motion pictures, or anything whatsoever connected with or appertaining to either of said motion pictures, is or has ever been community property and denies that the proceeds or any thereof either derived or to be derived therefrom, or from either of said motion pictures, either is or will be community property; denies that the total value of the community property of plaintiff and defendant is upwards of the sum of Ten Million ($10,000,000.00) Dollars, or is of the total value of any other sum in excess of the sum of Two Hundred Sixty-six thousand, nine hundred thirty-two dollars and sixty-three cents ($266,932.63).

Further answering said paragraph XVIII, this defendant alleges that as to that certain motion picture entitled *The Gold Rush* all right, title and interest in and to the said motion picture was originally owned by the Charles Chaplin Film Co., a copartnership composed of this defendant and Sydney Chaplin, and which copartnership has been in existence since on or about the year 1917 and which said copartnership on or about January 1, 1925 duly sold, assigned and transferred all of its right, title and interest in and to the said motion picture to the Charles Chaplin Film Corporation, a corporation, and said corporation has been, ever since said date, and now is the owner of all right, title and interest in and to said motion picture entitled *The Gold Rush*, together with the proceeds derived therefrom, except the right of distribution of the same, which said right of distribution is owned by the United Artists, a corporation, and that there is neither any community interest nor any property interest of this defendant whatsoever in or to the said motion picture entitled *The Gold Rush* or any proceeds derived or to be derived therefrom.

Further answering, and with particular reference to that certain motion picture referred to in the said paragraph as *The Circus*, this defendant alleges that the said motion picture is now in the process of production and that the same is incompleted and, as this defendant is informed and believes and therefore alleges, will not and cannot be completed until a long time subsequent to the filing of this answer if ever, and that to the best knowledge and belief of this defendant, will require at least three consecutive months of work before said picture is completed to that state of production that the same will be ready for cutting; that all right, title and interest in and to the last mentioned motion picture, to-wit, *The Circus*, is owned by the Charles Chaplin Film Corporation, a corporation and that this defendant and the plaintiff herein have no community interest whatsoever in or to said incompleted picture or anything connected therewith, nor has this defendant any separate property interest in or to said picture, and this defendant is further informed and believes, and therefore alleges that all proceeds which will be derived from said motion picture called *The Circus* is and will be the sole property of the aforesaid corporation, to-wit, the Charles Chaplin Film Corporation, except that portion thereof as will be paid by said corporation to United Artists, a corporation, for the distribution thereof, provided the same is ever distributed.

XIII.

Answering paragraph XIX of said complaint, this defendant admits that he has separate property situated in the State of California and elsewhere, but denies that the value of his separate property is upwards of the sum of $6,000,000.00, but on the contrary and in that connection alleges that the total value of both the separate property and the community property of this defendant is approximately the sum of $1,250,000.00, but no more than said approximate sum.

Denies that this defendant owns any separate property consisting of real estate, or that he has any community interest in any real estate situated in the County of Los Angeles, State of California, or elsewhere.

Denies that he is the owner or has any interest, either community or separate, in that certain real property particularly described in said paragraph XIX of said complaint, or in either of said parcels of property or any part thereof therein described.

XIV.

Answering paragraph XX of said complaint this defendant admits that from the time of said marriage until January 18, 1927, this defendant received a salary of $250,000.00 per year in connection with his services and activities as an artist and director in the motion picture business; but denies that this defendant receives or has received an annual income from other sources, or any other source, of upwards of $300,000.00 per year, or in any other sum in excess of an average yearly gross income of $162,055.78. And in that connection, this defendant further alleges that of said income a considerable portion thereof was received by this defendant as dividends on his stock in the Charles Chaplin Film Corporation, which said dividends were earned from the receipt by said corporation of the proceeds from the sale and distribution of that certain picture called *The Gold Rush*, but that the earning power of said picture has been practically expended, due to the fact that it is no longer a new picture and since the time of its original release, has been very widely distributed, but that in the future it will do very little business, and the aforesaid corporation will realize but very little profit from its distribution.

Further answering paragraph XX, and in connection with the aforesaid income other than salary, this defendant alleges that any money or other thing of value which this defendant receives or has received, other than his aforesaid salary, has at all times been, and now is his sole and separate property, and that the plaintiff has no interest therein, either community or otherwise.

Further answering said paragraph XX, this defendant alleges that he is not now, nor has he been since January 18, 1927, earning or receiving any salary whatsoever from any source.

XV.

Answering paragraph XXI of said complaint, this defendant denies that he has threatened to remove any property whatsoever, or any part thereof, from the jurisdiction of the above entitled court, or to otherwise or at all dispose of, conceal, transfer or encumber any property whatsoever for the purpose of defeating plaintiff's alleged right or rights, or claim or claims therein or thereto, either as his wife, or otherwise, or for the purpose of embarrassing, hindering, or delaying the satisfaction or payment of any order or orders made or which may be made herein, for the support or maintenance of plaintiff or the children of these parties, or either plaintiff or either of said children, or for suit money or other money, to enable plaintiff to prosecute this action, or to prevent the enforcement of any decree or judgment made or which may be made herein affecting plaintiff's alleged right or rights or claim or claims in or to any property whatsoever, or providing or which may provide for the permanent or other support or maintenance of plaintiff or of the children of these parties, or of either plaintiff or of either of said children. Denies that this defendant has disposed of, concealed, transferred or encumbered any property whatsoever in which the plaintiff has any interest whatsoever, for any purpose whatsoever or at all.

Denies that said defendant has intended to or has or does intend to or will, dispose of, conceal, transfer or encumber any property whatsoever in which the plaintiff has any interest whatsoever, either through or by or with the cooperation or instrumentality or assistance of any of his co-defendants, or by or through or with the cooperation or instrumentality of any person, firm or corporation whatsoever, or otherwise or at all.

Denies that any community property whatsoever or any funds or separate property of this defendant have been so commingled, or at all commingled, or have been so concealed, or at all concealed, in the name or names, or in the possession of the defendants, T. Kono, Alfred Reeves, The Chaplin Studios, Inc., a corporation, or the Charles Chaplin Film Corporation, a corporation, or either or any thereof, or at all, that on account thereof, or that on account of anything at all, it has been, or is, or will be necessary for the said defendant, or either or any of the aforesaid defendants, to render or make an account of any property whatsoever or any assets standing in their names, or the name of either or any of them, or in their possession, or in the possession of either or any of them, or under their control, or under the control of either or any of them, in order that the court may properly or at all determine the character, extent, or value of any property whatsoever, or for any other reason whatsoever, or that the court may determine the character, source or value, or the real, equitable or beneficial ownership of any property whatsoever or any assets whatsoever either held, owned or claimed by said corporations, or either of them, or by said other defendants or either or any of them, either in their possession, or in the possession of either or any of them, or under their control, or under the control of either or any of them, but in that connection, this defendant alleges that he is now and at all times has been ready and willing to make, render and file with the above entitled court a complete and accurate account and accounting of all community property owned by this defendant and the plaintiff and to cause said account and accounting to be duly, truthfully and properly made by a duly certified public accountant, which said certified public accountant may be designated by the above entitled court.

XVI.

Answering paragraph XXII, this defendant has no information or belief sufficient to enable him to answer, and basing his denial upon that ground denies each and every allegation contained in said paragraph XXII, and all thereof.

In particular this defendant denies that United Artists Corporation, a corporation, or The Chaplin Studios, Inc., a corporation, or Charles Chaplin Film Corporation, a corporation, or either or any of them has had, now has or will have, any money or property whatsoever, either received from the releasing of the picture *The Gold Rush*, or *The Circus*, or either of them, or for or on account of anything else whatsoever, which is community property of plaintiff and this defendant, or in which the plaintiff has any interest whatsoever.

XVII.

Answering paragraph XXIII of plaintiff's complaint, this defendant denies that he will continue to conceal, sequester and cover up, or to conceal, sequester or cover up the community property of plaintiff and defendant, or any part thereof, or at all, and the separate property or the separate property of the defendant, or any part thereof, or at all, and in this regard this defendant avers that he has at no time concealed, sequestered or covered up, either the community property of plaintiff and defendant, or any part thereof. Denies that a receiver should be appointed herein to take possession of and safeguard, or take possession of or safeguard all or any part of the community property of plaintiff and defendant, and all or all or any part of the separate property of the defendant, either within the jurisdiction of the above entitled court, or without the jurisdiction of the above entitled court.

XVIII.

Answering paragraph XXIV, this defendant denies that unless restrained by order of court from so doing, or otherwise, he will endeavor to or will harass or annoy plaintiff by attempting to take or by taking the minor children, or either thereof, of plaintiff and defendant, from the present custody of plaintiff, or by doing anything else whatsoever, except upon authority or permission of the above entitled court.

Denies that defendant, unless restrained by order of court from so doing, or otherwise, will harass or embarrass plaintiff by attempting to visit or annoy or speak to or communicate with plaintiff, or by doing anything else whatsoever, but in that connection this defendant admits that it is his desire to visit the minor children of plaintiff and defendant, and to have and enjoy their association.

XIX.

Answering paragraph XXV of said complaint, this defendant has no information or belief sufficient to enable him to answer thereto, and basing his denial upon that ground denies each and every allegation contained in said paragraph, and all thereof.

WHEREFORE, plaintiff prays:

FIRST: That a decree be denied to the plaintiff dissolving the bonds of matrimony.

SECOND: That the above entitled court inquire into all facts and circumstances necessary for the court to know and understand, to the end that said court may be enabled to make such order in respect of the care, custody, support, maintenance and education of the said minor children and each of them, as will in the opinion of said court, be for the best interests of the said children, and that accordingly and by reason thereof the custody and control of the said minor children be awarded to this defendant.

THIRD: That all relief prayed for by the plaintiff in her complaint and amended complaint on file herein, be denied and that the defendant be dismissed hence.

GAVIN MCNAB
LOYD WRIGHT
NAT SCHMULOWITZ
CHAS. E. MILLIKAN
Attorneys for said answering defendant.

IN THE
SUPERIOR COURT OF THE
STATE OF CALIFORNIA
IN AND FOR THE
COUNTY OF LOS ANGELES

No. D-52298

LILLITA LOUISE CHAPLIN,

Plaintiff,

vs.

CHARLES SPENCER CHAPLIN, et al.,

Defendants

CHARLES SPENCER CHAPLIN,
Defendant and Cross-Complaint,

vs.

LILLITA LOUISE CHAPLIN,
Plaintiff and Cross-Defendant.

CROSS-COMPLAINT

Comes now Charles Spencer Chaplin, defendant and cross-complainant above named, and for the cause of action against, and by way of cross-complaint against Lillita Louise Chaplin, plaintiff and cross-defendant above named, alleges:

I.

That cross-complainant is and for more than one year next preceding the commencement of the above entitled action and for more than one year next preceding the filing of this cross-complaint has continuously been a bona fide resident of the County of Los Angeles, State of California.

II.

That cross-complainant and cross-defendant intermarried at Empalme, in the State of Sonora, Republic of Mexico, on the 25th day of November, 1924, and ever since said date have been and now are husband and wife.

III.

For the statistical purposes required by Section 426a of the Code of Civil Procedure of the State of California, the cross-complainant alleges the following facts, to wit:

1. The place of marriage was Emplame, in the State of Sonora, Republic of Mexico.

2. The date of marriage was November 25, 1924.

3. The date of separation was November 30, 1926.

4. The number of years intervening from the date of marriage to the date of separation was two years and five days.

5. The number of children of the marriage was and is two.

6. The respective ages of said children are as follows: Charles Spencer Chaplin, Jr., aged about twenty-two months; Sydney Earl Chaplin, aged about thirteen months.

IV.

That cross-defendant has continuously been guilty of a course of conduct amounting to extreme cruelty toward cross-complainant and has treated cross-complainant in a cruel manner, and has during all of said period wrongfully inflicted upon cross-complainant a course of grievous mental suffering, humiliation, embarrassment and anguish of mind, some of the particulars of which are hereinafter set forth as follows:

1. That the cross-defendant revealed to the cross-complainant that she was infatuated with a certain young man; that the cross-complainant in all kindness, tolerance and understanding attempted to convince cross-defendant of the desirability of her ter-

minating said infatuation and therefore of not seeing said young
man again, but that cross-defendant persisted in continuing to see
and be with said young man, and, without the knowledge and
consent of cross-complainant, she, on several occasions, invited
him to her home while cross-complainant was away at his work;
that cross-complainant continued kindly to protest against her
continuance of any further contact with said man; that, notwithstanding cross-complainant's said objections, cross-defendant obstinately persisted in seeing said man; that arguments between
cross-complainant and cross-defendant in respect of said man con-
sequently frequently occurred, and that said arguments caused
cross-defendant to say to cross-complainant that she was nervous
and that the house she lived in was big and gloomy and that she
did not care to live in it any longer; that at said time, cross-defendant was in a delicate condition, being pregnant with said elder
child; that cross-complainant, being solicitous for his wife and
realizing her said delicate condition invited cross-defendant's
mother to live with her in order that cross-defendant might have
the company and comfort of her mother and in the hope that she
might abandon further contacts with said man; that shortly thereafter cross-defendant again insisted that she was not happy in the
house in which cross-complainant and cross-defendant then lived
together and she insisted that she live away from said house; that
said desire to live away from said cross-complainant's house was
prompted by her desire to continue seeing said young man; that
cross-defendant argued with cross-complainant that the atmosphere of said house was making her nervous and that it would be
better for both of them to live apart; that she did not love cross-
complainant and that he got on her nerves; that cross-complainant
realized that it was idle to object thereto, finally consented that
they try living apart; that immediately upon obtaining cross-complainant's said consent, cross-defendant insisted that cross-complainant express said consent before her physician, and she said
to cross-complainant that this suggestion from her was made for
technical reasons, because she did not want cross-complainant
thereafter to accuse her of deserting or abandoning cross-complainant; that said suspicion of cross-defendant that cross-complainant would ever regard cross-defendant's said temporary
living apart from him as a desertion or abandonment of cross-
complainant by cross-defendant and said insistence of cross-de-

fendant that cross-complainant should express his consent to their temporarily living apart before a witness caused cross-complainant grievous mental distress, humiliation, embarrassment and anguish of mind.

2. That thereafter cross-defendant, with her mother, lived for a period in a house separate and apart from said house of cross-complainant; that while said parties were thus living apart they kept in touch with each other, saw one another frequently, had meals together, went out together, and in all other respects continued harmoniously in their marriage relation, except in this, that cross-defendant continued to seek and to have the company of the aforementioned young man; that thereafter cross-defendant expressed the conviction that she preferred, after all, to be with cross-complainant and to forgo the company of said particular young man and that she wished to return to the house of cross-complainant and have his company and his comfort; that thereupon cross-defendant did, of her own free will and accord, return to cross-complainant's house and there live together with him happily until said elder child was born; that said living apart and said behavior of cross-defendant in continuing to have the company of said particular young man, caused the cross-complainant grievous mental suffering, humiliation, embarrassment and anguish of mind.

3. That from time to time the cross-defendant returned to cross-complainant's house, they lived together harmoniously as husband and wife and as companions and comrades; that cross-complainant sought the company of cross-defendant and tried to be with her as much as the nature of the work in which he was engaged permitted; that cross-complainant is engaged in the profession of acting for the screen and of making pictures therefor; that by dint of hard work cross-complainant has reached an eminent position in his said profession; that cross-complainant's work in his said profession, in itself and also especially by reason of the eminence he has attained therein, is extremely engrossing, difficult and time-consuming, and that in consequence thereof, for long, continual stretches of time, while a picture is being made, cross-complainant's time is not his own and he must be in attendance as a performer or otherwise in executive capacities while many persons are conjointly working with him in the creation of a picture; that, as a consequence, as cross-defendant at all times well under-

stood and realized, it frequently happened that cross-defendant had much time on her hands during which to divert herself as she chose; that from the return of the cross-defendant to the cross-complainant's house, the cross-defendant amused, diverted and entertained herself in various proper ways, including social intercourse with her friends and acquaintances of cross-complainant.

4. That about three or four months before the separation, cross-complainant discovered that the cross-defendant was associating with and frequently in the company of an automobile salesman, a person disliked and entirely disapproved of by cross-complainant, which dislike and disapproval had been communicated to cross-defendant; that cross-complainant by all proper means remonstrated with the cross-defendant against her association with said automobile salesman and against being seen with him in public places, dancing with him and drinking liquor, in her inviting him and others to the house of the cross-complainant and the cross-defendant, and at times when the cross-complainant was absent from such house; that cross-defendant deliberately defied the cross-complainant's suggestion, advice and remonstrance against such continued association with such automobile salesman and conduct with him, and persisted in continuing her association with such automobile salesman; that the continuance of such association between the cross-defendant and such automobile salesman and the cross-defendant's conduct caused adverse comment, gossip and rumors disparaging to the cross-defendant and cross-complainant, and their marriage relation, and that said comment, gossip and rumors came to the knowledge of cross-complainant and caused him grievous mental suffering, humiliation, embarrassment and anguish of mind.

5. That for a considerable period next preceding the time when cross-complainant and cross-defendant separated as aforesaid, cross-defendant habitually occupied almost all of her time dancing in hotels, cafes and beach resorts in and about the City of Los Angeles and other places, and thereby absented herself from her home and her said children to the grievous neglect of said children; that on numerous of such occasions cross-defendant did not return to her home until two or three o'clock in the morning; that on many of these occasions cross-defendant was accompanied by said automobile salesman; that she was frequently in the company of said automobile salesman and over the protests and against

the wishes of the cross-complainant, invited the said automobile salesman to the home of the cross-complainant and cross-defendant and entertained him and others thereat and at such times liquor was drunk to excess; that many times after such occasions, cross-complainant said to cross-defendant, in all kindness, that her said continual absence from her home and said consequent neglect of her children and her said dancing, through all hours of the night and day, and drinking liquor, were injurious to the welfare of said children and injurious to her reputation; that, notwithstanding the kind manner in which cross-complainant expostulated with cross-defendant in respect of said behavior and conduct and protested against the same on said occasions, or protested on other occasions against similar conduct of cross-defendant, cross-defendant habitually replied to cross-complainant, with irritation and anger, that she did not intend to change her mode of life to please him and that, if he did not like her conduct he could arrange with her for a divorce; that cross-complainant, to her suggestions of divorce, entered his protest and appealed to cross-defendant to consider the interests of their children; that finally, shortly prior to their said separation, cross-defendant declared to cross-complainant that she did not desire to live with him any longer and that she wished to be divorced from him, and that thereupon she asked cross-complainant coldly what financial arrangement he would make with her; that cross-complainant replied that he would provide for her abundantly and would give her more than she would be entitled to by law and that he would make such abundant provisions for her without any consideration whatsoever of any litigation; that cross-defendant then demanded to know what cross-complainant was worth; that cross-complainant replied that he did not see why that should be discussed at that time because, regardless of what he was worth, he would see to it that she was properly and fairly provided for.

6. That said mode of life thus engaged in by cross-defendant was totally disapproved of by cross-complainant and that cross-complainant communicated to cross-defendant his said disapproval and his reasons therefor; that cross-defendant did not change such mode of life but, on the contrary, she increased her indulgence in such vain and frivolous pleasures; that the cross-complainant is informed and verily believes that on various and sundry occasions the cross-defendant drank liquor to excess and

while under the influence of liquor her conduct became un-womanly, unseemly and undignified in speech and action; that, by her said conduct, she was thrown more and more often in contact with said automobile salesman hereinbefore mentioned, until finally she became infatuated with him, was constantly seen in public with him, and told several people that she was in love with him and very "crazy" about him; that cross-complainant again pointed out to cross-defendant the folly of her continuing said mode of life and continuing in her said relations with said automobile salesman and, with all consideration and kindness, tried to convince her that her said actions were bringing disrepute upon her, humiliation and mental suffering upon cross-complainant, pleaded with her that if she would not desist from such conduct out of any love she had for cross-complainant that at least she desist from said conduct for the sake of said children; that said pleadings of cross-complainant with cross-defendant were in vain.

7. That on a particular Sunday afternoon, the exact date whereof cross-complainant does not now recall, cross-defendant was preparing to attend a party to be given at a particular beach resort without the cross-complainant; that cross-complainant had heard of the planning of said party to which he was not invited; that cross-complainant again reasoned with cross-defendant in the manner hereinbefore mentioned and attempted to dissuade cross-defendant from attending said party and emphasized to cross-defendant that she should not, out of consideration for her children, attend said party without the cross-complainant; that cross-complainant again pleaded in vain and that cross-defendant insisted that she was going and asked cross-complainant what he could do about it; that cross-complainant told cross-defendant that he could not do anything about it except to try to dissuade her from going and that he could not force her or hold her down and said to her that the situation was becoming very serious; that cross-defendant replied, "Well, I don't care how serious it is, I am going;" that cross-complainant then said to cross-defendant that they must have some understanding about the situation existing in their relations and that said situation was becoming intolerable; that thereupon cross-defendant said to cross-complainant, "Well, what do you want, a divorce?" that cross-complainant replied to cross-defendant that this was a very serious and drastic step and that she should consider well and make up her mind thoroughly

before she decided upon this way out of such situation; that there-upon cross-defendant replied that she had already made up her mind, that their relationship was impossible and that she was not in love with cross-complainant; that thereupon there ensued be-tween cross-complainant and cross-defendant the conversation hereinbefore set forth with reference to a property settlement; that then cross-defendant said she had to hurry and go to the party and that she was already late therefor; that cross-complainant still tried to remonstrate with cross-defendant and asked her not to go to that party and suggested to her that it was a great pity that said salesman should break up their home and be the means of seri-ously injuring the welfare of their children; that thereupon cross-complainant suggested to and advised cross-defendant that she take a trip to Honolulu or to some other place in order to get away from her said associates, and in particular from said salesman and to break the habit she had formed of engaging in said mode of life; that cross-defendant refused to accept said suggestion or to follow said advice of cross-complainant; that thereupon, out of irritation with cross-complainant because cross-complainant con-tinued to try to dissuade her from attending said party, cross-de-fendant then said that it was all unfortunate and could not be helped and thereupon she left cross-complainant and went to said party; that sometime thereafter cross-defendant made up her mind that she would, and she did, take a trip to Honolulu.

8. Cross-complainant is informed and believes, and upon such information and belief alleges that while on the boat going to Ho-nolulu and likewise returning from Honolulu, and while cross-defendant was in Honolulu, she so conducted herself and engaged in such course of conduct as to cause passengers on the boat both to notice and to comment upon her conduct and to make uncom-plimentary remarks of and concerning her and her said conduct, which said observations and comment were reported to the cross-complainant and have caused him extreme mental anguish and sorrow and great humiliation.

9. That cross-defendant took with her, on the said trip to Hono-lulu, one of the children of these parties, and cross-complainant is informed and believes, and upon such information and belief al-leges that almost continuously during said trip she disregarded said child and frequently would go for hours without even going near the child or having anything whatsoever to do with him, to

such an extent as to cause the same to be observed and commented upon, which observations and comments were reported to the cross-complainant and which caused cross-complainant extreme mental anguish and suffering and great humiliation.

10. That, totally regardless of the material welfare of her children, of herself and of cross-complainant, cross-defendant gradually, during the period of said marriage, became increasingly extravagant in the spending of money in her personal appearance and, in this behalf, cross-complainant is informed and believes and therefore alleges the fact to be that while the said cross-defendant was in Honolulu she conceived the idea of entering proceedings for a divorce against this cross-complainant shortly following her intended return to Los Angeles, and for the purpose of carrying out her said scheme and plan it is further alleged in this regard that within a few days after cross-defendant's return from said trip to Honolulu she spent in excess of ten thousand dollars on clothes, shoes and perfumes for her individual use; that, on the day before cross-defendant left cross-complainant as hereinafter set forth, cross-defendant came into the room of cross-complainant and, while cross-defendant was in cross-complainant's room, as aforesaid, cross-complainant, having discovered said extravagant expenditure of over ten thousand dollars, mentioned the matter to cross-defendant and told her that such expenditure was ruinous and that she could not go on spending money in that way; that cross-complainant and cross-defendant quietly discussed the matter and he reasoned with her upon said subject matter and it was agreed that cross-defendant would try and be more careful and considerate in her expenditures for such commodities as clothes, shoes, perfumes and other objects of her personal apparel or use; that thereupon cross-defendant told cross-complainant that she would like to give a dinner and party that night at their home to just a few friends whom she had met on the boat on her return trip from Honolulu; that cross-complainant acquiesced, it being mutually understood that cross-complainant would be engaged in his work and would not be able to be present at such dinner; that, instead of giving a dinner at the house to just a few friends, as cross-complainant had been led to believe, as aforesaid, cross-defendant gave one dinner at said house to her mother and a number of friends and, on the same evening, gave another dinner for about twenty people at the Hotel Biltmore in the City of Los

Angeles; that, on said night, cross-complainant reached home at about eleven o'clock and, because he had been working hard all day, he immediately went to bed; that later, at about two o'clock in the morning, cross-defendant returned to said house with a large party of friends and they made a great noise and awoke the whole household; that before said company had been in the house very long, they were playing on the piano and on the organ and they also had the gramophone going, all at the same time; that said noise awoke the child which was in the nursery of said house, the other child then being away at its grandmother's home, and cross-complainant heard said child crying; that said noise continued for a long time, that couples were going in and out of the house and upon the lawn surrounding, and that he heard loud laughter and loud sounds of hilarity, to the great discomfort of cross-complainant and of said child; that cross-complainant bore with said proceedings patiently as long as possible, but that, as said noises continued and promised to continue indefinitely, cross-complainant at last called cross-defendant upstairs and remonstrated with her and told her that two o'clock in the morning was not a proper time to bring home a company of people seeking pleasure and entertainment when there was a young baby in the house, and that they were making altogether too much noise and that she should ask them to leave immediately; that cross-defendant immediately assumed a belligerent and defiant mood, but that cross-defendant then went downstairs and told her guests that they would have to go home; that, after said guests had left the house, cross-complainant tried, in all kindness, to discuss with cross-defendant what had just occurred, but that cross-defendant said to cross-complainant, in a hostile and belligerent tone of voice, that she did not wish to talk with cross-complainant, that she was tired and was going to bed, and that she did not wish to hear any of his preaching, and that thereupon cross-defendant abruptly left cross-complainant.

11. That on the following morning cross-complainant went to work before cross-defendant had gotten up, as was cross-complainant's usual practice, and early in the afternoon of that day, while cross-complainant was at his work, he was called to the telephone by one of his servants and was told that cross-defendant and her mother were packing trunks and making preparations to leave the home and to take the child away with them; that cross-complainant immediately left his work and repaired to his home;

that, on reaching his home, he discovered everything packed and that his wife had already gone; that he found his wife's mother still there and asked her the meaning of these proceedings; that cross-defendant's mother said confusedly that she did not know; that cross-complainant asked her, "Where is my wife?" but that cross-defendant's mother would not answer; that cross-complainant then went immediately to the nursery and found his child gone; that thereupon cross-complainant asked cross-defendant's mother, "Where is the child?" and she replied that it had been taken away; that the nurse of the children, who was standing near, then stated to cross-complainant that his wife and her mother had told said nurse that the children were never coming back; that, upon hearing this information, cross-complainant turned to the mother of cross-defendant and said, "You must leave my house and I wish to have my children and my wife back here immediately;" that cross-defendant's mother made some remark to the effect that "That is all right with me;" that thereupon she left the house; that later cross-defendant telephoned to the house and cross-complainant answered the telephone; that cross-defendant demanded to know whether her mother was there, and that cross-complainant told her that her mother had gone; that cross-complainant then said to cross-defendant that he wished her to return immediately as he wished to talk with her and that cross-defendant replied that she would be home in half an hour; that a little later cross-defendant again telephoned and said a man was coming to the house to call for her trunks and asked that said trunks be given to this man; that cross-complainant replied that nothing would leave the house until she had returned, and that cross-complainant wished to know what the meaning of all these proceedings was; that cross-defendant replied that if this was the way he felt about it, he had better go and see her lawyer, and that cross-complainant said, "Very well;" that a little later cross-defendant telephoned again because cross-complainant had refused to allow her trunks and things to leave his house, and that cross-defendant then said to cross-complainant, on his refusal to accede to her wish to move said trunks from his house, that she would send up the sheriff and give cross-complainant a lot of unsavory publicity if he did not allow the trunks to leave; that cross-complainant replied that he wished to have her and his children back at home; that cross-defendant thereupon abruptly hung up the telephone; that thereupon cross-defendant told newspaper reporters that she and cross-complainant had quarreled and separated and that, on the following day, cross-defendant's statement to said newspaper reporters was published in all the newspapers.

That the facts and circumstances hereinbefore in subparagraphs 10 and 11 set forth, were all a part of the execution of a preconceived plan of the cross-defendant to file an action for divorce and to force a divorce upon cross-complainant, which said plan was formulated and conceived prior to the trip of cross-defendant to Honolulu.

12. That since the said marriage and on various occasions, cross-complainant being unable to allege the exact dates, the cross-defendant absented herself from the home of cross-complainant and cross-defendant, without the knowledge or consent of cross-complainant and against his wish and desire, and while thus absent has become intoxicated in the presence of various persons, as cross-complainant has been informed and verily believes, and in this regard this cross-complainant is informed and believes and therefore alleges the fact to be that since the said marriage and on various occasions, the cross-complainant being unable to allege the exact dates, said cross-complainant consorted and associated with various persons whose names are not now known to this cross-complainant, all without the knowledge or consent of cross-complainant and against his wish and desire.

That on several occasions during the said marriage, cross-complainant being unable to allege the exact dates, the cross-defendant, secretly and clandestinely, appeared in various public places in the company of and as the companion of various persons, all without the knowledge or consent of cross-complainant and against his wish and desire.

13. That on January 10, 1927, this cross-defendant filed in the office of the County Clerk of Los Angeles County, State of California, a complaint for divorce; that the said cross-defendant voluntarily and without just cause and in wicked disregard for the future welfare and happiness of the elder of the two children of cross-complainant and cross-defendant, and with full knowledge that by so doing the said child would inevitably in the future be defamed, disparaged and stigmatized, and would, when grown, suffer reproach, humiliation and dishonor, included in the said complaint filed in the above entitled action an allegation by which

she published to the world that the said elder of the two children of these parties had been conceived out of wedlock. That said allegation in said complaint was made by the said cross-defendant with full knowledge and understanding that it was totally unnecessary for any purpose of stating in said complaint an alleged cause of action for a divorce against the defendant therein, this cross-complainant, and that said cross-defendant made said unnecessary allegation with utter and ruthless disregard for the future comfort and happiness of the said child, and solely for the purpose of wounding the feelings and sensibilities of this cross-complainant, and of coercing him into making an exorbitant property settlement with cross-defendant. That cross-complainant dearly loved and loves his said child, and the said unnecessary and wicked allegation so made by cross-defendant in her complaint in the above entitled action has caused cross-complainant to suffer and will continue to cause him to suffer grievous distress and anguish of mind.

14. That in said complaint for divorce filed in the above entitled action by cross-defendant, she wrongfully and falsely charged cross-complainant, among other things, with having attempted to commit, and with having solicited the commission of the crime defined by Section 288a of the Penal Code of the State of California; that said false charges were made in her said complaint by cross-defendant with the intent and purpose that they would cause cross-complainant to suffer and they did cause cross-complainant to suffer great humiliation, shame and mortification; that, furthermore, said false charges were made by cross-defendant in her said complaint for the additional intent and purpose that they would be given and they were in fact given wide publicity in all the newspapers, not only in the City of Los Angeles, but as well in the newspapers published and distributed throughout the United States of America and the world at large, and with the intent and purpose that such publication would cause cross-complainant to suffer intense humiliation, shame and mortification, and it did cause cross-complainant to suffer intense humiliation, shame and mortification; that, furthermore, said false charges were made by cross-defendant in her said complaint with the malignant purpose and intention to threaten, intimidate and coerce cross-complainant to pay to her an exorbitant sum of money as a property settlement and to pay the same to cross-defendant rather than to go to trial

on the issue raised by said false charges and in the hope that cross-complainant would raise and pay her said exorbitant sum in consideration of her abandoning her prosecution of her said action for divorce; that the said false, untruthful and wrongful charges and allegations were intended to cause and have caused this cross-complainant to suffer intense humiliation, shame and mortification and great and grievous mental anguish and suffering.

15. That said wicked and unnecessary allegation in her said complaint that the elder child of these parties was conceived out of wedlock, in its pitiless disregard of the welfare and happiness of said blameless and helpless child, together with said false charges of criminal conduct on the part of cross-complainant, have, under all the facts and circumstances hereinbefore set forth, caused cross-complainant grievous mental suffering and have so impaired cross-complainant's health that, as a result of cross-complainant's said impairment of heath, he has not been able, since the filing of cross-defendant's said complaint, to work at his profession of making motion pictures for the screen.

16. That at all times since cross-defendant entertained the fixed desire of having a divorce from cross-complainant, cross-complainant has been ready and willing to give cross-defendant all the share of the community property of said marriage to which she would be entitled under the laws of the State of California; that after the filing of cross-defendant's said complaint, cross-complainant authorized and instructed his attorneys to communicate to the attorneys of cross-defendant and his said attorneys did thereupon communicate to the attorneys of cross-defendant cross-complainant's willingness to give to cross-defendant all her share of the community property and his willingness that an accountant of high standing be mutually agreed upon to examine the books and accounts of cross-complainant for the purpose of determining the amount of such lawful share of cross-defendant; that cross-complainant is informed and believes and upon such information and belief alleges the fact to be that the aforesaid proposal was communicated to cross-defendant; that to this proposal said cross-defendant replied that she did not care whether or not there was any community property and that she proposed to get one million and a quarter out of cross-complainant; and said malevolent persistence of cross-defendant to extort said sum from cross-complainant intensified the great distress of mind suffered by

cross-complainant by reason of cross-defendant's prior intimidations hereinbefore set forth.

17. That for a greater portion of the time during the married life of these parties, and since the birth of the elder child of these parties, the cross-defendant has engaged in such a course of conduct as to make it impossible for her to devote more than a very little time to the children of the cross-complainant and cross-defendant and during said time she has deliberately and willfully disregarded said children and their care and welfare and has not bestowed upon them that care, attention or affection which is usual with a mother for and toward her children, all of which has caused the cross-complainant grievous mental suffering and anguish.

18. That cross-defendant, on various and sundry occasions has wrongfully and falsely charged cross-complainant and has made statements to third persons indiscriminately and maliciously charging cross-complainant with grave improprieties and has reflected upon the character, probity and integrity of cross-complainant by charging and asserting that cross-complainant had maintained and was maintaining illegitimate relations with various women and by such conduct the said cross-defendant has shown a complete lack of respect and trust and want of confidence in cross-complainant; that said charges and statements were and are and each of them was and is false and untrue and known by cross-defendant to be false and untrue at the said several and respective times when she made and uttered them; that said charges and statements were and are entirely without justification and that said conduct on the part of cross-defendant was intended to and did annoy, vex, torment and humiliate cross-complainant and did subject him to great shame and embarrassment, and caused him grievous mental suffering and pain.

V.

That all and singular the actions, conduct and behavior of cross-defendant, hereinbefore in paragraph IV set forth, constantly and repeatedly wounded and lacerated cross-complainant's feelings and caused cross-complainant constantly to suffer grievous and extreme anguish of mind and grievous mental pain and suffering; that all and singular said action, conduct and behavior of cross-defendant during the whole of said period did and does now absolutely destroy cross-complainant's peace of mind and happiness, endanger his health and unfit him from continuing his work in his said profession; that said conduct and behavior of cross-defendant has seriously impaired the health of cross-complainant; that all and singular said conduct of cross-defendant was calculated by her to and did render the proper discharge of the duties of married life impossible for cross-complainant and were and are such as utterly to defeat the legitimate objects of matrimony; that all and singular said conduct of cross-defendant was intentional, willful and without the consent and against the wishes of cross-complainant and was intended by cross-defendant to inflict grievous suffering upon cross-complainant and to outrage, wound and lacerate cross-complainant's feelings, that all and singular said conduct of cross-defendant has become a fixed and persistent habit of cross-defendant and is likely to be repeated if cross-complainant and cross-defendant should continue to live together.

VI.

That the cross-complainant is a fit and proper person to have the care, custody and control of the said children, both of whom are boys, and cross-complainant is ready and willing to receive their said care, custody and control as is ready, willing and able to do all things necessary for their best interests and their comfort and their proper education.

VII.

That there is community property of cross-complainant and cross-defendant of the total value of Two Hundred Sixty-six Thousand, Nine Hundred Thirty-two Dollars and Sixty-three cents, ($266,932.63).

WHEREFORE, cross-complainant prays that the bonds of matrimony heretofore and now existing between cross-complainant and cross-defendant be dissolved in the manner provided by law; that the above entitled court inquire into all facts and circumstances necessary for the court to know and understand, to the end that said court may be enabled to make such order in respect of the care, custody, support, maintenance and education of the said minor children and each of them, as will in the opinion of said court be for the best interests of the said children, and that accordingly and by reason thereof the custody and control of the said minor children be awarded to this cross-complainant. That cross-complainant further prays that said court also inquire fully into all matters in respect of the property and property rights of cross-complainant and cross-defendant to the end that the court may award to cross-defendant such property now in the custody or control of cross-complainant as she may be entitled to under the laws of the State of California in view of all the facts and circumstances relevant to the disposition of said question; that the court make such other order or decree as to the court shall seem meet and proper in the premises.

GAVIN MCNAB
LOYD WRIGHT
NAT SCHMULOWITZ
CHAS. E. MILLIKAN

Attorneys for Charles Spencer Chaplin, defendant and cross-complainant.
27 May 1927

IN THE
SUPERIOR COURT OF THE
STATE OF CALIFORNIA
IN AND FOR THE
COUNTY OF LOS ANGELES

No. D-52298

LILLITA LOUISE CHAPLIN,
Plaintiff & Cross-Defendant,

vs.

CHARLES SPENCER CHAPLIN, et al.,
Defendants & Cross-Complainants.

ANSWER TO CROSS-COMPLAINT

Now comes Lillita Louise Chaplin, plaintiff and cross-defendant in the above entitled action, and answering the cross-complaint on file herein, admits, alleges and denies as follows, to-wit:

I.

Admits the allegations contained in paragraph I of said cross-complaint.

II.

Admits the allegations contained in paragraph II of said cross-complaint.

III.

Admits the allegations contained in paragraph III of said cross-complaint.

IV.

As to paragraph IV of said cross-complaint, denies that cross-defendant has continuously, or otherwise or at all, been guilty of a course of conduct, or of any conduct, amounting to extreme cruelty to cross-complainant, and/or that she has treated said cross-complainant in a cruel manner; and denies that during all of the time alleged, or at any time or otherwise or at all, she has wrongfully inflicted upon cross-complainant a course of grievous mental suffering, humiliation, embarrassment and anguish of mind or any grievous mental suffering, humiliation, embarrassment or anguish of mind.

That as to the particulars of the alleged extreme cruelty set forth in said cross-complaint, cross-defendant answers as follows:

1. Alleges that she is unable to specifically answer the allegations in this paragraph of said cross-complainant contained, as they are alleged with reference to "a certain young man," or any particular man, for the reason that she is unable to ascertain from the allegations of said cross-complaint the identity of the man referred to.

Denies, however, that, during her marriage, she has ever been infatuated with any man, in any sense other than as an innocent, friendly preference; alleges that she is unable to ascertain from the allegations in said complaint contained in what manner, or how, it is alleged that she "revealed" said alleged infatuation to cross-complainant, and denies that she revealed, in any manner, as alleged, or otherwise, any infatuation for any man to cross-complainant, other than an innocent and proper friendship; and alleges that she has no recollection of so revealing any such friendship.

Denies that cross-complainant attempted to convince her, as alleged, or otherwise, of the desirability of terminating any infatuation for any man, or of not seeing any man; and denies that she persisted in continuing, or continued, to see and/or be with said man, or any man, except in a proper and friendly way, and always in company with other friends, without the knowledge and/or consent of said cross-complainant, or otherwise or at all; and denies that on several occasions or on any occasion, she invited said man or any man to her home, while cross-complainant was away or otherwise, except in company with other friends, and for a proper and innocent purpose. Denies that she obstinately, or otherwise, persisted in seeing said man except as above stated, and on proper and natural occasions of ordinary and usual diversions; and denies that there were frequent or any arguments between her and cross-complainant in respect to said man, or any man, except that said cross-complainant was unreasonably, and without provocation or cause, jealous or pretended to be of practically every man cross-defendant looked at or knew.

In this connection, cross-defendant alleges that cross-complainant wrongfully and without any cause accused her of being infatuated with and maintaining improper relations with nearly every man she met with any frequency at social gatherings; that on one occasion, he accused her of being infatuated with a man who passed the house where she was living, whom she had never met; that on another occasion, she had some friends to dinner, consisting of a mother, her son and the son's fiancée; that, as usual, cross-complainant was not at home for dinner and that he told her the next morning that he had looked through the windows the night before and knew who had been there, and accused her of being no better than a prostitute for having said man at her home for dinner; that cross-defendant's relations with said man were such that she had never been in his company excepting when either his mother or his fiancée was present.

Denies that cross-defendant ever at any time complained to cross-complainant about living in her home because it was gloomy and/or because she was nervous on account of any quarrels with cross-complainant over any man, or her association with any man; and denies that cross-complainant invited her mother to live at said home in any hope that cross-defendant might abandon further or any contact and/or association with the unnamed and unidentified man referred to in said cross-complaint or any man.

In this connection, she alleges the fact to be that at said time she was several months along in pregnancy, as alleged in said cross-complaint and that, during the greater portion of said time she was so sick on account thereof that she was unable to sit up; that cross-complainant was with her scarcely at all, night or day; that there was no one in said house but Japanese servants, who treated her as an interloper and with contempt; that one day she complained to cross-complainant about this condition and tried to persuade him to come home oftener for dinner and in the evenings; that it was on this occasion and under these circumstances that he had cross-defendant's mother come and stay with her.

Admits that at the times set forth in this paragraph of said cross-complaint, cross-defendant insisted that she was not happy, and that she was not happy in the house where she and cross-complainant lived. In this connection, she alleges that practically all of said time she was alone in said house, until her mother came to stay with her, as aforesaid; and that a greater portion of said time when cross-complainant was at home she was in tears or a state of nervous hysteria on account of his cruel and inhuman treatment.

Denies that she ever at any time, until the separation alleged in said cross-complaint, expressed a desire or insisted that she live away from the home of said parties or that she and cross-complainant live apart, or that it was better for them to live apart; and denies that during said time, or at any other time, she had any desire to live away from cross-complainant's house in order to continue seeing the unknown and unidentified man referred to in said cross-complaint, or any other man. And denies that cross-complainant has or ever had any ground, reason or foundation for the alleged motive attributed to cross-defendant in leaving said house at said time; and that said allegation as to said motive is false and untrue and known by cross-complainant to be false and untrue.

In this connection, cross-defendant alleges the fact to be that she left said house and took up her temporary residence apart from cross-complainant solely because she was advised by two doctors to do so, in order to escape the physical effects of his cruelty upon herself and her unborn baby; that said course was pursued upon the unsolicited suggestion, in the first instance, of a doctor friend of cross-complainant who was at said house one evening and witnessed the effect upon cross-defendant of cross-complainant's cruel treatment of her; that even then, she refused to leave said house and live elsewhere on account of the fear that said suggestion was not made in good faith but was a trap to compromise and prejudice her; that she did not leave said house until her own family-doctor was called into consultation, and until a statement was signed by said doctors jointly to protect her from any charge by cross-complainant of any improper motive or purpose in leaving said house.

Admits that the atmosphere of said house not only made her

nervous, but that, in connection with the previous mental suffering inflicted upon her by cross-complainant as alleged in the complaint on file herein, she was in a constant state of physical terror and mental anguish; but denies that there were ever any arguments with cross-complainant upon any subject, excepting pitiful and futile appeals to him to cease condemning and mistreating her for a situation which she could not escape and for which she was not responsible.

Denies that at said time, she argued with cross-complainant on the subject or ever stated to him that she did not love him and/or that he made her nervous. In this connection, cross-defendant alleges that at said time she loved cross-complainant with the romantic devotion and infatuation of a sixteen-year-old girl for her first and only sweetheart; and that solely on account of said love she bore his abuse and cruelty and complied, to the best of her ability, with his selfish and unreasonable demands to be protected from adverse public criticism at her expense.

Admits that cross-complainant consented in the presence of said two doctors to the temporary removal of cross-defendant from said house to protect her from any charge of desertion on his part; but denies that said removal was for the purpose of trying living apart or for any reason or purpose except as above set forth.

Denies that cross-defendant suggested or insisted that cross-complainant express his consent to her leaving said house for the purpose alleged in said cross-complaint, or for any purpose other than as above alleged. Alleges further in this connection that said suggestion, from the doctor whom cross-complainant brought to said house, that cross-defendant remove temporarily therefrom, was acquiesced in so promptly and willingly by cross-complainant as to constitute reasonable and probable cause for her aforesaid fears regarding the good faith of said suggestion.

Denies that her insistence that he express or the expression of his consent to her leaving said house in the presence of said doctors caused cross-complainant any grievous mental distress, humiliation, embarrassment and/or anguish of mind. Alleges that cross-complainant's whole attitude in connection therewith was one of apparent and manifest satisfaction and pleasure to get cross-defendant out of said house.

Alleges upon information and belief that if cross-complainant suffered any grievous mental distress, humiliation, embarrassment or anguish of mind, on account of said occurrence, that the same was not caused by the expression of his consent to said removal before said witness but was caused by the admission of his own lack of ordinary humane consideration for a mere child in a pregnant condition, which was necessarily implied in the expression of such consent.

2. Admits that while said parties were living apart as aforesaid, they "kept in touch with each other," but denies that they saw one another frequently. In this connection cross-defendant alleges the facts to be, that during said time, which covered a period of several months, she telephoned her husband daily and, as a rule, several times a day; that on most of said occasions her communications with him were through his Japanese valet; that during said time, according to her best recollection and belief, he had dinner with her at said house only twice; admits that during said time he came to see her and took her out but denies that such visits were on an average of any oftener than once a week; and alleges that on practically every such occasion, he told her that such visits were only for the purpose of keeping up appearances so that the financial success of the picture which he was then making would not be jeopardized on account of adverse public opinion.

Admits that the relation of said parties at said time as above set forth was a continuation of their previous marriage relation, (as alleged in said cross-complaint) with respect to their social and personal relations.

Admits that said relation was harmonious to the extent that cross-defendant was always agreeable and pleasant toward her husband and while in his company, but not otherwise; and alleges that she never, at any time during their marriage relation, quarreled with him on any subject; but denies the implication in said allegation that the marriage relation of said parties was ever a normal, harmonious or happy one.

Denies that during the time cross-defendant lived apart from her husband as aforesaid, she continued to seek and/or have the company of the unidentified and unknown "young man" referred to in said cross-complaint; and that she sought and/or had the company of any man during said time, excepting the company of her husband, at long intervals as aforesaid. Cross-defendant admits that, during said time, a very few of her men friends came to see her but not as the "company" insinuated by the allegation in said cross-complaint. In this connection, cross-defendant alleges, without reservation or exception, that during said time no man, other than a member of her own family, ever visited her at said house, except in company with, and as the escort of, women friends, and only at times when her mother was present.

Denies that she ever expressed the conviction to cross-complainant or any one else that she preferred to be with cross-complainant and/or wished to forgo the company of any man, or any particular man, in any sense as implied by insinuation and innuendo in the allegation of said cross-complaint, that the company of any other man had ever been preferred to that of cross-complainant; and denies that she ever expressed to cross-complainant, or anyone else, the wish to return to the house of cross-complainant in any sense as implied by said allegation, but not specifically alleged, because she has been away and had remained away from said house, as a matter of personal preference or because she had preferred the company of any other man to that of cross-complainant.

Admits that in returning to said house she wished and desired the company and comfort of her husband, and alleges that she was entitled to have and enjoy such company and comfort, in the aforesaid delicacy of her physical condition; but denies the implication arising from the language of the cross-complainant in this particular that any prior attitude of her husband toward her justified the expectation of enjoying such company and comfort; and alleges that she never entertained such expectation, or gave expression to such a wish, on that account.

In this connection, cross-defendant alleges that the allegation in said cross-complaint that she returned to the home of her husband at said time because she had decided to give up her association with some man whose identity is not disclosed, and whose identity cross-defendant does not know and is unable to ascertain, or of any man, is false and untrue and that it is made deliberately, and with full knowledge, on the part of cross-complainant, that it is false and untrue. Cross-defendant further alleges that it is a fact and that cross-complainant well knows it to be a fact that at said time he had insisted and was insisting and demanding that cross-defendant go away, in hiding, to give birth to her baby in order to carry out his ideas of protecting himself and in utter disregard of her convenience and comfort and the safety of herself and of said baby; that at said time he had made all arrangements for the birth of said baby as aforesaid; that cross-defendant, on account of her great love for her husband and on account of his aforesaid insistence and demands, and because of her willingness, on that account, to do anything in conformity with his wishes and for his protection, or the protection of his career, had consented to carry out said plans so made by cross-complainant for the purpose as aforesaid; that on the day when cross-defendant was to have left the house where she was temporarily living as aforesaid, in compliance with said demands and plans of cross-complainant, her labor pains came on unexpectantly and so violently that she rushed to the home of her alleged solicitous husband, at the risk of her own life and that of her baby, not for his company and comfort in her extremity or his solace in her fear of travail due to her pain and the inexperience of her youth, but to ascertain from him what he wanted her to do in this newly arisen emergency, in order that she might best service and protect his own greatness and the financial success of his picture.

Alleges, if cross-defendant had any convictions with reference to her preference of the company of her husband over that of any other man, as alleged only by implication in said cross-complaint, that at said time, her physical condition, together with the mental condition brought about by the prospect and fear of having to bring her firstborn into the world like a thief in the night, in order to satisfy the alleged solicitude of an indulgent husband and father, were such as to justify cross-defendant, by her denial, in making the implied admission that she failed to express said convictions at said time.

Denies that after cross-defendant's return to the house of cross-complainant as aforesaid, she lived there happily until the elder child of said parties was born, or lived there happily otherwise or at all. And alleges in this connection that after cross-defendant's return to said house under the circumstances above alleged, cross-complainant wrongfully and brutally subjected her, in carrying out plans solely designed and unreasonably and selfishly conceived, to protect himself and his financial interests, to the most harrowing ordeals and excruciating experiences conceivable; that on account thereof, cross-defendant nearly lost her life from hemorrhages after said baby was born. That cross-defendant submitted to said plans and went through said ordeals and suffered said experiences and physical dangers solely on account of her love for cross-complainant and her willingness on that account to make any sacrifice which he represented to her was necessary to protect him and his interests.

Denies that cross-defendant's living apart from her husband as herein alleged caused him grievous mental suffering, humiliation, embarrassment and anguish of mind, or any mental suffering, humiliation, embarrassment or anguish of mind. And alleges that after said baby was born and before it was safe for cross-defendant to be moved, on account of the birth of said baby, cross-complainant wanted her again to remove from said house, whereby she was subjected to and suffered great and grievous mental anguish and whereby and on account whereof, her life and her health and the life and health of said baby were seriously endangered. Denies that cross-defendant's continuing to have or having the company of the "particular young man" referred to in said cross-complaint, or of any man, during said time caused cross-complainant grievous mental suffering, humiliation, embarrassment and anguish of mind or any mental suffering, humiliation, embarrassment or anguish of mind, for the reason that cross-defendant's "association" and "company" with any and all men during said time was nothing more than the casual association of friends and was free from any and all suggestion of indiscretion or moral turpitude.

3. Denies that from the time cross-defendant returned to cross-complainant's house or otherwise or at all, they lived together harmoniously as husband and wife excepting for brief and widely separated intervals; and alleges that the lack of harmony in said relation was solely due to cross-complainant's inconsiderate, cruel and inhuman treatment, as more specifically alleged and set forth in the complaint on file herein. Denies that at said time or at any time during the entire marriage relation of said parties, they ever lived together as companions and/or comrades. Denies that cross-complainant sought the company of cross-defendant and/or tried to be with her as much as the nature of the work in which he was engaged permitted or otherwise or at all, and alleges that it was cross-complainant's habit, during the entire time that said parties lived together, to spend the time when he was not working away from her and in the company of others; admits the allegations contained in said cross-complaint on page 5, with reference to

cross-complainant's work, down to and including line 22,[1] but denies that said work was so engrossing as to require his attention, or that he engaged in said work, to such an extent that it was accountable for his absence from home on Sundays and holidays, and until one and two o'clock in the morning, during practically the entire marriage of said parties; admits that cross-defendant had her time on her hands when her husband was engaged in his work, but denies that this time, or the time when he was away and not at work as aforesaid, was engaged in diversions; alleges that she was pregnant for approximately 18 months out of the 24 that she was married, gave birth to two children and had them to care for, and during approximately 20 months of said 24, made substantially all of her own clothes; alleges that she never complained and does not now complain of any absence of her husband from his home and family due to or on account of his work; admits that she realizes and knows substantially the portion of his time which cross-complainant devoted to his alleged work and the portion thereof which it was necessary and proper to devote thereto.

4. Admits that before the separation of said parties, she knew several automobile salesman, in various degrees of acquaintanceship; alleges that she has no knowledge, information or belief as to any particular automobile salesman which cross-complainant had in mind in making the allegation in this paragraph contained or as to what associations, proper or otherwise, it is alleged she had with any automobile salesman, or the nature of any such associations which it is alleged that he discovered sufficient to enable her to specifically answer said allegations, and upon that ground, she denies each and every, all and singularly, the allegations in said paragraph contained with reference thereto.

In this connection, she further alleges that one automobile salesman whom she knew at said time and with whom her relations were the most casual and purely of a business nature, has been approached recently, according to her information and belief, by persons claiming to be representatives of cross-complainant, and wrongfully and falsely accused of having had improper relations with cross-defendant on such a nature as to seriously reflect upon her character and reputation, and urged to make a written statement admitting said relations and promised in consideration

---

1. See page 220.

of doing so material and favorable consideration from cross-complainant; and further alleges upon information and belief that practically all of her acquaintances and those with whom she has come in almost any kind of personal contact during the past two years, even to the Hawaiian beach boys at Honolulu and the oilers on the *S. S. City of Los Angeles* have been sought out by such persons and offered financial reward or compensation for any evidence or information derogatory to or seriously injure her reputation and character.

Alleges that she has no information or belief sufficient to enable her to specifically answer the allegation in said paragraph contained as to cross-complainant's "dislike" and/or "disapproval" of the automobile salesman which he had in mind in making said allegation, or of any automobile salesman among her acquaintances; or as to what cross-complainant "disliked" or "disapproved of" in said or any automobile salesman, and upon that ground, she denies each and every, all and singularly, said allegations. Denies that cross-complainant's dislike and/or disapproval of said, or any, automobile salesman of any character or kind, was ever communicated to her by cross-complainant; and denies that he every by all, or any, proper or other means, or otherwise or at all, remonstrated with her or in any way commented upon her association with said or any automobile salesman; and denies the existence of any justification whatever for the improper and unfounded insinuation and innuendo contained in said allegations, reflecting upon the character of cross-defendant as a wife and mother, with reference to her associations with an unidentified man; denies that her associations with the automobile salesman in cross-complainant's mind, or with any other automobile salesman or any other man, ever called for or justified any remonstrance on account thereof, as insinuated in said allegation, or otherwise or at all; alleges that her associations with any and all automobile salesman of her acquaintance, and with each and every of them, never at any time involved anything improper, and that no act or conduct of cross-defendant in connection therewith was either improper or inconsistent with either a friendly or business relation.

Alleges that said allegation is trivial and tenders no issue of extreme cruelty or grievous mental suffering in that no act of impropriety and no improper association or conduct is charged or alleged with anyone; that on account of the insidious character of said allegation and the improper and unfounded insinuations and implications contained therein and the unwarranted inferences intended to be drawn therefrom, the public press has misconstrued and published said allegations as charges of infidelity against cross-defendant by cross-complainant, to her great humiliation, damage and mental suffering.

Alleges that cross-defendant has no knowledge, information or belief as to the allegations contained in said paragraph of said cross-complaint with respect to any adverse comment, gossip and/or rumors regarding her alleged association with any man other than cross-complainant, on account of the uncertain and indefinite character thereof, and upon that ground denies each and every, all and singularly, the said allegations in said cross-complaint contained; and denies that any such alleged adverse comment, gossip and/or rumors, or any adverse comment, gossip and/or rumors, disparaging to either or any of said parties, and/or their marriage relation, came to the knowledge of cross-complainant and/or caused him grievous mental suffering, humiliation, embarrassment and/or anguish of mind, or any mental suffering, humiliation, embarrassment and/or anguish of mind; and alleges that at no time was there anything in cross-defendant's conduct or association with any unidentified automobile salesman, or any man, to justify or warrant any adverse comment, gossip or rumor, disparaging to her or her husband or their marriage relation, or otherwise or at all.

Alleges that said allegations in this connection do not charge any specific misconduct, or any specific act, in respect to the alleged association, or any association, with anyone, and cross-defendant is unable on that account to fairly meet or answer the veiled and improper insinuations contained therein; that they do not specify or define the nature or character of the alleged comment, gossip and/or rumors alleged to have come to the knowledge of cross-complainant, and do not specify in what manner or in what respect they were adverse or disparaging to cross-defendant, her husband and/or their marriage relation; that the terms "disparaging" and "adverse" have a wide latitude of meaning, from that implying trivial criticism or disapproval to an implication of the grossest immorality and misconduct; that used in connection with cross-defendant's association with a man other

than her husband, even without any direct allegation that said association was improper or otherwise, the natural construction, by
way of implication and inference, is one seriously reflecting upon
the character of cross-defendant; that said allegations of said
cross-complaint subject cross-defendant to this serious reflection
upon her character, without charging anything which she is able
to answer or controvert, except that she associated with and was
in the company of another man, and with nothing to indicate, excepting cruel and reckless insinuations, that this association was
not merely one of ordinary social intercourse, open and free from
any impropriety.

Alleges that a demurrer to said cross-complaint and a motion to
strike out such allegations therein would entail a delay in the trial
of said action, which cross-defendant is desirous of avoiding; that
for said reason, she has elected to answer said cross-complaint in
the most specific and comprehensive manner possible, in view of
the nature, character and form of the allegations therein contained.

5. Denies that for a considerable period of time next preceding
the separation of said parties or at any time cross-defendant habitually, or otherwise or at all, occupied almost all of her time or any
of her time excepting as hereinafter alleged, dancing in hotels,
cafes and/or beach resorts in and about the city of Los Angeles or
any other place, or otherwise or at all. Denies that she thereby
absented herself from her home and/or her children on account
thereof except as hereinafter alleged, and denies that on said account, or any account, she, during said time or at any time, griev-
ously or otherwise or at all neglected her children. Alleges that
she is unable to ascertain the meaning intended by the allegation,
"habitually occupied almost all of her time;" admits, however,
that she is fond of dancing and of the ordinary and proper diversions and pleasures usually enjoyed and indulged in by people of
her age; and admits that during said time, on many occasions, she
attended parties at proper and respectable places and danced at
said parties. Denies the implication in said allegation that she indulged in said pastime to any extent inconsistent with the amount
of her leisure time or inconsistent with a proper, considerate and
motherly consideration for and attention to her children. Alleges
that upon each and every occasion when cross-defendant has not
had said children actually with her that her first consideration has
been to provide, and she has provided, for them to be left in the

charge of thoroughly competent and reliable persons. Denies the apparent implication in the term "beach resorts" that she has visited improper or questionable places of amusement, and in this connection alleges that she has never visited any resort, club or other place of amusement or entertainment at any beach, unaccompanied by her husband, excepting the Santa Monica Swimming Club, of which cross-complainant is a member; that she, during said time, only visited said last named place unaccompanied by her husband once; that at said time, she went to said place in the afternoon with a woman friend to whom she had been introduced by cross-complainant himself, and that at said time, said woman friend and cross-defendant sat on the sand and sewed and talked and did nothing of any more consequence or importance.

Further alleges that on every occasion when she has attended teas or dinner dances at the respectable hotels in Los Angeles as aforesaid, or has gone to said places for the purpose of dancing, or otherwise, that she has been accompanied by her mother, excepting on one such occasion; and alleges that on all such occasions, without exception, she has been one of a considerable party of friends.

Denies that on numerous of such or any occasions, cross-defendant returned to her home at 2:00 or 3:00 o'clock in the morning or at any other unseasonable or unusually late hour, and alleges, according to her best recollection and belief, that she never returned home at any such an hour, but that if she were ever out that late on any occasion, it was a rare and unusual condition and exception for which there was a good, proper and adequate reason and justification.

Denies that on many or any of these occasions, she was accompanied by any person subject to the description of an automobile salesman and/or by any man whomsoever, even in the sense or to the extent that she was escorted to or from any place of amusement by any such man.

Admits that on every occasion when she has indulged in the innocent and proper pleasure and pastime of dancing as aforesaid, men have necessarily constituted a part of said company, and admits that on some of said occasions, a gentleman who was an automobile salesman was present; denies, however, that at any time said automobile salesman or any other gentleman in said company was any more in the company of cross-defendant than of any other woman present, or that there was anything in said meetings other than the ordinary and proper association of friends, and that nothing transpired on any of said occasions other than the indulgence in an innocent and proper pastime. Denies that she was frequently, or otherwise or at all, in the company of any automobile salesman or any man except as above alleged and set forth, and denies that over the protests and/or against the wishes of cross-complainant, or otherwise or at all, she invited any automobile salesman, or any man whomsoever, to the home of said parties and entertained him and/or others except as hereinafter alleged; and denies that at any such time or times, liquor was drunk to excess by cross-defendant at all, and/or by any of her guests to her knowledge.

In this connection, cross-defendant alleges that at only one time during the marriage of said parties did she entertain a party of friends at her home when men were included; that at the time referred to, she gave a luncheon, with the consent and approval of cross-complainant, at which said luncheon there were approximately fourteen guests; that at said time a gentleman of cross-defendant's acquaintance who was an automobile salesman was present; but that upon said occasion was the only time that said automobile salesman or any automobile salesman, excepting purely for business purposes, was ever invited to or entertained in her said home by her. Denies the implication in said allegation that cross-defendant served intoxicating liquor to guests of hers in said home at any time; and alleges that during said time she never, on any occasion or at any time, without exception, served intoxicating liquor to any guest or guests in her said home or at any social function given by her elsewhere; alleges, however, that on the occasion of the luncheon above referred to, a woman guest to whom she had never been introduced by cross-complainant, brought some wine to said luncheon; that cross-defendant drank two glasses of said wine, and no more, and that no one present, to her knowledge, drank any of said wine to excess.

That in addition to the time set forth, when there were men acquaintances of hers in her said home, she alleges that on several incidental occasions, young men have come to her home, either in company with or to escort home girl friends of hers who were calling, but that at no time has any man or men of her acquaintance ever come to her said home alone, nor has any such man or men ever come to her said home in company with other girls excepting for the purpose of, and as, a proper and friendly call.

Denies that at any time cross-complainant, in kindness or otherwise, said to cross-defendant that her continual absence, or any absence, from her home and/or the consequent or other neglect of her children and/or her said dancing, or otherwise, through all or any hours of the night and/or day and/or drinking liquor were injurious to the welfare of her children and/or injurious to her reputation.

Alleges that the allegations last above denied are immaterial for the reason that they are nothing more than a recitation of cross-complainant's opinion in respect to the effect upon cross-defendant of statements of facts assumed in the recitation to have existed, without the allegation of any fact sufficient to justify the said opinion or the said assumption; that said recitation, however, contains the insinuation and implication, and nothing more, that cross-defendant was a woman of the night life and a drunkard; that cross-defendant denies said insinuation and implication and alleges that the same is false and untrue and without foundation or justification; and further alleges that said allegation has been and is deliberately made in the full knowledge that there is no foundation or justification therefor and with the sole intent and purpose of injuring cross-defendant's reputation and thereby prejudicing her in the prosecution of her suit for divorce, by an ingenious insinuation and implication of facts which are not alleged and which there is no evidence to support.

Denies that cross-complainant ever expostulated with cross-defendant in respect to her alleged behavior and/or conduct and/or protested against the same on any occasion, and denies that she ever, with irritation or anger, or otherwise, stated that she did not intend to change her alleged mode of life to please him and/or that if he did not like her alleged conduct, or any conduct, he could arrange with her for a divorce; and also denies the insidious and improper implication by said allegation that there was, on the occasions alleged, or on any occasion, any ground, foundation or reason for any expostulation or protest on the part of cross-complainant, as alleged or otherwise or at all, with respect to cross-defendant's conduct, other than in respect to purely natural and innocent indiscretions properly and justly attributable to cross-defendant's youth and inexperience.

Alleges that cross-defendant at all times and on all occasions, endeavored to carry out and perform to the best of her ability any and all suggestions of cross-complainant with respect to her conduct in every particular; and denies that at any time or for any reason, she ever manifested an attitude with respect to a divorce as alleged in said cross-complaint, or similar thereto; denies that at said alleged time or at any time, cross-complainant entered his, or any, protest and/or appeal to cross-defendant to consider the interests of their children with respect to her alleged suggestions concerning a divorce or with respect to any suggestions or conversations regarding a divorce; and alleges, in this connection, that at no time during the entire married life of said parties did cross-complainant alter, change or modify his attitude with respect to their marriage relation, as more particularly alleged and set forth in the complaint of plaintiff on file herein, to the effect that he never intended to permit, and would never permit the continuation of said relation only until such time as it was most convenient and practical for him to have it dissolved; and alleges that in order to protect said children and herself, she submitted to the acts and conduct of cross-complainant and endured the mental suffering alleged and set forth in her complaint on file herein, in an honest and sincere hope that cross-complainant might abandon and change said attitude and intention, and on that account that she refrained from leaving cross-complainant and instituting proceeding for divorce as long as possible; denies that at any time during said marriage relation, cross-defendant stated to cross-complainant that she did not wish to live with him any longer and/or that she wished to be divorced, except on the 29th day of November, 1926; and denies that thereupon, as alleged or otherwise or at all, she asked cross-complainant, coldly, or otherwise or at all, what financial arrangement he would make; denies that at said time, cross-complainant replied that he would provide for her abundantly and/or that he would give her more than she would be entitled to by law and/or that he would make abundant provision for her without any consideration whatsoever of any litigation, or otherwise or at all; denies that at said time, cross-defendant then demanded or asked to know what cross-complainant was worth; denies that cross-complainant replied that he did not see why that should be discussed at that time, because, regardless of what he was worth, he would see to it that she was properly and fairly provided for, or otherwise or at all.

Further in this connection, cross-defendant alleges that there is no materiality in the allegations denied as aforesaid and that the only purpose of said allegation is by implication and innuendo to create a false and untrue impression that the sole motive and purpose of cross-defendant, in her marriage with cross-complainant and in her prosecution of this action, was and is an unscrupulous desire to profit financially thereby.

Admits that at about said time, there was a conversation between said parties with respect to a divorce and a property settlement; alleges that the subject was brought up by cross-complainant and that at said time, he told her that after the completion of the picture, *The Circus*, upon which he was then working and which he expected to complete in a few months, would be the most opportune and practical time for her to get a divorce in order to best serve his convenience and interests; that as aforesaid, cross-complainant had been, during the entire time of their marriage relation, insistent in his demands that at such time she would have to separate herself from him and secure a divorce; that in said conversation, cross-complainant specified a certain definite sum which he stated he was willing to pay cross-defendant in full of hers and the children's rights to support and maintenance; that he suggested that she go to Paris to secure said divorce and that he would pay all of the expenses incidental thereto; that at said time he asked her if she would be satisfied with said settlement and she stated that she did not know, but that she thought the rights of herself and her children should depend, to some extent, upon the amount of the community property; that at said time, cross-complainant flew into a rage and said, "What do you expect; half of my earnings since I married you?" That thereafter, said parties continued a discussion of said subject and said cross-complainant persuaded and induced cross-defendant to go to San Francisco and consult her uncle and attorney, with respect thereto, and that said cross-defendant went to San Francisco for said purpose, at the aforesaid suggestion and request of said cross-complainant, and said cross-complainant paid the expense of her said trip for said purpose; that upon her return to Los Angeles, cross-defendant brought her uncle and attorney back with her for the purpose of discussing the details of any property settlement with said cross-complainant; that said cross-complainant refused to see said attorney or discuss said subject with him but advised cross-defendant to tell him that when the said picture was completed, he would pay the expenses of said attorney to go to New York and discuss the details of said property settlement with Nathan Burkan, the attorney of cross-complainant at said place; that there was no further discussion upon said subject between cross-defendant and cross-complainant thereafter, and said parties continued their cohabitation as man and wife under the same conditions and circumstances as had existed prior thereto; that the aforesaid offer of cross-complainant as a settlement of the property rights of said parties was coupled with the condition that cross-complainant should give up her youngest baby, and that cross-complainant should have the care, custody and control of the said child, then less than one year old; that cross-defendant verily believes that said condition was attached to said offer of settlement solely for the purpose of taking an unfair advantage of her natural motherly love and affection for said child in order to secure for cross-complainant a settlement of her property rights and a discharge of his obligation to support her and said children, as cheaply as possible.

That the aforesaid attitude of cross-complainant, with respect to a divorce, notwithstanding his previous attitude in reference thereto, for the first time fully convinced cross-defendant that he was determined to terminate said relation and deprive her of the protection which said marriage afforded her and her reputation on account of the publicity which had been given to the relation of said parties prior to said marriage, as more specifically alleged in the complaint on file herein.

Denies that cross-complainant ever communicated to cross-defendant his total, or any, disapproval of her alleged mode of life, or any mode of life and/or conduct on her part other than as hereinbefore stated, and denies that there was ever any reasonable cause, reason or justification for any such communication or disapproval; denies that any mode of life and/or conduct on cross-defendant's part, as alleged in said cross-complaint, ever existed; but admits that after cross-complainant's aforesaid attitude with respect to a divorce between said parties and on account thereof, and on account of the further fact that during said time was the first and only time during the marriage relation of said parties that cross-defendant was not either pregnant or caring for a very small infant, that she did increase her indulgence in such vain and frivolous pleasures and pastimes as dancing, attending teas and going to theaters with her mother and friends. Denies that on various and/or sundry, or on any, occasion or occasions, the cross-defendant ever drank liquor to excess; alleges that she has no knowledge, information or belief as to what her conduct would be or would become while under the influence of liquor in any degree or to any extent, excepting under the circumstances and as hereinafter stated; and denies that she ever at any time or on any occasion ever became, in any sense or to any degree, under the influence of liquor so that her conduct became or was unseemly, unwomanly or undignified in speech and/or action, or otherwise or at all.

In this connection, cross-defendant alleges the fact to be that prior to her marriage to cross-complainant and for approximately one year and eight months of the two years which they were living together as man and wife, she had never taken a drink of intoxicating liquor in any form and had never smoked; that after said marriage, at the private social gatherings to which cross-complainant took cross-defendant, as a rule intoxicating liquor was served and the women smoked cigarettes; that on said occasions up to and until the time aforesaid, cross-defendant consistently declined drinks of the character aforesaid, when offered to her, and consistently declined the offer of cigarettes; that cross-defendant never at any time since the marriage of said parties has cared for and does not now care for intoxicating liquor in any form; that cross-complainant many times has tried, without success, to induce her, prior to approximately four months before their separation, to drink with him at their home and has chided her for not taking a drink and smoking cigarettes when out with him, upon the ground that her said conduct was not being "a good fellow;" that on or about four months before the separation of the said parties as aforesaid, cross-defendant took her first drink at her home in company with her husband, and at his suggestion and solicitation; that thereafter, on very rare occasions, she drank wine with him as aforesaid but never at any time to such an extent as to become intoxicated; that thereafter and when cross-defendant had tasted intoxicating liquor only a few times as aforesaid, cross-complainant took her to the home of one of his friends for dinner; that at said time, cross-defendant was offered a drink of something which she does not now know and did not at the time know the name of; that cross-defendant demurred at taking said drink and was urged to do so by some of those present, including her husband; that cross-defendant thereupon took said one drink, and no more, while she was at said dinner party as aforesaid, and that said drink was the first drink she had ever taken in anyone's company except that of her husband alone; that immediately upon taking said drink, she became ill and was compelled to lie down in one of the bedrooms and was unable to eat any dinner; that cross-defendant did not at the time know and does not now know whether the effect produced by said drink was in the nature of intoxication or whether it merely made her ill because she was not accustomed to it; that while cross-defendant was ill as aforesaid, cross-complainant did not come in to see her and showed no solicitation or consideration for her condition; that thereafter she asked him why he thought said drink had made her sick and he replied, in a slurring and contemptuous manner, "Sick nothing; you were drunk." That if cross-defendant was intoxicated at said time and under said circumstances, it is and was the only time she was ever intoxicated.

Cross-defendant admits, in this connection, that during the last three or four months that she and cross-complainant lived together as husband and wife that she has drank intoxicating liquor while in the company of friends where liquor was being served; but that on none of said occasions and at no time other than as aforesaid has she drank said liquor because she cared for it or in any excess or to such a degree as to produce intoxication; that on the occasions when plaintiff has drank intoxicating liquor as aforesaid, she has done so only on rare occasions and at intervals of considerable time, and has at all times done so only in a spirit of frivolity and not because of any habit, desire, craving or inclination to drink said liquor or to experience the effects thereof; that she has never acquired and does not now possess the habit of drinking or using intoxicating liquor in any sense of the term. Cross-defendant alleges and verily believes according to her best information, recollection and belief that the times when she has taken a drink of intoxicating liquor, from the time that she first took a drink thereof, as aforesaid, up to the present time, would average not oftener than once in two or three weeks; that any information conveyed to cross-complainant, as alleged in said cross-complaint, that cross-defendant drank liquor to excess and while under the influence thereof became unwomanly, unseemly and/or undignified in speech and/or action, is false and untrue; and cross-defendant alleges that if such information were conveyed to cross-complainant, he was too well acquainted with her aforesaid attitude toward drinking intoxicating liquor to have believed said information, and that on account of his said acquaintance, he never had any reasonable ground or justification for believing such information.

That many times during said marriage relation, cross-complainant, well knowing cross-defendant's aforesaid attitude toward drinking intoxicating liquor, and her aforesaid lack of taste therefor, has commented upon the same on various occasions before other people, and has stated in published interviews that his wife had no taste for intoxicating liquor and had no inclination to indulge in the drinking thereof.

Alleges that the extent to which cross-defendant drank intoxicating liquor as aforesaid was no foundation or justification for, and did not cause cross-complainant any concern or mental suffering; that as a rule cross-complainant and all of his friends drank intoxicating liquor as an ordinary and usual thing to a very much greater extent than cross-defendant has ever drank the same; that on the 29th day of November, 1926, when cross-defendant entertained some of her friends at a supper dance at the Biltmore Hotel with cross-complainant's consent and approval (after which supper and dance the facts occurred which precipitated the separation of said parties, as hereinafter more specifically alleged), cross-complainant had his Japanese valet, at the request and suggestion of cross-defendant, make the necessary reservations and arrangements for said supper at said hotel; that said Japanese servant never at any time during her marriage relation with cross-complainant showed cross-defendant any consideration as the mistress of their said home, and treated her in respect thereto with the utmost contempt and indifference; that in making the arrangements for said supper dance as aforesaid, said Japanese servant came to her and asked her if she wanted to serve any intoxicating liquor at said supper and told her if she did that he could get it for her; that cross-defendant advised said servant that she did not want to serve any intoxicating liquor, and alleges that said servant well knew that she had never served intoxicating liquor to her guests; further alleges in this connection, on information and belief, that the aforesaid offer of said Japanese servant to get intoxicating liquor for her was with the full knowledge and at the suggestion of cross-

complainant and for the sole and only purpose of thereafter criti-
cizing her and charging her with impropriety, if she had accepted
said offer.

Denies that by her alleged conduct, or any conduct, or on account of any fact or circumstances, she was thrown more often,
or at all, in contact with any automobile salesman or other man
whomsoever, except that, on account of her increased freedom
and convenience, as above stated, and solely for that reason, she
was able to see and did see more of her friends and acquaintances,
and alleges that her increased diversions, as alleged and admitted
at said time were in no way connected with or on account of her
infatuation or other interest in any man; denies that finally or otherwise or at all, she ever became or was infatuated with any automobile salesman or other man unless said allegation is intended
to mean and does mean the innocent, proper and friendly preference for certain men friends and acquaintances over others; that
upon the aforesaid assumption, she admits that she had such pref-
erences but that there was never at any time anything improper in
her relation with said men friends or acquaintances or any one or
more of them, and that her relations with any and all of such men
friends and acquaintances was of such nature, at all times and on
all occasions, that at no time was she ever in the company of any
of her men acquaintances alone, either at her home or elsewhere.
Denies that she was ever constantly, or otherwise or at all, seen in
company with the man referred to in said cross-complaint, or any
other man, except as members of a party of friends; and that such
occasions occurred no more frequently than to constitute the reasonable and proper indulgence by cross-defendant in reasonable
and proper recreation and diversion, and in the reasonable and
proper association with her friends and social acquaintances. Denies that she told several people, or any person, that she was "in
love with" and/or "crazy about" the man intended and referred to
by cross-complainant, or any other man, in any sense or manner
to indicate anything serious or improper in such remarks. In this
connection, she alleges that she might have jokingly, with reference to any one of several of her acquaintances, remarked that she
was "crazy about" them, but that she has no recollection of any
such statement and alleges that if any such statement or statements
were made, they were made under such circumstances and in such
a manner as to clearly indicate the frivolity thereof. In this connec-

tion, cross-defendant further alleges that she does not remember stating, in the presence of certain of her girl friends that she was "just crazy about" a certain movie actor; but that she had never met said man and does not now know him and that said remark was intended to mean, and only did mean, that she admired and enjoyed him on the screen. Again denies that cross-complainant ever discussed with her, in any manner or form, her relation with any automobile salesman or any other man and/or that he tried to convince her that her alleged actions, or any actions with any man were bringing disrepute upon her and/or humiliation and/or mental suffering upon cross-complainant; and denies that he ever at any time pleaded with her to desist from such conduct on account of her love for cross-complainant and/or for the sake of her children; and denies that the alleged pleadings, or any pleading of such a character, were in vain; and again alleges that there was never any reasonable foundation, cause or occasion for any such alleged pleadings or attitude on the part of cross-complainant as alleged, or otherwise, for the reason that cross-defendant's conduct with any and all men of her acquaintance at any and all times during the marriage relation between the said parties, never has been and never was such as to warrant the bringing upon her of any disrepute or of reasonably causing her husband any humiliation and/or mental suffering, nor of such a character as to justly reflect upon her or her children in any way, manner or form injurious to her or said children.

6. Denies that on a particular Sunday afternoon as alleged or on any afternoon, or otherwise or at all, cross-defendant was preparing to attend a party at a particular or any beach resort, without cross-complainant. Denies that she ever prepared to attend and/or ever attended any party at, or was ever at any particular or any beach resort during the entire marriage relation of said parties excepting as hereinabove alleged, without her husband; and/or that she ever attended any beach resort or club or other place of amusement or entertainment, at any beach, excepting the Santa Monica Swimming Club, with her husband, and that she only attended the Swimming Club mentioned with her husband on a very few occasions. Denies that cross-complainant ever heard of the planning of any party such as alleged and denies that cross-complainant ever reasoned with or spoke to cross-defendant in any manner with reference to attending any such party and/or that

he ever suggested or emphasized that she should not attend any such party out of consideration for her children, or otherwise or at all, because the cross-complainant had not been invited, or otherwise or at all. Denies that cross-complainant pleaded in vain, or otherwise or at all, with cross-defendant, with respect to attending any such party, or any party whatever, and denies that she insisted that she was going and asked cross-complainant what he could do about it, or made any remark of similar import or character with reference thereto; and denies that at said time, or at any time, she ever stated to cross-complainant that she was not in love with him; and denies generally and specifically the other allegations in said paragraph contained down to and including the word "therefor" in line 7,[2] without more particular specification, upon the ground that said allegations constitute a mere recital of immaterial and insinuating details. In this connection, however, cross-defendant specifically denies the insinuation by implication that she was in the habit of attending parties unaccompanied by her husband and contrary to his wishes, and to which he had not been invited, for some unnecessary or improper reason, to his great disappointment and concern.

In this connection, cross-defendant alleges that at no time during the marriage relation of said parties did the ordinary, usual and normal relations exist between cross-defendant and cross-complainant in respect to the aforesaid matters; that said cross-complainant never attended any of the parties or social gatherings of cross-defendant and her friends; that he never, excepting for the purpose of appearances, as above alleged, made her a party to, or included her in, his social activities or his normal and usual associations with his friends; that he told her on many occasions that he did not want to participate in any of her diversions or pleasures and did not want to meet, and would not meet, any of her friends; that pursuant to said determination and attitude, he refused to meet, and has never met, with one or two exceptions, friends of cross-defendant, even when such friends were guests in her home and he was present in said home at said time; that on account thereof, cross-complainant's alleged and implied concern over not being invited to the party alleged, or any party, is false and untrue and known to be so both by cross-complainant and

---

2. See page 224.

every friend and associate of cross-defendant, and the implied reflection therein upon cross-defendant is cruel, unfounded, vicious and unmanly. With respect to the allegations in said paragraph contained, beginning with line 7 on page 10,[3] cross-defendant denies that cross-complainant, at said time and in respect to her attending said party as therein alleged, or at any time or with reference to any such an occasion, tried to remonstrate with her and/or ask her not to go to said party, and/or did suggest to her that it was a great or any pity that said salesman should break up their home and be the means of seriously injuring the welfare of their children. In this connection, cross-defendant alleges that on account of the fact aforesaid, she is unable to ascertain the party referred to in said cross-complaint which it is alleged she planned to attend and did attend said party; for that reason, she does not know and is unable to ascertain from said allegations whether or not any automobile salesman of her acquaintance was at the party alleged by cross-complainant, and upon that ground she denies that any automobile salesman of her acquaintance was present at the alleged party referred to by cross-complainant; alleges that if said, or any, salesman was present at any party which cross-defendant had planned to attend, or which she did attend, that said salesman, or any such salesman, or any such man at said party never had and never could have had, on account of cross-defendant's relations with any such men or associations with any such man, anything to do with any breaking up of the home of said parties, nor, on account thereof or otherwise, of seriously or otherwise, injuring the welfare of their children. That the insidious and insinuating assumption and implication in the allegation of the recital referred to, is intended to connect and does connect cross-defendant with some man not her husband, in a manner to give rise to the inference that her relations with said man were improper and involved moral turpitude on her part, without charging her with any impropriety or any act involving moral turpitude; that said allegations are, on that account, a cruel, unfounded, unwarranted, vicious and unmanly reflection upon the mother of cross-complainant's children, and deliberately made, as cross-defendant verily believes, with the sole intent and purpose, and regardless of the interests and welfare of said children, of injuring and ruining

---

3. See page 224.

the reputation of cross-defendant and subjecting her to public scorn and contempt, to prejudice her in her efforts to recover in this action a proper, just and equitable amount of money from cross-complainant for the support and maintenance of herself and said children.

Admits that cross-complainant suggested to cross-defendant that she take a trip to Honolulu or some other place, but denies that said suggestion had any connection with and/or any relation to, any conversation between said parties with respect to cross-defendant attending any party and/or with respect to her associations with any person or persons and/or with respect to any mode of life and/or conduct, on her part. In this connection, she alleges the fact to be that cross-complainant was always irritated because she and the said children were around him in his home; and that, on many occasions, he expressed such irritation to her and told her that it caused him such a feeling of restraint that he was unable to do his work; that upon one occasion when he had told her this, he made the suggestion that she go away on a trip to some place; that at said time, he specifically stated: "Go away some place farther than Coronado or Catalina and take a good long vacation." Cross-defendant alleges that this suggestion was made, as she verily believes, because he wanted to escape and avoid her requests for him to visit her and the children when she was away on her summer vacations. That in the course of said conversation, cross-defendant herself suggested that she go to Honolulu, and cross-complainant said, "That will be a fine place for you to go. You have never been there and you would enjoy that trip." That thereupon, cross-defendant planned and made arrangements for said trip, and planned to take both of her babies with her; that when cross-complainant found out that she had so planned to take said children, he objected to it upon the ground that it would give rise to gossip and newspaper comment to the effect that they had separated, and insisted, on that account, that she leave one of said babies at home, that, for said sole and only reason, cross-defendant took with her, on said trip to Honolulu, only the elder of said children. Alleges, upon information and belief, that cross-complainant's sole purpose and object in urging and persuading cross-defendant to go away and stay away for a considerable time was in the effort and endeavor to put her in a position where she might commit some indiscretion, and to have her watched while she was away, in the hope and for the purpose of securing evidence against her for divorce; that she is informed and believes, and upon such information and belief states the fact to be, that cross-complainant engaged and had detectives following her and watching her at all times while she was away on said trip; that said detectives watched every movement of cross-defendant during said time and reported every detail of her actions to said cross-complainant, even to the extent of advising him of the minute detail and fact that while she was in the stateroom of a woman passenger, with the door thereof wide open, a man friend of the woman's came in, and that while he was there, said woman stepped out of the stateroom to get something in the next room, and left cross-defendant and said man together in said stateroom, with said door open, as aforesaid, for a time not exceeding about a minute in duration; that practically all of the people with whom cross-defendant came in contact upon said trip, even the beach boys at Honolulu, have since said time been approached by persons purporting to be representatives of cross-complainant, and urged, with the suggestion of financial reward, to make signed statements derogatory to her and reflecting upon her character; that said conduct on the part of cross-complainant has humiliated cross-defendant and caused her grievous mental suffering and has injured her reputation and has thereby cast a reflection upon her children without foundation, justification, cause or excuse.

7. Alleges that there is nothing contained in paragraph 8 of said cross-complaint material to or constituting extreme cruelty or from which a finding of grievous mental suffering could be made; that cross-defendant does not pretend, or claim, to be fortunate enough to escape uncomplimentary remarks as to her conduct; that she is unable to specifically answer said allegations for the reason that they contain no intimation of what the conduct referred to was, or what the character of the uncomplimentary remarks was. However, cross-defendant denies the insinuation contained in said allegation by implication that there was anything improper or justifying any criticism of her conduct other than that criticism which might justly be founded upon considerations of personal taste and opinion.

8. Admits that cross-defendant took with her on said trip to Honolulu the elder of her two children, as aforesaid. Alleges that she is unable to ascertain what is intended or meant by "disregard-

ing" said child, or what the causes of the observations and/or comments thereupon were, and alleges that said allegations in said paragraph of said cross-complaint contained are immaterial and uncertain to such an extent as to require no answer on the part of cross-defendant; that said allegations could not, and do not, as a matter of law, constitute any ground or cause for mental suffering, anguish and/or humiliation on the part of cross-complainant.

Cross-defendant alleges the fact to be, with reference to the care of said child, that her mother and a personal friend, as a nurse, accompanied her upon said trip, and that at all times said child had the care, devotion, attention and consideration of a normal and natural mother and grandmother, in addition to the care of said nurse; that cross-defendant's said mother is greatly devoted to cross-defendant's children; that she has been with said children almost constantly since they were born and that she has personally undertaken the care and supervision of all matters affecting the welfare of said children; that if cross-defendant at any time, as alleged, was away from said child on said trip, for a time which might have seemed to others unreasonable, it was because cross-defendant knew that said child was in the care of her mother at said time and that her own presence was, on that account, unnecessary.

9. Cross-defendant admits that during the period of the marriage of said parties, her expenditure of money for clothing and other personal effects increased, but denies that said increase was extravagant or constituted any extravagance. Alleges that she is unable to ascertain from the allegations in said paragraph contained how the expenditure of in excess of ten thousand dollars, as therein alleged, for clothing, shoes, perfumes, etc., could have any relation to or affect in any way the carrying out of any purpose or scheme, conceived in Honolulu or elsewhere, to obtain a divorce from cross-complainant. Denies that within a few days after her return from Honolulu, or after her return from Honolulu at all, she expended in excess of ten thousand dollars, or any other considerable sum, for clothing, shoes and perfumes, or for any other purpose, for her individual use. Admits that prior to going to Honolulu, she supplied herself with a wardrobe, which, including her expenditures for Christmas presents for that year, amounted to something in excess of ten thousand dollars. Denies that this was extravagance and alleges that up to this time, cross-

defendant had made all of her own clothes and at said time had no clothing or wardrobe fitting to her station in life and commensurate with the position of her husband; that at the time of her marriage, she had no trousseau; that shortly prior to the time of said expenditures, remarks of various people had come to her knowledge to the effect that she looked shabby and looked like she made her own clothes; that prior to that time, she had bought all of her clothes, met all of her other incidental expenses and bought her automobile out of a very meager weekly allowance; that at the time cross-defendant was preparing to take said trip to Honolulu, she had no clothing as aforesaid, fitting her station and position, or which were proper for her to wear in going upon such a trip and coming into contact with many people as the wife of cross-complainant; that on that account, the expenditure alleged represents practically cross-defendant's total expenditures for said purposes during the entire two years that she was married; that on or about said time, cross-complainant had on deposit, in cash, in the banks of Los Angeles and Hollywood alone, approximately $2,650,000.00; that on that account cross-defendant is unable to ascertain in what manner the expenditure of said sum of money for such purpose could or did affect the material welfare of her children and upon that ground, alleges that the same has not and did not affect any material welfare or said children.

In this connection, cross-defendant further alleges, as an indication of her economy, that while she was in Coronado, shortly before her trip to Honolulu, it was necessary for her to purchase a new hat for herself, and that in the purchase of said hat, she went to the basement of one of the stores in San Diego and purchased said hat, expending therefor the sum of $2.00; and that said hat constituted her best hat for a considerable portion of time thereafter; that while she was in Coronado, as aforesaid, it was necessary for her to purchase a bed for the younger child; that cross-defendant was not able to purchase said bed out of her allowance, on account of the increased expenditures incidental to her being away from home; that in order to purchase said bed, it was, on that account, necessary for her to get the money from cross-complainant; that at said time, cross-complainant refused to permit cross-defendant to expend the money necessary to purchase a new bed and mattress for said baby, which he was advised by cross-defendant would cost about $20.00, upon the ground that said amount was too much to spend for said purpose; that cross-defendant was told she would have to find something cheaper; that on account thereof, she was required to and did go the rounds of the junk shops and second hand furniture stores in San Diego, to find and purchase a second hand bed and mattress for said baby, which she found and purchased as aforesaid, for the sum of $11.00; alleges that cross-complainant's alleged and implied consideration for the material welfare of his children, in respect to the expenditure of money, was at all times during said marriage relation confined to cross-defendant's expenditure of money and not his own; that in 1925, for a Christmas present, cross-complainant gave cross-defendant a diamond studded lady's watch, costing $1900.00 and purchased at Cartier's, New York; that at said time, he told her he could not afford it, that it was spending too much money but that he wanted to give it to her so it would appear that their relations were harmonious; that many times thereafter, cross-complainant referred to the purchase of said watch, stating that it was an extravagance and that he could not afford it and he should not have given it to her; that, according to cross-defendant's information and belief, he purchased another lady's diamond studded watch, from the same firm and at the same time, for which he paid $3800.00; that cross-defendant received, as her Christmas present, the $1900.00 watch and has never been advised by cross-complainant, and has no information or knowledge as to who received the $3800.00 present.

Admits that cross-defendant and cross-complainant had a conversation with respect to the amount which she had spent for clothes before going to Honolulu; that at said time, cross-defendant reminded cross-complainant of the fact that she had no clothes with which to take such a trip and that it was advisable for her to appear to reasonable advantage; that up to that time she had made her clothes and had put him to very little expense on account thereof, but that said clothes were not fit and proper for her to wear; that at said time cross-complainant said: "Well, why don't you keep on making them? You look well enough." Admits that at said time, cross-complainant made various and sundry remarks about being ruined on account of said expenditures, notwithstanding the amount of his bank deposits as aforesaid.

Admits that cross-defendant requested the permission of cross-complainant to entertain some friends met on the boat returning from Honolulu at a supper party at the Biltmore Hotel, but denies that there was any suggestion with reference thereto that she desired to give a dinner at her home, and alleges that at said time, she requested cross-complainant to permit his Japanese valet to arrange for said supper party at the Biltmore Hotel and that pursuant to said request, said Japanese valet did make all of the arrangements for said supper. Denies that there was any mutual understanding, or otherwise, that cross-complainant would be engaged in his work and on that account would not be able to be present at such supper. Admits that there was a mutual understanding that he would not be present at said party, but alleges that said understanding was solely due to, and on account of the fact that it was cross-complainant's fixed habit and policy to attend none of the social gatherings of cross-defendant and her friends, and to meet none of said friends and she had no reason to believe that there would be any exception to said habit and policy on this occasion. Alleges that she has no information or belief as to the time when cross-complainant reached home on the evening that she gave said supper party and upon that ground, denies that he reached home at said time, about eleven o'clock, and upon the same ground denies that he came home at said time because he had been working hard all day; denies the implication in said allegation that his work was so arduous that it was necessary for him to forgo the pleasure of being with his wife and her friends at their social gatherings and/or on that account that it was necessary and/or his habit to come at such an early hour as eleven o'clock at night and retire; and alleges in this connection that if his work was so arduous on that day as to necessitate his coming home as early as eleven o'clock at night, it was the first time in several months that cross-defendant has any knowledge of, that its arduous character had that effect. Denies that cross-defendant returned to said house with a large or any party of friends at about two o'clock in the morning, or at any other or different time than at about the hour of 12:30 o'clock, which was a seasonable and proper hour under the circumstances. Alleges that cross-defendant and her guests at said supper party danced at the Biltmore Hotel during said evening and left said hotel and came directly to the home of said parties for the reason that some of her guests desired to see the home of cross-complainant on account of his prominence as a moving-picture actor; that cross-defendant entertained a natural wifely and girlish pride in the manifestation of this interest in her husband's home and took them home with her on that account; that said guests apologized for making said request on account of the time, and stated that they would stay only a few minutes. Alleges that it was a rare and exceptional occasion for cross-complainant to be home as early as the time when cross-defendant arrived home with said guests as aforesaid; and that cross-defendant believed and had every reason to believe that he would not be at home, or disturbed in any way. Admits that at said time, some of said guests innocently commenced playing some of the musical instruments in said home, upon the belief and assurance of cross-defendant that it would disturb no one; but denies that there was any unusual noise in connection therewith; and alleges that neither cross-defendant nor any of said guests made any more noise or did anything unusual or out of the ordinary, in view of the fact that they had no knowledge or idea that cross-complainant was at home and had retired. Denies that said noise awoke the child, or any child, of said parties in the nursery of said house, or elsewhere, and denies that cross-complainant heard said child crying at said time; and alleges that if he was able to hear said children, or either of them, crying in his room when they were in said nursery, it is the first knowledge that cross-defendant has ever had of that fact; and that if he was concerned, as alleged at said time, over the crying of said child, it was the first and only time that he ever manifested that character of concern or solicitation regarding either of said children. Denies that said or any noise continued for a long time or that there was anything loud or unusual in the conduct and demeanor of said guests and/or that anything in the conduct of said guests, or any noise produced or caused by said guests, caused cross-complainant discomfort or annoyance justifying his hereinafter alleged boorish, ungentlemanly and insulting conduct; and alleges that said conduct was not due to, or on account of, any lack of consideration on cross-defendant's part, or any impropriety on the part of her guests, but was solely due to, and on account of, a most miserable and unjustifiable contempt for his wife and her feelings. Alleges in this connection, that said occasion was the only time during the two years that said parties were married that cross-defendant had ever brought guests home with her at night under any such circumstances; and alleges that her position in said home, and the domineering attitude of cross-complainant toward her as only the nominal mistress thereof was such that she would not have dared to have done so on said occasion had she thought he was home at said time, for fear of some such humiliation as that which she subsequently suffered on account thereof. Denies that said noises continued and/or promised to continue indefinitely, and in this connection alleges that cross-defendant and her said guests had not been in said house more than fifteen minutes until cross-complainant called her upstairs, as alleged in her complaint. Denies that cross-complainant remonstrated with her in any manner or form, as alleged in said cross-complaint, or otherwise or at all, excepting to say, "Get that wild bunch out of here and get them out quick. What do you think this is, a whorehouse?" Denies that at said time, she immediately or at any time, or otherwise or at all, assumed a belligerent and/or defiant mood or attitude; and alleges, as also alleged in said cross-complaint, that she immediately, meekly and peremptorily dismissed her said guests from her home, notwithstanding the great humiliation involved therein; and further alleges that cross-defendant's said conduct at said time and under said circumstances, in so complying with the aforesaid unreasonable, domineering and insulting demands of cross-complainant, indicated anything but a belligerent and defiant mood. Denies that after said guests left said house, or otherwise or at all, that cross-complainant tried in all or any kindness, or otherwise or at all, to discuss with cross-complainant what had just occurred, except as hereinafter alleged. Alleges the fact to be that she went to her room and cross-complainant came to the door of her said room and, in a very surly, domineering and threatening manner, told her to come into his room, that he wanted to talk with her; that the demeanor and attitude of said cross-complainant at said time was so threatening that cross-defendant became and was afraid to go into said room and had her mother come to the door of said room and stand outside of said door; that at said time, cross-complainant commenced to violently and unreasonably upbraid and condemn cross-defendant for awakening him, and refused to accept cross-defendant's explanation that she did not think he was at home or expect him to be at home, and that her guests only wanted to see his home; that at said time, cross-defendant's shame and humiliation in being compelled to dismiss her guests from her home as aforesaid, for no cause or reason, apparent to them, and cross-complainant's unreasonable, violent, insulting and abusive conduct in respect thereto, caused plaintiff to believe, and she did believe, that any further cohabitation with him was and had become impossible, and that at said time, cross-defendant advised cross-complainant of her aforesaid belief; that he thereupon so completely lost his head, on account of a realization that his aforesaid conduct had driven his wife into the determination to leave him, and his cruel, inhuman, inconsiderate, indecent and felonious treatment of her would thereby become public, that he picked up a loaded revolver and told her that he would kill her if she left him, or gave any publicity to their domestic affairs, as more specifically alleged in the complaint on file herein.

10. Alleges that the allegations contained in this paragraph of said cross-complaint are merely a recital of trivial and unimportant details and that said recital is made, according to cross-defendant's information and belief, for the sole and only purpose of giving the public impression that cross-complainant was really concerned over the departure of his wife and babies, rather than with the fact that their departure under such circumstances, would defeat his own plans, as hereinafter alleged, to get rid of them cheaply and quietly. Alleges that at said time, said cross-complainant had previously planned and determined to compel cross-defendant to separate from him, with said children, and obtain a divorce in such manner and upon such grounds as should be dictated by him, upon the threat that in no other way would she receive from him an adequate or proper provision for the support of herself and said children; that at said time cross-complainant cared nothing about cross-defendant and said children leaving said home, but in fact, that it was his desire, wish and obsession to get rid of them; that he feared, however, unfavorable and injurious public criticism and comment if said separation and divorce were not brought about in accordance with his own plans, and the real facts of the case suppressed; and that the aforesaid fear at said time constituted his only concern. Further alleges, that in order to accomplish the aforesaid purpose and carry out the aforesaid plan, cross-complainant, in addition to the aforesaid threat, coerced, intimidated her and fraudulently imposed upon cross-defendant's youth, inexperience and mother love, by holding the threat over her that if said divorce were not arranged and carried out according to his wishes, and the property rights of herself and babies

settled upon his terms, that cross-defendant's right to the custody of her babies, would be contested and resisted; that on account of said threats she was induced to, and did, continue living with him and to tolerate his aforesaid cruel and inhuman treatment, and to endure the humiliation, mental suffering and anguish caused thereby as aforesaid, awaiting his convenience and pleasure, until said cohabitation could be endured no longer, and until cross-complainant threatened to kill cross-defendant as aforesaid.

With respect to the last paragraph of No. 11 of said cross-complaint, cross-defendant denies that the facts and/or circumstances referred to in said paragraph of said cross-complaint were all or any of them a part of the execution of a preconceived or any plan of the cross-defendant to file an action for divorce and/or to force a divorce upon cross-complainant, and denies that said plan or any plan for said purpose was formulated and/or conceived prior to the trip of cross-defendant to Honolulu, or at any other or different time, or otherwise or at all. Alleges in this connection that up to the time of cross-complainant's aforesaid conduct with reference to cross-defendant's guests in said home and his threat to take her life if she did not further submit to his tyranny and cruelty until such time as he was ready to permit her to obtain a divorce, as alleged in the complaint on file herein, she had no intention or idea of doing anything but accepting and complying with the dictation of cross-complainant with respect to said divorce and the separation of said parties, as a matter of necessity, in the belief that in that way alone would she receive any adequate provision for her support and the support of said children. Cross-defendant admits that cross-complainant's aforesaid suggestions and propositions with reference to a property settlement for the aforesaid purpose, coupled with the condition that she give up her youngest baby, so alarmed and concerned her that a few weeks prior to the actual separation of said parties, and upon the advice of her attorney, she had taken steps to protect herself and her interests and her right to the custody of said children by procuring more concrete and positive evidence for divorce against said cross-complainant, to be used in the event that said cross-complainant should refuse to make proper provisions for the support of cross-defendant and her children or should insist upon taking said children, or either of them, away from her.

11. Alleges with reference to paragraph 12 of said cross-com-

plaint that cross-defendant does not know and is unable to ascertain from the allegations of said cross-complaint in said paragraph contained any materiality of said allegations with reference to the fact that cross-defendant absented herself from the home of said parties without the knowledge or consent of her husband and against his wish and desire. With respect to said portion of said allegations, cross-defendant alleges that she has never had any knowledge or intimation that leaving her said home at any time or on any occasion other than when she separated from cross-complainant on the 29th day of November, 1926, was without his wish and/or desire; that she has no knowledge, information or belief as to the times or occasions referred to in said allegations when she is alleged to have absented herself, as therein alleged. Denies, however, the insinuation contained in the allegation that any absenting of herself was "without the knowledge or consent" of her husband and/or that cross-defendant "surreptitiously or secretly" at any time or on any occasion left said home or absented herself therefrom; and alleges, in this connection, that at all times and on all occasions when she has left said home and/or absented herself therefrom for any purpose whatsoever, it has been openly and without any effort to, intention of, or reason for concealment; that cross-complainant himself was home so little that he was not affected by any absence therefrom on the part of his wife and had on that account no opportunity of knowing, of his own knowledge, when she was absent or for what purpose or under what circumstances; that according to cross-defendant's information and belief, any information obtained by him as to her absence from said home has been received through the maintenance of a system of espionage for the sole purpose of securing evidence against her for divorce.

Denies that while absent from her home, as alleged in said cross-complaint or otherwise or at all, she has ever become intoxicated in the presence of various or any persons or person; and denies that said cross-complainant has been so informed and/or that he verily believes any such information to be the fact; but alleges that if he has been so informed by any person or persons that said information is false and untrue and without any foundation, and has come to him solely on account of his maintenance of a system of espionage as aforesaid. Admits that since the marriage of said parties and on various and numerous occasions, cross-defendant has associated with various persons, both the names and identity of whom are unknown to cross-complainant, and admits that said association has been on various occasions without his knowledge and/or without his consent; but alleges that she has no information or belief as to his wish and/or desire in respect to said association, except as next hereinafter alleged, and upon that ground, denies that said associations were against his wishes and/or desires. In this connection, cross-defendant alleges that her associations with practically all of her friends and acquaintances were without her husband's knowledge, and most frequently with people whose names he did not know, but only for the reason that he took no interest or concern in knowing anything about the names of such persons or in knowing anything about her association with them; alleges that said associations with her friends and acquaintances as aforesaid, as a rule were without his consent but solely for the reason aforesaid and the further reason that said associations were always and without exception open, innocent and proper in every way and that nothing in connection therewith, on that account, involved or necessitated the giving or asking of his consent; that his attitude with respect to such matters was one of such utter indifference that he would not even permit cross-defendant to talk with him about them or about matters of similar interest to her; that if said associations were against the wish and/or desire of cross-complainant, he never communicated or indicated his wishes and/or desires in respect thereto to cross-defendant; and if his wishes and/or desires were against said associations, there was no reasonable or proper ground for any such attitude. In this connection, however, cross-defendant recalls that her husband did object to her association with one woman; that said woman was a very intimate friend of her husband's, and prior to her meeting said woman, they had many arguments over his insistence that cross-defendant should meet her; that after meeting said woman, upon cross-complainant's insistence and demand as aforesaid, cross-complainant made many very slurring remarks about her which cross-defendant felt at said times were without justification; that her associations with said woman were not of such a character or to such an extent as to amount to anything, whether the reason for cross-complainant's opposition thereto was justified or not; alleges that there is no allegation in said paragraph contained, that cross-defendant's associations with any of the per-

sons with whom she is alleged to have associated, were improper
or of such a character as to reasonably justify any opposition
thereto on the part of cross-complainant; and in this connection,
cross-defendant denies the insinuation and innuendo wrongfully
implied by said allegations, that there was anything improper in
her said associations, or in the character or reputation of the persons with whom she associated, to justify or warrant the designa-
tion of said associations as a "consorting with various unknown
persons."

Denies that on several occasions, or any occasion, during the
said marriage relation, cross-defendant secretly and/or clandestinely appeared in various or any public places in the company of
and/or as the companion of various or any persons without the
knowledge and/or consent of cross-complainant and/or against his
wish and/or desire. Denies the insinuated and implied allegation
that there was anything improper in cross-defendant's alleged appearances in public in the company of and with companions indefinitely and obscurely referred to in said cross-complaint, as
intended to be conveyed by the allegation that said appearances
were "secretly and clandestinely" made; alleges that cross-defendant does not know, and is unable to ascertain from said allegations, how she could appear with her friends and acquaintances
"secretly and clandestinely" in public, and states that she is unable to answer said allegation upon the ground that the same is
ambiguous and absurd.

12, 13 and 14. That with respect to the paragraphs numbered 12,
13 and 14, cross-defendant alleges that the allegations contained
therein refer solely to charges made against cross-complainant in
cross-defendant's complaint for divorce on file in this action; that
the truth of said charges, and cross-defendant's justification on
that account for making them, is a question of fact to be hereafter
determined in this proceeding, and that the making of charges as
aforesaid does not constitute extreme cruelty and is not ground for
a cross-complaint in this action; that said allegations contain in
addition to the facts aforesaid merely a recital of argumentative,
immaterial and incompetent matters, and matters of opinion; that
cross-defendant is advised and believes, and upon such information and belief, alleges the fact to be that said allegations have no
place and serve no legitimate or proper purpose in a cross-complaint for divorce, and that said fact is well known to cross-com-

plainant; that the allegations, recitals and narrative in said paragraphs contained have been and are knowingly made for the wrongful and improper purpose of prejudicing public opinion against cross-defendant in respect to her integrity, motives and justification in bringing her action for divorce against cross-complainant, and to thereby prejudice her in the prosecution of said action to the financial advantage of cross-complainant; that for the aforesaid and above mentioned reasons, no further answer is deemed necessary to said allegations than to deny generally and specifically each and every, all and singularly, the material allegations in said paragraphs contained.

More specifically answering paragraph 13 of said cross-complaint, however, cross-defendant alleges that long prior to the filing of her complaint in this action, cross-complainant had so wrongfully, stubbornly, dishonorably and unjustly refused to carry out his promises of marriage to her that, solely on account thereof, and in spite of her efforts to prevent it, the fact that cross-defendant had been seduced by cross-complainant and was pregnant with child had become and was generally and publicly known, to the great and irreparable injury and damage of both cross-defendant and said child; that cross-complainant is himself solely accountable and responsible as aforesaid, for the general and public knowledge of the fact that said child was conceived out of wedlock; that he only consented to give his alleged dearly beloved child an honorable name and a legitimate birth in order to himself escape punishment for a felony; that the legitimacy of the birth of said child, and the fact that it is legally entitled to bear its father's name, even with the wholly unavoidable reflection, as far as she is concerned, upon its and her good name as aforesaid, are solely and wholly due to her great material sacrifices and mother love for said child; on account whereof the father of said child has caused her to suffer, even since the consummation of said marriage, unspeakable mental torture; that at no time since the birth of said children has cross-complainant manifested any normal filial or paternal interest in or consideration for said children; that after the separation of said parties, cross-complainant, well knowing that said children and their mother were penniless, with millions in cash to his credit in the banks, wholly failed to provide her with enough money to properly care for and maintain said children; that the above entitled court has held the allegation in said complaint referred to in said paragraph of said cross-complaint, to be material, proper and necessary in the statement of cross-defendant's cause of action, notwithstanding cross-complainant's alleged opinion that they were unnecessary, and ruthlessly and wickedly alleged on that account; that insofar as their proper maintenance and support are concerned, said action for divorce is prosecuted for the joint benefit of the said children and their mother; that it has been necessary by and in said action for cross-defendant to force cross-complainant to properly recognize and respond to his obligations to said mother and children; that cross-defendant is informed and believes, and upon such information and belief alleges the fact to be that cross-complainant's only present interest in said child is to get rid of his obligation to support and educate it as cheaply as possible; and that in furtherance of said purpose and to accomplish said object, he has made the allegation in said paragraph contained, in an attempt to wrongfully, maliciously and selfishly prejudice its mother in the prosecution of her said action, in order to save himself money at the expense of said children, and in utter disregard of his obligations to them, and of their welfare and advantage.

Alleges upon information and belief that it is not any reflection upon his child that has caused cross-complainant grievous mental suffering, as alleged, but because he had been charged with cruelly, brutally and unmanfully treating its mother while she was pregnant with said child as a result of the seduction alleged, and whose only offense was to insist that he marry her and give that child a name; and the fear that he may be required to part with money hoarded without proper recognition even of his obligation to the government under whose protection he made it, on account of the degree and character of that cruelty.

Alleges upon information and belief that before bringing an action to enforce payment of money for the support of herself and children, it is not necessary or customary, as indicated by the allegation in said cross-complaint, for a wife to first submit her complaint to her husband for his approval, especially where he has left the state and removed his property therefrom in an effort to defeat their claims; that allegations of misconduct in an action for divorce are not ordinarily complimentary, and that the wife is not required to previously consult her husband or his legal advisers, in order to permit them to pass judgment upon the extent to which facts should be suppressed, in order to save hurting the husband's feelings unnecessarily; that when a mother is borrowing money to support a millionaire husband's children, she is not subject to discipline by the courts as an unnatural mother, because, in furtherance of the financial interest of her children, she charges their father, in his opinion, with more and greater cruelty than necessary to merely obtain a divorce.

Denies the assumption that cross-defendant ever entertained any fixed desire of having a divorce from cross-complainant except and until the filing of her complaint in this action, and denies that since said time, or at any time, cross-complainant has been ready and/or willing to give cross-defendant all or any of the share of community property of said parties to which she is entitled under the laws of the State of California, or otherwise, or at all. Alleges that said allegation is immaterial and serves no other purpose than the statement of an irrelevant attitude of cross-complainant's mind for the purpose of influencing public opinion. Cross-defendant admits, in this connection, however, that cross-complainant has stated that he was willing to make a proper division of the community property of said parties but that said statement has been at all times based upon his arbitrary constructions as to what the said community property consisted of, and in said construction of cross-complainant as to what the said community property consisted of, cross-complainant has insisted that cross-defendant permit him to carry out and perpetrate a fraud upon her rights and upon the rights of her children, with respect to said property, by the false and fraudulent pretense that various corporations organized, conducted and controlled by him are, in fact, separate entities and not merely instrumentalities for holding in their names the separate and community property belonging to said cross-complainant; that in the manipulation of said corporations, cross-complainant has caused portions of the stock thereof to be issued to parties other than himself, upon the pretext and false and fraudulent representation that the issuance of said stock represented, and does represent, a beneficial interest in said corporations and the property thereof, on the part of the persons to whom said stock has been issued, when in truth and in fact, according to cross-defendant's information and belief, all of the stock certificates issued to others than cross-complainant for stock in the said corporations has been at all times in the surreptitious possession and under the secret and absolute control of cross-complainant; that cross-complainant is the sole and only beneficial owner of the stock of said corporations and of all the property and assets thereof; that he has at all times pretended to cross-defendant that the only community property belonging to him was a pretended salary paid to him by one of said corporations; that a determination of the community property belonging to said parties must necessarily involve a determination of the character and beneficial ownership of the stock of said corporations.

That the allegations in paragraph 16 of said complaint contained with respect to cross-complainant's alleged attitude with respect to a settlement of the property rights of said parties and all offers of settlement in respect thereto have been made without a satisfactory or any determination of the questions involved in this action with respect to the real status of said corporations; that in view of said facts and conditions, cross-complainant's recital of his offers of compromise and settlement and of his intention and consideration in respect thereto have no proper or relevant place in said cross-complainant and are obviously made for the sole and only reason and purpose of covering up cross-complainant's aforesaid efforts and attempts to defraud his wife and children of their rights and make it appear that he has been willing and desirous of doing the fair, proper and manly thing by them.

Cross-defendant denies that anything is or can be involved in a suit for divorce and a legal adjudication of property rights between husband and wife which, in any sense, can justify a statement on oath that such a suit is an attempt to extort money; and alleges that the statement of such an opinion in the verified cross-complaint on file herein is improper, prejudicial and a flagrant distortion of the purposes of pleadings in civil action, in an attempt to gain an unfair, unconscionable, unethical and dishonorable advantage over a woman and two children, by holding the plaintiff in said action, and the mother of said children, up to public scorn and contempt, by the statement of incompetent personal opinions as allegations of fact, and without any reasonable foundation or justification for such opinions.

Admits that she has been unwilling to accept, for herself and children, an inadequate, improper and unfair provision for their support and maintenance, without regard to the allegation of cross-complainant's incompetent personal opinion with reference to her legal rights. Admits that she has declined to permit cross-complainant to decide her case by permitting him and his legal advisors to determine the questions of law and fact involved; and alleges in this connection that whatever his own feelings of contempt for the law and the courts may be on account of his alleged genius, cross-defendant, for various reasons, has preferred and now prefers to have the courts try and determine the merits of her case; and denies that by this manifestation of confidence in the justice of her cause and in the integrity and competency of the courts to make a fair, just and equitable adjudication thereof, she is chargeable with extortion, blackmail, wickedness, gold-digging, perjury and/or lack of motherly love and consideration for her children.

16. Denies that for a greater or any other unusual or improper portion of the time during the married relation of said parties, cross-defendant has engaged in such a course of conduct, as alleged, or otherwise or at all, so as to make it impossible for her to devote more than a very little time to the children of said parties, or so as to interfere in any way with a proper care, consideration and attention to said children; denies that during said time she has deliberately and/or willfully or otherwise or at all, disregarded said children, and/or their care, and/or welfare; and denies that she has not bestowed upon them that care and/or affection which is usual for a mother for and/or toward her children, and denies that cross-complainant has been caused grievous or other mental suffering and/or anguish on account thereof; and in this connection alleges that, in addition to the services of a nurse provided by cross-complainant, said children have at all times had the personal supervision, care and attention of cross-defendant, her mother and her grandmother; that said three women have every love, affection and consideration for said children, and are far more competent, experienced and capable of determining all matters in respect to their proper care and what is best for their welfare than cross-complainant; and alleges that cross-complainant was not at home a sufficient portion of the time to know anything about the care, attention and consideration bestowed upon said children by cross-defendant, and that he is solely dependent upon information, in respect thereto, furnished him by servants who were hostile to cross-defendant and who were trying to get any information, for cross-complainant, at his suggestion, derogatory to cross-defen-

dant; further alleges that cross-complainant is unqualified, as an expert or otherwise, to pass judgment upon the sufficiency and adequacy of the care, attention and consideration bestowed upon said children by their mother. And alleges further in this connection that said children have at all times been in perfect health and that the care and attention reflected by the physical condition and training of said children is the best refutation of the truth of cross-complainant's allegations of neglect on the part of their mother.

17. Alleges that the allegations contained in paragraph 18, down to and including line 24,[4] are too indefinite and uncertain to enable cross-defendant to specifically answer the same; that she does not know and is unable to ascertain from said allegations what various women are intended thereby; and denies that by such or any conduct cross-defendant has shown a complete or other lack of respect and/or trust and/or want of confidence in cross-complainant; alleges that on account of the uncertainty of said allegation as aforesaid, cross-defendant is unable to state whether or not the charges and statements in cross-complainant's mind were false and untrue, but denies that she ever made any statement or change to any person or persons or under any circumstances regarding cross-complainant in this respect without reasonable and probable cause for believing the same to be true or without said statements and charges being merely the repetition of general gossip and rumor; denies that any statements or charges as alleged or otherwise, made by cross-defendant with respect to cross-complainant's relations with other women were intended to and/or did annoy, vex, torment and/or humiliate cross-complainant, and denies that the same subjected him to great or any shame and/or embarrassment and/or caused him grievous or any mental suffering and/or pain.

Admits that cross-defendant has had no respect, trust or confidence in cross-complainant in respect to his relations with other women, or with respect to his relations, of the character alleged, with cross-defendant; alleges that cross-complainant has boasted to her of such relations with other women to such an extent as to indicate an absolute lack of shame or embarrassment on account thereof, or on account of anything that might be said by anybody with respect thereto; alleges that notwithstanding cross-defendant's said opinion of cross-complainant in this respect, the same

---

4. See page 231.

has been such a matter of humiliation to her that she has been disposed on all ordinary occasions to keep her knowledge of his said attitude to herself, rather than to publish it.

Alleges in this connection that many facts and circumstances have come to cross-defendant's knowledge during her marriage relation with cross-complainant reasonably indicating that his relations with various other women were improper and illicit; and alleges, upon information and belief that on a certain day in the month of July, 1925 at about 10:30 o'clock P.M. of said day, as near as cross-defendant is able to fix the time, cross-complainant committed adultery with a certain woman, whose name and identity cross-defendant does not know, of her own knowledge, at Hollywood, California, in the bungalow of cross-complainant situated on the northeast corner of the lot of the Chaplin Studios, Inc., located at Sunset and La Brea Streets in said city; and further alleges on her information and belief that cross-complainant has on diverse other days and at other times, prior and subsequent to said last mentioned time, committed adultery with said woman at and in said bungalow, and at and in the home of cross-defendant and cross-complainant, located at 1103 Cove Way, Beverly Hills, California, and at various and diverse other places in said County of Los Angeles and elsewhere; and alleges that each and all of said acts of adultery were committed without the consent, connivance, procurement or previous knowledge of cross-defendant, and that she has not lived or cohabited with cross-complainant since she became cognizant of the commission of any of the several acts of adultery hereinabove alleged.

V.

Denies that the actions, conduct and/or behavior of cross-defendant, as alleged in paragraph IV of said cross-complaint, or otherwise or at all, constantly and/or repeatedly or otherwise, or at all, wounded and/or lacerated cross-complainant's feelings and/or caused cross-complainant constantly or otherwise to suffer grievous and/or extreme anguish of mind, and/or grievous mental pain, and/or suffering, and denies that said or any action, conduct and/or behavior of cross-defendant during the whole or any portion of said period did, and/or does now, absolutely or otherwise destroy cross-complainant's peace of mind and/or happiness or endanger his health or unfit him for continuing his work in his said profession; denies that said or any conduct and/or behavior of cross-defendant has seriously or otherwise impaired the health of cross-complainant; denies that said or any conduct of cross-defendant was calculated by her to and/or did render the proper discharge of duties of married life impossible for cross-complainant, and/or were such as utterly or otherwise to defeat the legitimate, or any objects of matrimony; denies that said or any conduct of cross-defendant was intentional, willful and/or without the consent and/or against the wishes of cross-complainant; and denies that it or anything was intended by cross-defendant to inflict grievous suffering on cross-complainant and/or outrage, wound and/or lacerate his feelings. Denies that said or any conduct of cross-defendant has become a fixed and/or persistent habit and/or is likely to be repeated if cross-complainant and cross-defendant should continue to live together.

Alleges in this connection that the conduct referred to in said paragraph and as alleged in paragraph IV of said cross-complaint, amounts to nothing but the allegation of usual, proper, ordinary and trivial conduct on the part of cross-defendant so coupled with insinuations and implications of impropriety as to make it appear that cross-defendant's conduct has been improper without any allegation of that fact, with the sole exception that she is charged with having overindulged in "frivolous and vain" pleasures in the opinion of cross-complainant, and that she has become intoxicated in the presence of various unnamed persons.

VI.

Denies that cross-complainant is a fit and/or proper person, morally or otherwise, to have the care, custody and/or control of said children, or either of them; and alleges that cross-complainant is unfit morally, and because of the lack of a normal, paternal interest in and affection for said children, to have their care, custody or control.

Denies that he is or has ever been, ready and/or willing to receive the care, custody and/or control of said children, or either of them; admits that he is able, but denies that he is willing, to do all or anything necessary for their best, or any, interest, and/or comfort, and/or education.

Alleges that the attitude and conduct of cross-complainant, both

before and after the separation of said parties, conclusively indi-
cates that he is willing to do only those things for the best interest,
comfort and education of said children made necessary by compulsion of law or public opinion; upon information and belief that
cross-complainant has been and is the father of other children, and
that his attitude toward said other children, in the respects alleged
and otherwise, has been and is so heartless, indifferent and unnatural that the very thought of the welfare, interest and proper education of her babies being left to the voluntary consideration of
their father, fills cross-defendant with maternal fear and trepida-
tion.

VII.

Alleges that the allegations in this paragraph contained are uncertain and ambiguous in that cross-defendant is unable to ascertain therefrom whether the total value of certain community
property in cross-complainant's mind, is of the value alleged, or
whether the allegation of the total value of the community property referred to is intended as an allegation that said property constitutes the total of the community property of said parties.

Denies that the total value of any specific community property
is $266,932.63, for the reason that cross-defendant has no infor-
mation or belief as to the nature and character of the community
property referred to; and denies that the community property of
said parties does not exceed in value $266,932.63.

Admits that the balance of a pretended salary received by cross-
complainant from one or more alter ego corporations, is approximately the sum alleged; but denies that said balance constitutes
all the community property of said parties.

In this connection, alleges, upon information and belief, that all
of the receipts and assets of the Chaplin Studios, Inc., a corporation, and Charles Chaplin Film Corporation, a corporation, derived from the motion pictures *The Circus* and *The Gold Rush* are
receipts and assets produced and earned as the result of the personal skill and labor of cross-complainant, together with the in-
vestment of his own separate funds, and the community funds of
said parties, and that no person, firm or corporation other than
cross-complainant, has any beneficial interest in or claim to any of
the assets of said corporations, or either of them; that the aforesaid

portion of the assets and receipts of said corporations, and each of them, is affected by the community property interest of cross-defendant, and an undetermined part of said portion constitutes and is community property; that the value of the entire community property of said parties is far in excess of the alleged sum of $266,932.63.

Further alleges upon information and belief that the allegation in said paragraph of said cross-complaint contained, with reference to community property, is deliberately and intentionally evasive and equivocal, so as to have the general effect and appearance of a direct statement on oath of the total value, extent and amount thereof, without making any such a direct allegation; that said allegation is a deliberate and intentional subterfuge, to make it appear that cross-complainant's alleged offers of settlement are fair and untainted by the fraud aforesaid, and in order to gain public sympathy for him, and to prejudice cross-defendant in the prosecution of her claim against him for the support of herself and children.

WHEREFORE, cross-defendant prays that cross-complainant be denied any affirmative relief as prayed for in his said cross-complaint; that cross-defendant be granted the relief prayed for in her complaint; and for such other and further relief as shall be meet and equitable in the premises.

EDWIN T. McMURRAY,
YOUNG & YOUNG,
BY EDWIN T. McMURRAY
Attorney for Plaintiff and Cross-Defendant.
1 July 1927

IN THE
SUPERIOR COURT OF THE
STATE OF CALIFORNIA
IN AND FOR THE
COUNTY OF LOS ANGELES

No. D-52298

Lillita Louise Chaplin,

Plaintiff,

vs.

Charles Spencer Chaplin, et al.,

Defendants.

ORDER

This cause coming on to be heard this 17th day of January, 1927, in the matter of the application of plaintiff for alimony pendente lite, attorneys' fees, costs and expenses, plaintiff being represented in court by her attorneys, Messrs. Young & Young and Edwin T. McMurray, and it appearing that no appearance having been made on behalf of the defendant, and that the order to show cause was not served upon the defendant and that defendant was and is out of the state, and had departed from the state; that property has been heretofore taken into the hands of the Receivers appointed in this cause, and is now in the hands of said Receivers and under the control of the Court, belonging to defendant, which consists of separate real property and money, which is the community property of defendant and plaintiff; and that defendant has counsel representing him in this jurisdiction, and in the City and County of Los Angeles, and that defendant has had, and now has actual notice of this proceeding and the time set therefor through said counsel; and the Court being fully advised in the premises and having considered oral and documentary evidence introduced on behalf of plaintiff's application;

IT IS HEREBY ORDERED, ADJUDGED AND DECREED:

That the defendant, Charles Spencer Chaplin, pay to the plaintiff for the support and maintenance of plaintiff and the two minor children of plaintiff and defendant, the sum of $8,000.00 forthwith, and the sum of $4,000.00 on the 15th day of February, 1927, and a like sum and amount upon the 15th day of each and every month thereafter until the final determination of said action, or the further order of the Court; and that the defendant pay to plaintiff forthwith on account of attorneys' fees, and costs and expenses to enable her to prosecute said action, the sum of $6,400.00, and

IT IS HEREBY FURTHER ORDERED: that if said sums are not paid as herein provided upon the making and signing of this order, or if reasonable security is not deposited in Court by defendant at said time to secure the payment of the sums provided to be paid in said order, that any money in the hands of the Receivers be, and it hereby is, applied to the satisfaction of said order.

DATED: this 17th day of January, 1927.

WALTER GUERIN
Judge

IN THE
SUPERIOR COURT OF THE
STATE OF CALIFORNIA
IN AND FOR THE
COUNTY OF LOS ANGELES

No. D-52298

LILLITA LOUISE CHAPLIN,

Plaintiff,

vs.

CHARLES SPENCER CHAPLIN, et al.,

Defendants.

ORDER—ALIMONY, ATTORNEYS' FEES, etc.

THIS CAUSE came on to be heard on the 17th day of January, 1927, in the matter of the application of plaintiff for alimony pendente lite, attorneys' fees, costs and expenses, that plaintiff be granted custody of the two minor children of plaintiff and defendant, Charles Spencer Chaplin, pendente lite, and that said defendant be restrained, pendente lite, from annoying and molesting said plaintiff; said plaintiff being represented in Court by her attorneys, Edwin T. McMurray, Esq., Messrs. Milton K. Young, Lyndol L. Young, William K. Young and L. R. Brigham, of the firm of Young & Young; and

It appearing that no appearance has been made on behalf of said defendant, that the order to show cause on the above application was not served upon said defendant; that said defendant was, and is, out of the State of California, and has departed from the State of California; that property has heretofore been taken into the hands of the Receivers heretofore appointed in this cause, and is now in the hands of said Receivers and under the control of the Court; and that defendant has had, and now has, actual notice of this proceeding and the time set therefor, through said counsel; and the Court being fully advised in the premises, and having considered oral and documentary evidence introduced on behalf of plaintiff's application.

IT IS HEREBY ORDERED, ADJUDGED AND DECREED that said defendant Charles Spencer Chaplin pay to the plaintiff for the support and maintenance of plaintiff and the two minor children of plaintiff and said defendant, the sum of $8,000.00 forthwith, and the sum of $4,000.00 on the 15th day of February, 1927, and a like sum and amount upon the 15th day of each and every month thereafter until the final determination of this action or the further order of the Court; that said defendant pay to plaintiff forthwith, on account of attorneys' fees, the sum of $4,000.00, the sum of $2150.00 for and on account of the premiums on the bonds heretofore filed in this action by said Receivers and the bond filed by plaintiff in connection with her application for the appointment of said Receivers, and on account of costs and expenses, to enable her to prosecute said action, the sum of $250.00, and that the matter of further allowance, if any, to plaintiff on account of attorneys' fees and costs be continued pending further hearing thereon by the Court; and

IT IS HEREBY FURTHER ORDERED, ADJUDGED AND DECREED that the said plaintiff have the sole and exclusive custody of said two minor children of plaintiff and said defendant, pendente lite; and

IT IS HEREBY FURTHER ORDERED, ADJUDGED AND DECREED that said defendant Charles Spencer Chaplin, and his representatives, agents, attorneys and servants be, and each of them is, hereby restrained, pendente lite, from annoying, harassing, or in any manner whatsoever molesting said plaintiff.

DATED: January 19, 1927.

WALTER GUERIN
Judge

No. D-52298

LILLITA LOUISE CHAPLIN,

Plaintiff,

vs.

CHARLES SPENCER CHAPLIN, et al.,

Defendants.

ORDER—MAKING PERMANENT PENDENTE LITE, RESTRAINING ORDER OF JANUARY 11, 1927.

THIS CAUSE came on to be heard on the 17th day of January, 1927, on the order to show cause on behalf of plaintiff why the restraining order heretofore made on the 11th day of January, 1927, against the defendants Charles Spencer Chaplin, The Chaplin Studios, Inc., a corporation, Charles Chaplin Film Corporation, a corporation, United Artists Corporation, a corporation, T. Kono, Alfred Reeves, First National Bank of Los Angeles, a corporation, Bank of Italy, a corporation, Security Trust & Savings Bank of Los Angeles, a corporation, Farmers & Merchants National Bank, a corporation, and the representatives, agents, servants and representatives of Charles Spencer Chaplin, should not be made permanent pendente lite; plaintiff being represented in Court by her attorneys, Edwin T. McMurray, Esq., and Messrs. Milton K. Young, Lyndol L. Young, William K. Young and L. R. Brigham, of the firm of Young & Young, and the defendant United Artists Corporation, a corporation, and Samuel Goldwyn served and sued as Doe Two, by Messrs. Loeb, Walker & Loeb, and it appearing from the affidavit of service attached to said order to show cause, that service thereof has been regularly and duly made upon the defendants First National Bank of Los Angeles, a corporation, Bank of Italy, a corporation, Security Trust & Savings Bank of Los Angeles, a corporation, and Farmers & Merchants National Bank, a corporation, United Artists Corporation, a corporation, Loyd Wright, sued and served as Doe One, and Samuel Goldwyn, sued and served as Doe Two; and

It appearing that no appearance has been made on behalf of the other defendants upon whom service has been made; that no appearance has been made on behalf of the defendant Charles Spencer Chaplin; that the order to show cause has not been served upon the said defendant, and that said defendant was, and is, out of the State of California, and has departed from the State of California; that the real property specifically described in said order to show cause and other property has been heretofore taken into the hands of the Receivers heretofore appointed in this cause, and is now in the hands of said Receivers and under the control of the Court; and that defendant has had, and now has, actual notice of this proceeding and the time set therefor, through said counsel, and the Court being fully advised in the premises, and having considered oral and documentary evidence introduced on behalf of plaintiff's application,

IT IS HEREBY ORDERED, ADJUDGED AND DECREED that said restraining order be, and the same is, hereby made permanent, pendente lite.

DATED, this 19th day of January, 1927.

WALTER GUERIN
Judge

IN THE
SUPERIOR COURT OF THE
STATE OF CALIFORNIA
IN AND FOR THE
COUNTY OF LOS ANGELES

No. D-52298

LILLITA LOUISE CHAPLIN,

Plaintiff,

vs.

CHARLES SPENCER CHAPLIN, THE CHAPLIN STUDIOS, INC., a corporation, et al.,

Defendants.

ORDER FIXING AMOUNT OF BOND ON APPEAL FROM ORDER APPOINTING RECEIVERS AND STAYING EXECUTION THEREOF.

Application having been made to this Court for an order fixing the amount of a bond to be filed by The Chaplin Studios, Inc. for the purpose of staying the execution of an order appointing Receivers in the above entitled action pending appeal from the said order so appointing said Receivers, and good cause appearing therefor,

IT IS HEREBY ORDERED that the amount of the said undertaking to be executed on the part of The Chaplin Studios, Inc., as appellant, to stay proceedings upon and pending the appeal from the said order so appointing the Receivers in the above entitled action be and the same is hereby fixed in the sum of $1,000,000.00.

AND IT IS HEREBY FURTHER ORDERED that upon the execution and filing of said undertaking that the execution of the said order appointing Receivers be stayed pending the appeal from the said order so appointing said Receivers.

January 19, 1927.

WALTER GUERIN
Judge of the Superior Court

IN THE
SUPERIOR COURT OF THE
STATE OF CALIFORNIA
IN AND FOR THE
COUNTY OF LOS ANGELES

No. D-52298

LILLITA LOUISE CHAPLIN,

Plaintiff,

vs.

CHARLES SPENCER CHAPLIN, et al.,

Defendants.

NOTICE OF MOTION FOR AN ORDER PERMITTING PLAINTIFF AND MINOR CHILDREN TO OCCUPY DWELLING.

To Charles Spencer Chaplin and The Chaplin Studios, Inc., a corporation, defendants above named, and to Messrs. Gavin McNab, Loyd Wright, Charles E. Millikan and Nat Schmulowitz, attorneys of record of defendant, The Chaplin Studios, Inc., a corporation; and to Messrs. W. I. Gilbert and Herman Spitzel, Receivers in the above entitled action:

YOU AND EACH OF YOU ARE HEREBY NOTIFIED and YOU AND EACH OF YOU WILL PLEASE TAKE NOTICE HEREBY: that on Tuesday the 15th day of February, 1927, at the hour of ten o'clock A.M., or as soon thereafter as counsel can be heard, in Department 20 of the above entitled court, said department being the courtroom of the Honorable Walter Guerin, the plaintiff above named will make a motion for an order permitting plaintiff and the two minor children of plaintiff and defendant, Charles Spencer Chaplin, to move into and occupy the dwelling heretofore occupied by plaintiff and defendant, Charles Spencer

Chaplin, prior to their separation as alleged in the complaint on file herein, at 1103 Cove Way, Beverly Hills, California, and for an order restraining said defendants, Charles Spencer Chaplin and The Chaplin Studios, Inc., a corporation, their employees, agents, servants and attorneys or anyone acting for them, or either of them or in behalf of them, or either of them, from interfering with, disturbing or molesting in any way the occupation of said dwelling by plaintiff and said minor children until the further order of the court.

Said motion will be made upon the following grounds, to wit;

1. That said defendant has left the State of California and is now beyond the jurisdiction of the above entitled court, without making adequate or any provisions for a suitable dwelling or home for plaintiff and said minor children.

2. That the said dwelling is the dwelling of the defendant, and was the dwelling of plaintiff and said children during the marital relation of the parties to said action, and up to the 30th day of November, 1926; that plaintiff is without means or income to provide a suitable dwelling and home for herself and said minor children.

3. That said dwelling is now unoccupied, save and except by servants and caretakers of said defendant, Charles Spencer Chaplin.

4. That plaintiff was compelled to leave said dwelling and home on or about the 30th day of November, 1926, on account of the extreme cruelty of said defendant, Charles Spencer Chaplin.

5. And that plaintiff is entitled to occupy said dwelling under the provisions of Section 157 of The Civil Code of the State of California.

Said motion will be based upon the affidavit of the plaintiff, Lillita Louise Chaplin, and the pleadings, files and records of the above entitled action.

DATED: February 11th, 1927.

EDWIN T. MCMURRAY
YOUNG & YOUNG
MILTON K. YOUNG
LYNDOL L. YOUNG
WILLIAM K. YOUNG
L. R. BRIGHAM
BY LYNDOL L. YOUNG
Attorneys for plaintiff.

IN THE
SUPERIOR COURT OF THE
STATE OF CALIFORNIA
IN AND FOR THE
COUNTY OF LOS ANGELES

No. D-52298   Dept. 20

LILLITA LOUISE CHAPLIN,

Plaintiff,

vs.

CHARLES SPENCER CHAPLIN, et al.,

Defendants.

INTERLOCUTORY JUDGMENT OF DIVORCE

This cause came on regularly to be heard on the 22nd day of August, 1927, before the Superior Court, in Department 20 thereof, the Honorable Walter Guerin, Judge Presiding, Messrs. Edwin T. McMurray, Bradner W. Lee, Jr., and Kenyon F. Lee, appearing as attorneys for plaintiff herein, and Messrs. Gavin McNab, Loyd Wright, Nat Schmulowitz, and Charles E. Millikan, appearing as attorneys for the defendant, Charles Spencer Chaplin, herein.

And it appearing to the Court that the defendant, Charles Spencer Chaplin having duly served and filed his answer in this action on the 2nd day of June, 1927, and said cause having been duly set for trial, and evidence having been introduced at the hearing of said cause, and it appearing that said plaintiff and said defendant have entered into a property settlement agreement in writing, dated the 19th of August, A. D. 1927, providing, among other things, for the settlement of their various property rights, claims and interests, and making provisions for the care, custody and control, support and maintenance of their minor children, Charles

Spencer Chaplin, Jr., and Sydney Earl Chaplin, and the evidence being closed, and said cause having been submitted to the Court for its consideration and decision:

NOW, THEREFORE, said Court having made and filed herein its findings of fact and conclusions of law;

IT IS HEREBY ORDERED, ADJUDGED AND DECREED, that the said plaintiff, Lillita Louise Chaplin, is entitled to a divorce from the defendant, Charles Spencer Chaplin, upon the ground of defendant's extreme cruelty; that when one year shall have expired after the entry of this interlocutory judgment, a final judgment and decree shall be entered, granting a divorce herein, wherein and whereby the bonds of matrimony heretofore existing between said plaintiff and said defendant shall be dissolved.

IT IS FURTHER ORDERED, ADJUDGED AND DECREED that the permanent custody, care and control of the said minor children and each of them of the plaintiff and the defendant be, and the same is hereby awarded to the plaintiff, Lillita Louise Chaplin, subject however, to the right on the part of the defendant, Charles Spencer Chaplin, at any and all reasonable times to visit with and enjoy the companionship of the said children and each of them, or either of them; that the said children shall not, nor shall either of them be removed from the State of California by either of the parties hereto without first obtaining the written consent of the other party, or upon order of the above entitled court after due notice of the application therefor, and in this regard the court hereby reserves the right to modify this decree[1] with reference to the care, custody, education and/or control of the said children and each of them, or either of them, as may seem necessary or proper.

IT IS FURTHER ORDERED, ADJUDGED AND DECREED that the said agreement hereinbefore referred to, entered into on the 19th day of August, 1927, between Lillita Louise Chaplin and Charles Spencer Chaplin is in all respects, reasonable, adequate, just, fair, equitable and proper and the court hereby ratifies, approves and confirms the same and it is hereby further ordered,

---

1. This decree was modified by order of the court on 15 September 1932 to further read, "Minors Charles Spencer Chaplin, Jr. and Sydney Earl Chaplin to be employed, apprenticed, hired out etc. only upon written consent of both plaintiff and defendant."

adjudged and decreed that the said plaintiff, Lillita Louise Chaplin and said defendant, Charles Spencer Chaplin are and each of them is bound irrevocably by all the terms, covenants and conditions contained in said agreement.

The Court reserves the right to hear and determine the report, account and application for discharge of the Receivers acting in this case, and to authorize the payment of such fees to said Receivers and each of them as may be proper.

Done in open court this 23rd day of August, 1927.

WALTER GUERIN
Judge of the Superior Court.

NOTICE—CAUTION

This is not a Judgment of Divorce. The parties are still husband and wife, and will be such until a Final Judgment of Divorce is entered after One (1) year from the entry of this Interlocutory Judgment. The Final Judgment will not be entered unless requested by one of the parties.[2]

---

2. Plaintiff was granted a final judgment of divorce from defendant on 24 August 1928.

Index

abortion, Grey offered half million dollars to have, 146
Actman, Irving, 117
adultery, 127–128, 141, 280
"Age of Innocence, The," xvii, 14n19, 30
Aguirre, Henry, Jr., 118, 118n14, 119
Ambassador Hotel, 178
Arnold, Danny, 120, 120n17, 123
Arrast, Henri d'Abbadie, d', 35, 35n7
Asquith, Anthony, 71, 71n2, 72
Asquith, Elizabeth (Princess Antoine Bibesco), 71, 71n2
Asquith, Herbert Henry, 71
Attenborough, Richard, 123

"Baby, Oh Where Can You Be?," 111
Baker, Nellie Bly, 23, 23n32
Baker, Phil, 112, 112n7
Bank of Italy, 151, 153, 156, 159, 160, 207, 289, 290
Barrymore, John, 66, 66n41, 67, 72–73, 75
Beauharnais, Josephine de, 44, 44n21, 66, 94–96
Becker, Roland, 109, 111
Beebe, George, 105
Beethoven, Ludwig van, 93

Benny, Jack, 111, 111n2
Bergman, Henry, 23, 23n31
Bergh, Julia, 115
Berle, Milton, 117, 117n11
Best, Albert, 120
Big Parade, The, 43n18, 46, 66n40
Biltmore Hotel, entertaining at, 191, 225–226, 256–257, 266
birth prevention as desire of defendant, 133–134
blackmailer, plaintiff accused of being, 134
Boardman, Eleanor, 46, 46n23, 65–66, 86–87
Bookends, 123
Brahms, Johannes, 93
Brandstatter, Eddie, 68
Brigham, L. R., 162, 287, 289, 294
"Bring Back My Mother to Me," 111
Brownlow, Kevin, 123
Burkan, Nathan, xix, 53, 53n33, 101, 253
Burnell, Charles S., 118
Burtnett, Earl, 65
Butler, David, 114

Cantor, Eddie, 111, 111n3
Carey, William, 90, 90n3
Carpentier, Georges, 112, 112n8, 113, 116

About the Author

Jeffrey Vance, a student of the art of Charles Chaplin and the silent cinema since childhood, is a writer, historian, and lecturer whose friendship and close collaboration with Chaplin's second wife, Lita Grey Chaplin, led to the completion of this volume. Mr. Vance holds a Master of Arts degree in English Literature from Boston University and works in the film industry as an archivist. This is his first book.